When Hope Can Kill

How Hope Keeps you with the Wrong Person – Reclaim Your Soul for the Right Person

Revised Edition

By Lucy Papillon, Ph.D.

FEP International, Inc.

When Hope Can Kill

How Hope Keeps You with the Wrong Person – Reclaim Your Soul for the Right Person

By Lucy Papillon, Ph.D.

Copyright © 1998, 2006

Title of First Edition: When Hope Can Kill: Reclaiming Your Soul in a Romantic Relationship. Everywhere Press, 1998.

Lucy Papillon

Published by FEP International, Coralville, Iowa

Printed in the United States of America

ISBN 0-9769689-6-7

Second Edition, January 2007

Printed in USA

http://www.fepint.org/when-hope-can-kill/

Grateful acknowledgment is made for permission to include the following copyrighted material:

Excerpt from "East Coker" in *Four Quartets,* copyright 1943 by T.S. Eliot and renewed 1971 by Esme Valerie Eliot, reprinted by permission of Harcourt Brace & Company.

For Colored Girls Who Have Considered Suicide/When The Rainbow Is Enuf, by Ntozake Shange. Copyright©1975, 1976, 1977 by Ntozake Shange. Reprinted with permission of Scribner, a Division of Simon & Schuster.

Pathway of Roses, by Christian Larson. Published by Newcastle Publishing Co., Inc., North Hollywood, California Copyright 1994

Voices From the Caves-The Shamans Speak, by Bill Worrell, Shaman Arts, Inc., 1997.

CONTENTS

With gratefulness

I dedicate this book

Both

to my children,
Benjamin and James Robert,
who I gave life to once
but who have given me life
many times.

And

to my soul
that had to withstand so much
yet
can still stand
for me
as I move
beyond my brokenness
and
no doubt
will stand for me
no matter what.

I said to my soul, be still, and wait without hope
For hope would be hope for the wrong thing; wait without love
For love would be love of the wrong thing; there is yet faith
But the faith and love and the hope are all in the waiting.
Wait without thought, for you are not ready for thought:
So the darkness shall be the light, and the stillness the dancing.
T.S. Eliot

Acknowledgements

There are a number of people to whom I owe a great deal of gratitude. First, a book in progress, especially one as personal and raw as mine, can feel quite fragile; it is of immeasurable assistance to have readers who are sensitive and yet honest. Because my sister was a discerning judge of the strengths and weaknesses of the first draft, *When Hope Can Kill* is an even more revealing account of both my own and others' journeys out of agony than it otherwise could have been.

There is no finer editor than Marie Hunt – incisive, patient beyond human capabilities, and devoted to bringing out the best values of the manuscript from the day she first saw the revised version of my book.

Ultimately, I must give great thanks to the publisher, Andrew Doan, M.D. Ph.D. From the first day I met him, he trusted me, he believed in me, and he was willing, beyond all reason, to dwell in possibility with me that we could revise the book in such a way that it would bring even more of a healing message than what occurred in the original edition – to all who were willing to begin their journey out of suffering. I know that Andrew understood what I wanted to convey to everyone who read the book as well as the necessity for it, so I was assured he would make it all happen. I could never have found him on my own. God sent him to me.

Introduction to Revised Edition

It is fascinating to me to look back to see where I was when I first wrote this book and where I am now. I don't recognize myself in lots of ways. I was fresh out of this relationship I speak of and still reeling from the consequences of it in many ways. I know, now, so much more than I knew then, even though I knew a great deal then. I also have had an enormous amount of responses about the importance and the impact that the message of this book has had on people across the world.

I know more fully now, though, that if a soul is being jeopardized, unmasking the unnamed agony is of primary consideration. By originating the concept "soul mugging," I unravel this mystery of all who falter in treasuring their soul within a relationship, which can become an insidious pattern, desecrating to the human spirit. So many people have asked me to succinctly describe what soul mugging is. It is a profound spiritual and psychic trauma to the critical life core of one's existence (which is the soul). Soul mugging is often a lifelong pattern which one unknowingly perpetuates through interaction. It distorts reality. Even simple actions on one's behalf become incomprehensible. Soul mugging entraps you and holds you captive, creating devastating, ongoing suffering. I know now that I have revealed to thousands, perhaps millions, the valuable, unparalleled discoveries based on my personal and clinical experience, such as showing how hope has a pivotal role in perpetuating this profoundly damaging occurrence. I interweave psychological and spiritual principles to complement my original theories on susceptibility to soul mugging. I do challenge you by introducing innovative approaches such as questions, dialogues, and exercises to empower you to reclaim full possession of your soul.

It totally warms my heart to imagine that people understand that "soul mugging" is much more prevalent than most are willing to admit. And it isn't just verbal disrespect and defiling from others that they describe, it is often what people are doing to themselves, due to their unwillingness to follow what they most want to give to themselves. Now, that is a powerful statement of what so many of you are doing to you, isn't it? You don't even have to be in a relationship to experience what I have named "soul mugging." You know what it is because you carry it with you wherever you go. It is you, isn't it, that is not willing to honor you, to listen to you, to welcome what your soul is saying it needs? You just keep doing the same things while secretly wanting something different.

I am writing this revised edition for several reasons, one of which I've already mentioned. I am not who I was in 1996 when I first communed with so many of you. I also know even more clearly how important it is for the message that this book conveys to be spread even further around the world than it was back when it was first published. In addition, I have discovered that this book is definitely not just for those in romantic relationships, it is for all of you who are in relationships of any kind – with supervisors, employers, fathers, mothers, older siblings, children or friends who treat you less than what you deserve, and, of course, mostly, the relationship you are in with yourself.

I want to let you know that what seemed like the end of my life, I mean that literally, became, over time, the most beautiful, extraordinary beginning of my life that I could ever have imagined. I was brand new when I awakened from the shock of that situation and its "last episode." I had to be, I had died to what-had-been and miraculously found I was birthing myself into what-could-be, what had to become possible, if I wanted to continue living.

At first it was an "if" because I was breathing without even caring if I took another breath. I was walking around, even though I had no idea where I was going nor did I want to make a plan about that or anything else. As far as I was concerned at the time, I had no future and it meant nothing to me that I was a blank slate.

Now I can look back and see that this blackest darkness was actually what saved my life, what brought me to another level of living, a deeper, more profound spiritual understanding of what life is and what my life, in particular, could be. I had used hope to keep me stuck and found that it was the most deadly contributor to my suffering. I had used hope to keep me in a relationship that was defiling my soul. Hope had prevented me from making important decisions on behalf of myself.

As I keep awakening more and more each moment to what life can offer, I often use the marvelous metaphor of the caterpillar who has no idea that as a caterpillar that dark, tightly woven chrysalis was actually going to be a place for birth rather than death. The caterpillar, that former self, thought of the chrysalis as death, but it was actually the beginning of a lighter, larger, greater experience of life for the butterfly. Your darkest hour can actually be the light that saves your life, moving you beyond what you could even have ever imagined.

Breaking through any of these old patterns of behavior, these things that have kept you stuck, prevented you from going for those impossible dreams that are actually, of course, totally possible since they are "of God," is what this book offers you. You don't have to stay paralyzed by your circumstances, thinking they define you. You don't have to stay in situations that don't honor all of who you are, you don't have to be exposed to those who disrespect you even though you've been taught that you are to take what you get, because you think you probably deserve it.

No, you are not those circumstances; no, you are not what others have defined as who you are. No, you don't deserve to be treated less than the beloved of God, and no, you are not limited to one room when there is a mansion waiting for you to discover.

Open you up to new vistas, new perspectives, breaking through the limited ways of seeing your life right now and not when you feel you can. That will not happen. I discovered that by taking the long path. Stop walking the way that leads you into more pain, more muggings, more suffering.

I have seen, over the ten years since this book first came out, what an un-boundaried world we live in. It is filled with abundance, with choices, with opportunities, really, with miracles. The catch is you have to be awake to access these in your own life.

You had to go to sleep in order to continue to stay in a relationship of any kind that no longer serves you. You stay in it because: It is safe (though of course it isn't, because you aren't meant to be constrained, constricted, truncated by any situation). It is comfortable (which it isn't, because you are noticing daily a nudge deep within that is calling you to be more than what you are, to be an expanded being, one that is adventurous and truly goes after what you want). It is secure (which it isn't, in truth, because you are always on the edge of running, not away from the relationship as much as toward your true heart's desire. It just seems "silly, stupid, unwise, ridiculous" after all these years – so you stay). It is the right thing to do (which it isn't, because you aren't being true to either one of you; you want out, and if you feel that way, on some level, so does the other person, whether it is an employer or a spouse). It is fine (What is fine? It isn't fine that in the secret place within your heart you dream of a different life, and grand experience, before you die). It is too costly, not in the financial sense alone but in all that you have built in this situation you are in (Costly? What price have you already paid for not having what you truly and deeply want, when are you going to let you have what you have dreamed of, desired and wished for your life?). It is selfish (This is my favorite one, for it reeks of a false righteousness, for who really and fully loses as you stand firm in what a good person you are, except you?). And what I heard the most – I can't do this to the other person (What favor are you pouring onto them by staying due to obligation and loyalty rather than freeing both of you to find the aliveness, the *joie de vivre* that you came into this world to have? It is your birthright as a child of the Most High).

I am clear that it isn't whether you stay or go, whatever kind of relationship you are in at this moment but that you become radically honest with yourself about what you are gaining and what you are losing by your choices. The reason that last rationalization for staying in any relationship is so prevalent is that you, if you are saying it, aren't being honest with yourself or the other person. If "loyalty" is your reason, then be loyal to the innermost part of you and be honest to the other, for that other couldn't want someone who stays, not because of a true desire, but because of a value that has long ago been ripped apart by circumstances that occur when one evolves, expands, allows spirit to enter and take over their lives. A higher value is to honor the calling, the purpose for which you were born and that is always to embrace the most profound you that you are conscious of by taking all of who you are into account. You must not truncate you for a false sense of being that "good person." It won't get you what you want and a relationship of any kind will not flourish with that kind of in-authenticity as its basis. It just won't.

You only have this one, precious life to live, and you are settling for less than you deserve if you don't allow you to have what you know you want. Is it okay with you to deprive you of the richness, the aliveness, the greatness, the splendor and most of all, the fulfillment of your heart's greatest desire?

I am writing this revised edition to urge all of you to look deep within yourselves and to ask your soul – are you living the life that you came into this world to live, not from the outside world's judgments of you or the achievements you've gained through your hard work and years of pushing yourself? I am asking you to ask that essence, that place in you where all wisdom resides, that sanctuary where only you and your soul dwell: am I really honoring who I am by how I am being from the inside out? Is my soul fulfilled by the choices I'm making or is it all about appearances? How is that going to feel in ten years, twenty years when I look at my life and what I have chosen? Who cares then about how loyal I've been, how much I've sacrificed for the sake of "keeping myself out of the fires of Hell?"

Who knows if there is a Hell later; what I know is that you make a hell or a heaven here by the ways you live moment to moment – not by following some external rules but rather by tuning into your soul and letting it be your guide, your ever-present truth-sayer for every step you take, every decision you make and every move you go through as you awaken to all that is possible and has always been possible for you to experience.

It is your life, are you going to live it for others? It is your one life, are you planning to get your reward in heaven or make your heaven on earth by following your heart instead of your head?

It is all up to you. Choose wisely, for your choices make all the difference in whether you live an abundant life or a life filled with an emptiness you can't ever escape.

In ten years, I've seen both, those who decided for their soul's fulfillment and those who chose for their "reward" in the after life. Many show up in my practice with deep sadness, even though they keep reaching for one more achievement in the world. They think they can fulfill themselves, not by going where their heart leads them but rather where their head tells them they need to go.

Chapter One

You're Nobody Till Somebody Loves You

My Story

The seed that is to grow
Must lose itself as seed
And they that creep
May graduate through
Chrysalis to wings
Wilt thou, then,
O mortal,
Cling to husks
Which falsely seem to you
The Self?
– Anonymous

"This is a freeway, Jonathan. Don't stop right here... please!"

I was getting more nauseated by the minute, both from fear and from the frantic stopping and starting.

"Get serious. I'll stop anywhere I want. Stop that controlling stuff, right now! I mean it, you idiot. Don't you know better than to try to do that by now?"

He turned sharply into the next lane, barely missing a moving van. I noticed I was hanging onto the purse in my lap, as if that could assuage the terror I was feeling.

"Quit hurting me, you're slamming me against the head rest with your stops and starts. Just go off the next exit and let me drive. You've had too much to drink."

I'd said it, the one thing I knew would set him into a full-on rage. It had slipped out, I was petrified now.

"Oh, so now you're going to try to tell me I'm drunk. You are just an unbelievable bitch. I should never have taken you on this trip. I won't make that mistake again. And besides, you are going to regret you ever opened your mouth. I'll make sure of that."

I was beyond sick to my stomach now. I was barely sitting up. As soon as he started yelling, it confirmed I'd crossed the line. He just kept piercing me with his knife-like words. I had no defense against what he was saying. He had gone straight into my soul. He might as well have literally cut me deeply. I was certainly bleeding internally with a sense of loss, not just of him, but of my self. I'd given me over long ago and now, the more I was with him, the more it became clear that what I thought was the solution to my having given me up only deepened my loss of me.

You're going to hit that tree, Jonathan. Watch out! What are you doing?"

I ducked, thinking I could save my soul by saving the part of my body getting ready to be hit directly by a tree.

1

"Listen, you sorry substitute for a real woman, get out of the car, just get out! I can't stand to look at you one more second."

Oh my, I thought, *how can I tolerate this pain? It is only getting worse and now he is throwing me out.* I noticed I'd stopped breathing. It seemed safer that way. Just lose consciousness, and then maybe the pain will stop for awhile. It was indescribable, the mass mixture of feelings I was having, mostly terror and enormous pain, invading every cell of my body. I had nothing left of me, just an overwhelming sense of despair. What I had always been able to use was escaping me now – the life-sustaining force of hope. It had pulled me through other less traumatic moments, couldn't it assist me now? I couldn't find it. I was devastated to realize that my arduous but infallible task of finding hope in every situation was failing me now. I couldn't secure a spot in his heart, no matter what I said. He was gone.

"It's dark, Jonathan. I have nowhere to go."

I was raw from hurting so deeply and for so long, not just tonight, but many nights during the past years. It was hopeless, what a concept, me without hope. That had never happened.

"That's not my problem. Just leave. You make me sick. Get the hell out of this car. Now."

This romantic partner was supposed to fill the gaping hole that I had had in my soul for many years. He was to save me from having to face such a vacuous hole. I had counted on it, I had hoped for it, in fact, hope was the most prevalent feeling I had called on over these many years, it was etched into my heart as the one thing I could count on to pull me through anything. It was failing me now. How come?

My story is one of rediscovery. I knew that what I had lost had to be found, but I didn't know where to begin my search. I had given up my precious essence, my soul, so long ago, hoping that I would get love, be loved, feel I was lovable. Now, where was I to begin to learn how to get acquainted with that soul, embrace it and treasure it?

If you find yourself in this same dilemma, I ask that you stay with me through the whole process, every small step of the way, for what I know for certain is that you too will discover what *I* had to open to: that the barren place within me could eventually be a place filled with abundance. It took enormous faith. You must find that faith within you, too, faith that it is possible to regain your own soul and make it the foundational place from which everything else emerges.

Let me start my story at the beginning of this relationship, even though the giving up of my soul to get love began much earlier in my life.

The Role of Perpetual Hope for a Perfect Romance

One Saturday morning, I walked into a conference room where many people had already gathered. I had no idea that my life was about to completely change. I had been hoping for the perfect man, and, if by magic, he appeared. One of my friends had invited me to this seminar, not a seminar I was particularly interested in, but she said that the leader was someone I needed to meet.

He was not someone I had ever heard about, though in my friend's circles, he was quite well-known, popular as a facilitator and one of the top-rated speakers across the country in his field. She knew I liked a certain type of man and she was confident he was going to take my attention away from the content and be totally placed on him.

She was right. I saw him from afar as he walked towards the podium. He stopped to speak with several people and I definitely saw how much others were drawn to him. I must say I was too, though I hadn't heard him say a word. It was immediate, though, the attraction. I felt it throughout my body. I didn't often have much of a reaction to men. In fact, it was rare that I bothered, for most just were not of interest to me. I'd rather read an interesting book than spend an evening with someone who didn't thrill me in some important way.

He did.

As Jonathan began to speak, I felt my heart expanding and my face getting hot. I knew I was turning red and I was afraid others might notice. My heightened state of physical excitement contrasted with a strangely different sensation: a calming sense of relief. I said to Jonathan in my mind: *I've been waiting for you all my life. I just didn't know where you were.* I looked at my friend with a look she immediately responded to, "I knew it! You see now why you had to say yes to my invitation?"

I did find I was surprisingly flustered. The intense and instantaneous impact Jonathan had on me made my mind race with a thousand scenarios. I did not hear a word he said. I was thinking about how I could approach him at the end of the session. *Would he want to meet me?* I asked myself. I was so nervous by the time the seminar ended that I had to rush to the restroom. My anxiety had wreaked havoc on my stomach.

Then my friend said that Jonathan wanted to meet me. Surely she was kidding. That felt too good to be true. I made it back into the conference room just as people were leaving.

Jonathan walked over to me, held out his hand and welcomed me as a visitor. I was certain he held onto my hand longer than someone usually does. Any sign was important to me at this point. My friend made formal introductions and then moved away. *Oh no,* I thought frantically, *She's gone. There's no buffer. It's just he and I now.*

Jonathan and I discussed many areas of the new and controversial perspectives he was bringing into corporations. We talked about his projects, my projects, and some of the ideas I was working on.

On a parallel level, though, the tone of our voices, our eye contact, and our body language were not just intimate, but absolutely steamy. We connected on a primal level. At times I could sense that our eyes conveyed – joy, yes, but recognition, relief and, uncontained flowing emotion.

Jonathan would not be every woman's dream, but he was just right for me. I liked the way he held his body and the way he listened to people when they asked him questions. His sandy-colored hair was perfect. He was neat, but just a tad rumpled – not too put together for me to be drawn to him. The combination of his quiet smile, his confidence, and his rapport with people made him my fantasy man.

As if locked together, Jonathan and I engaged in conversation for almost an hour. Abruptly, a security guard rushed in to tell Jonathan that the corporate jet was waiting. We quickly traded business cards and said we would talk on the phone. He did call and we talked about schedules. It turned out that the next time we could even say hello in person was at an airport as we both came from different speaking engagements. So several days and many daydreams later, I saw him again.

We were both at O'Hare Airport in Chicago trying to get back to the West Coast. Checking in for a Los Angeles flight, I spotted Jonathan. He was about twenty feet away, head to one side, his gaze piercing through me, but in a soft, quizzical way. He walked over to me. "Hey you," he said, "My assistant ticketed me for San Francisco, even though I was supposed to go to L.A." We hugged and chatted. Then he said, "Wait a minute. I'm changing my ticket to your flight right now. How about waiting in this line with me?"

We were inseparable after that flight. I found more and more things that made him the perfect man for me. It was not his looks that captivated me, although I loved the way he looked. It was his heart. There was an innocence, a purity to it, that mesmerized me. How could a man this prominent in his field still have such an exquisite part of him intact, as if he had never been touched deeply by another woman? I intuitively knew he had worn armor, just the way I had, and yet I saw straight through that metal plate over his heart. This incredible man had captured my heart before the flight was over.

As we got to know each other he talked of how different from other women I was, how he could see through my eyes into a soul that yearned to breathe free, to be cared for, to be attended to on every level. How could he know this? He was seeing me as I was simultaneously seeing him, not just the visible aspects, but deeply hidden parts. It was exhilarating.

Jonathan could make me laugh so hard that tears would roll down my cheeks and my stomach would ache. He would make up characters and act them out, using anything handy, such as the hotel curtains, as a prop. Being with Jonathan was joyous, passionate, indescribable to others, and certainly the most fulfilling union I could have imagined.

The first time we spoke of marriage we were sitting on a park bench in a beautiful part of town. The creek was flowing; the trees were sparkling as the wind blew the leaves at exactly the right moments. Jonathan and I had been having a picnic and were lingering over our last glass of champagne. He said "I know we've only been living together for two months, but in my heart I've known you all my life. You finally showed up in person. I thank God for that miracle. I want to know if you would be willing to spend the rest of your life with me as your husband."

I was beyond thrilled. I was ecstatic. I had already found a dress I wanted to wear when we married, but I didn't know he was going to ask me so soon. I guess I thought I was more in love than he was, even though in every way he had shown me he was devoted.

I answered him, "I love you so much. I wish you could feel how I feel as my love overflows towards you. You have no idea how often I envision our lives together forever. You are right. You were shown to me in a dream I once had, but having it become a reality is still more than I can believe at times."

My Wilting Dream

The first time I overheard Jonathan be rude in phone conversations with his office staff, I was astonished. He used such a different tone of voice than I had ever heard. I cringed for them. I couldn't recognize this as being part of my Jonathan. I was sure that he could never talk to me that way, so I made no further attempt in my mind to reconcile this part of him.

Eventually, though, Jonathan's behavior toward me began to change. The first time this happened it was with no warning. He said to me, with tremendous venom in his voice: "You make me sick. Get out of my sight." Startled, I thought, *Could this be Jonathan? How could this be? How could these words come from a man who had just told me how deeply in love he was? He said he'd never experienced such a depth of intimacy. He said I was crucial to his life.* With pain, I remembered witnessing his demeaning treatment of his staff.

I tried to disregard these insulting outbursts and explain them away. Each time I hoped he would never say things like this again. I needed to stay totally convinced that I had a secure place in his heart.

I also began to notice that Jonathan was very unpredictable. Often he was very welcoming of me, other times he dismissed me, as if I weren't someone he liked, much less loved. One evening he and I were at a party. He was talking to a couple who had been to several of his training sessions. He was discussing some of his new material with them when I approached him. At first, he didn't even look in my direction. When he did, he gave me a look that I could not have misinterpreted. His expression screamed, *Go away. You don't belong here.*

His abrupt dishonoring of me cut me more deeply than I imagined it could. I was devastated. I was completely unprepared for this treatment. We had been so close all afternoon – building a fire, talking about future plans, and then reluctantly pulling ourselves away from our bliss to come to this party. What had happened? I was dismayed and humiliated. I said to myself, *I was wrong to have intruded on him.*

I only saw it as my own mistake and so, as I tried to analyze it, I found my head throbbing. I wanted to go away, slip off into the night and disappear. *I really messed up. I should have known not to join him at that moment. Now the whole weekend's ruined. I wish I had brought a separate car, then Jonathan wouldn't have to bother with me.* I kept repeating these damning thoughts, hating myself more and more. I was convinced that somehow I could have prevented this scene.

That pivotal incident was the first major tarnish in the magic luster I had felt since I first met Jonathan. Until that time, even though he was unpredictable, I had always told myself that I was his priority. From that day on, though, I was much more fearfully aware he might unexpectedly explode, triggering those horrible feelings. I wanted to make certain that didn't happen again. I began to become more hyper-vigilant of my behavior, I wasn't as spontaneous as I had been. I didn't know it then, but I was beginning to diminish my light, my own sense of self that was tenuous to begin with. Now, I was beginning to tell I needed to be even more careful, more perfect, more cautious.

There were other seemingly small things that widened this chasm in the blissful nature of the relationship. Although troubling to me, I kept thinking I could keep them from happening by making changes in my behavior. It was up to me. I felt it was all my fault that any of it was happening. And I made up my mind that I was up to the challenge. I believed our love, and especially my hope, would sustain me.

Another rupture in my vision of this perfect match came a month later when I went on a trip with Jonathan. He had to give three training sessions in four days, so I didn't get to see much of him. But I thought he would want to spend his free time with me.

The second day of the trip he said, "You know, I wish you hadn't come along. I need space to relax. Can't you lose yourself somewhere? I can't unwind looking at your face. Maybe later I can stand having you around. Just get lost."

His jarring words pierced me to the marrow, leaving me feeling like a heap of fragmented bones, shattered by his words that fractured what I was trying my best to keep as a perfect world for us. Again I started digging that hole in my soul. I blamed myself, thinking, *I'm too demanding, and I have nothing to offer. I can see why he's sick of me. How could he stand me?* I paused, searching inside myself to reignite my spark of hope. I had to keep hoping that I could change enough to make the relationship blissful again.

Even after several more incidents, I was still blind to the way I was repeatedly re-injuring myself. I experienced many humiliating scenes with Jonathan which prompted more inner dialogue about how much I hated who I was. This hatred was then reinforced by the desecrating remarks Jonathan made. Jonathan was actually echoing words I had already uttered to myself. All that did was increase my self-hate and dig a deeper hole in my soul.

My Life-Altering Moment

My hand gripped the door knob, just as I was about to leave for a conference. I tried to fight off the chilling effect of my inner thoughts. Eventually nausea swept over me. I kept repeating, *This can't be. I want to be dreaming. I can't believe I have done this to myself. How could I have missed what was happening?* Soon I was shaking with sobs.

My relationship for the past two years had satisfied deep longings. I had searched hard for years to find ways to fill these. I just knew I'd found the perfect answer. I had had a gaping soul need that was finally being met by a man. He knew instinctively just how much I needed him, when to supply my needs and how to keep me captivated by controlling the amount of soul-giving nourishment he provided.

I would reach a point of enormous emptiness and like magic he was there to provide the sustenance I thought I had to have. His ability to keep me on edge and poised to please him was uncanny. I am not proud of how needful I was of his physical, emotional, and intellectual attention. In fact, I am humiliated to make public that he became virtually indispensable to my sense of being. I had never experienced anything close to the intensity of this need.

These feelings were validated and reinforced by the satisfaction that our closeness brought. In this relationship I thought I had at last found everything I wanted. I felt special, precious, completely embraced beyond my imagination. We had a strong bond between us. It was the first time in my life I had experienced a relationship so satisfying. I was confident that my soul would become whole in this relationship.

But the day before, I had unexpectedly had a life-altering awareness. It was the first day of spring. I listened to the last patient of the day describe an extremely painful interaction with her husband. As she spoke, the struggles of so many other patients came to mind. No matter what I might have done, I could never have been prepared for what she said next:

"I feel as if I'm not here – even as I'm talking to you. It seems as if I've vanished. I can't feel my self, my Spirit, my soul. I can't trust my feelings. I don't know how to think anymore. Some days I try to distract myself by keeping busy. Other times, I feel as if I don't even exist."

I gasped, almost audibly. Her plight was not extremely different from that of other patients, but I was astonished that she used words almost identical to the ones I had come close to forming about myself. Until now I had closed them out before they rose to full consciousness. Now I found it difficult to continue focusing on what she was uttering between her sobs. I was consumed in that moment by her revelation and my pain. I could no longer dodge what I intuitively knew about myself.

Now as I was recovering from my sobs, I realized just how damaged I felt. I feared I could never love again. Jonathan had taken my soul, my being, my essence. I felt depleted and robbed, I pinched myself to see if I actually existed. And I didn't even care.

I continued to suffer for a long time. I felt stripped of my honor, torn from my being. Yet I resisted fully acknowledging the unacknowledged. I had not yet named the immense pain I was in.

Finally I decided to call my unnamed horror "soul mugging." It began when I started robbing my soul of its essential truths.

As I gained insight, I knew I had turned over to others the final say about who I was long before I met Jonathan, and I had continued to do that in my relationship with him. My soul had thus been deprived of its own unique journey, as well as its resilient strength and its innate richness.

My Mirage of Hope

I had hoped that my relationship with Jonathan would be fulfilling if I just loved him enough. Yet the gaping hole in my soul was made wider and deeper as I relied on hope. While I thought hope was saving me, it was actually killing me. I was falling deeper into this hole as I simultaneously expected to be climbing out of it. This was a strange contradiction for me to experience.

Hope imprisoned me by giving me the false expectation that Jonathan's love could make me whole. It actually made a hole so deep it was nearly impossible to get out of. My hoping for the best created a chasm in my soul, robbing me of my essential self. Now with the full impact of what I had done with my soul, I was horrified and thrown into despair. I felt there was no way out of my tightly wound web. I needed the reassurance of Jonathan's love and attention all the more. I held onto the hope that by fixing myself I would somehow get just his love and not his scorn. In this way, hope helped me to spin the tight web in which I had become trapped. I could not find my way out. Hope deceived me as I pursued the false vision of a different tomorrow. There was a profound void within my self which was getting wider and deeper every day. I was using hope to deepen this void, and my inappropriate use of hope was making it more difficult to find my way out.

I also felt desperate. I increasingly relied on the hope that I would never have to feel humiliation and self-hatred again. I believed I was responsible for making sure I did everything possible to keep things loving between Jonathan and me, no matter what it took. Unfortunately, it took giving up valuable parts of myself, in fact, losing my soul to do so.

While I continued to fortify myself with hope, I could not start restoring the hole in my soul. I also could not stop the rampant damage I was exposing myself to. Through hope I lived a lie, and I paid heavily for it.

I mistakenly believed that if I stood by my man during difficult times and loved him enough, we could ride out any storm. I hoped he would feel so full, complete, secure and strong in my love that we would triumph over even the most challenging times in our relationship. I hoped for the best. Hope had been my friend and had sustained me through difficult times since childhood. Hope had been there when all else failed. I had no understanding, consciously, that by hoping to fill my void with a man's love and attention, I was actually increasing the void. Unknowingly, I was killing my soul. It was anguishing. I felt:

Haunting blankness ... vast absence ... eerie stillness ... infinite blackness ... blinding whiteness ... sterile void ... un-positioned ... unlinked ... unnamed ... soulless. An enormous hole in my soul was preventing my wholeness.

Hope had completely let me down. I was left with no road map to follow. I was compelled to write this book for you who are suffering, too. I know your blackness, your torment and your need for a guide to find your way out.

The Way Soul Mugging Developed

I made up a phrase to convey how it felt when Jonathan defiled my essence. I decided to call this behavior soul mugging, because it affected me exactly that way. If I had named it verbal abuse it would not have let you know, and much more to the point, given you a phrase to use for yourself in stating exactly how it felt to you and how it felt to me to receive these dismissive, disrespectful, devaluing comments and behavior from another person. Verbal abuse also doesn't connote that this pattern takes place within oneself way before you get into a relationship with another. I use the phrase soul mugging to mean a profound spiritual and psychic trauma in the critical life core of my existence. For me, and most often for all others, it is a lifelong pattern which I now know I unknowingly perpetuated through my interactions with Jonathan. I see now how soul mugging distorts reality. Even simple actions on my behalf became incomprehensible. Soul mugging entrapped me and held me captive, creating devastating, ongoing suffering.

How, you might ask, could a smart, attractive, highly successful woman have missed recognizing this downward spiraling? After all, I had had other intense, meaningful relationships in my life. Why was something so terribly wrong now? Only after fully committing to working through changes in my self and by more completely understanding the dynamics of a soul-mugging relationship could I make sense of it all. I eventually understood that two main factors create a fertile environment in which soul mugging can take place.

The first factor was my particular vulnerability due to conclusions I formed at an early age such as needing another person to tell me I was valuable. One of the most devastating characteristics of this was my willingness to relinquish the most sacred part of me, my soul – a part I had not yet fully developed and did not fully own or value. Jonathan's particular lifelong configuration of characteristics likewise contributed to his being drawn into a relationship with me. Some of these included his never having had an intimate relationship like we were developing, he kept saying, and his desire to be cared for, listened to and attended to in ways, even as a child, he'd not experienced. Jonathan was the oldest of three siblings and had to be the caretaker throughout his childhood, so my wanting to focus on his every desire was very appealing to him.

The second factor is that, together in our relationship, with our particular backgrounds and needs, we were mutually pulled into an intricate pattern of interactions and behaviors. The distinct qualities we brought to our romantic relationship fostered the circumstances for soul mugging to develop. Moreover, Jonathan completely captivated me.

You might also ask why would I put up with, much less explain away, his desecrating insults and demeaning behavior? Because, despite my achievements and success, I felt I had no value as a person. From childhood, I believed I lacked something basic and crucial. Without my father's approval, nothing I did mattered. I perceived that if I didn't exist for him, then I didn't exist for myself either. From very early in my life I was starving for his love.

As in many traditional families where the father is the head of the household, my father was the one to please. Validation came from him. Mother seemed not to have a voice of her own. She likewise looked to my father for approval.

I was constantly seeking my father's recognition and approval. I didn't know at the time that no person could ever fill my huge need. I just kept trying and the void kept growing bigger by the day. I could not let myself acknowledge how large this void had become or that my every action was guided by trying to fill it. I believed it could be satisfied only by my father, who I perceived was emotionally unavailable to me. Since he was always at work, I concluded that he didn't value me enough to give me his time.

I despaired of ever finding enough to offer him. Each day when he returned home from work I waited to get even a moment of attention. Sometimes I got fussed at: "What are you doing? I'm tired." I never went anywhere else for attention. He was it. And he was not giving it to me. I made gifts for him, especially at Christmas. Each year I hoped that this time I would receive my much needed attention and nourishment. Nope. Not ever. I remember Christmas afternoons as the saddest times of my childhood.

I believed I had to be perfect or I had no chance at love. I continued on a deep level to feel that I had no inherent value. Indeed, I became not a person, but merely a reactor to my environment. I competed fiercely with my sister, who always seemed to have my father's favor. If I could surpass her achievements some of the time, this was my best hope to get the love I yearned for.

As a child I remember thinking, *I hope today will be different. I only want to be loved. Why doesn't anyone care that I have to kill what's inside of me to get any of what I want? I must try harder to fit in, to please, and to become as invisible as possible.*

It seemed that in my adult life, I had sought out a man like my father. Jonathan displayed certain behaviors that reminded me of my father. One particularly devastating scene with Jonathan occurred one evening after he had returned from a business trip. He came into the house without speaking a word to me. He seemed not to notice that I had a candlelight dinner on the table. Within minutes, he walked through the kitchen saying in an angry tone: "Why have you done all this? I thought we would just go down to the local place and eat something light tonight. I'm exhausted, it's late and you don't seem to remember that at those times eating a meal like this is the last thing I want to do. Never mind, I'll just go down there by myself and take some of my work with me. I need to catch up on the stacks of stuff that pile up when I'm gone. I'll see you later."

I am of no value to him, I thought, and that is killing me inside. I do things to create a sense of importance in his life and he gets mad. I am of no use. I hate how I feel, and I hate even more what I have become: a nothing. I went to bed and cried into the pillow for what seemed like hours. I had finally just fallen asleep when Jonathan returned, not to the bed, but to the sofa to do more work. I heard the front door open and then lights go on in the living room. I wished I could just die.

Of what use am I alive? I felt I was of no use to my father, and now I'm certainly of no use to Jonathan. The thought was too much to take in. My head hurt terribly. I could not keep feeling. I wanted numbness. Finally, I made myself get up and take some aspirin for my headache. As I lay back down, I knew I would not sleep. I never could turn my thoughts off long enough to get any peace.

I was at a loss, done in by my own behavior, trapped by my own self-defeating ways. I had no idea that there might be options. When I was young, I never blamed my father. I blamed myself for not being lovable enough to deserve his time. Nothing I did seemed to make a difference. Now with Jonathan I was doing the same thing – blaming myself. I just kept digging a deeper and deeper hole in my soul, starving myself to death for love that was not forthcoming. My goal to be loved was thwarted over and over. In addition, hope was etching more deeply than ever the hole in my soul.

I increasingly reverted back to what I was taught early in life. I learned not to trust my own perceptions of things such as anger on a parent's face or a strident tone in their voices. I gradually filtered these important signals out of my conscious awareness. They only created problems.

Thus I placed a blindfold over my eyes and made a binding decision that I was not to understand things either literally or intuitively. So, I began then to mug my soul whenever I thought I saw something. "Be quiet," I said to my soul. "Don't you dare see that; it will only get you in trouble. Make up something else. It is about your problem with life, with people, with isolation, anything, but don't believe what is in front of you."

I also tried to stop knowing. Each time I did confirm something, I would mug my soul for seeing such a prohibited truth. "Stop it now," I told my soul. "Don't you know the rules? The rules are not to see, so stop perceiving anything you instinctively, intuitively might know." I severed my connection with my intuition, stopped reading meaning into subtle expressions and signs of annoyance. I stopped because I was punished or at least contradicted if I called things the way I saw them. I did my best to shut my inner self down.

It was then that I became a victim of my own denial. I was very young. And I was forever after that denying what I knew. I would say to myself that I was wrong or that I was to blame if things didn't turn out right, so I needed to change in some way. Then I would see things differently. I literally gave up my own judgment, intuition and sense of being attuned to the way I experienced and observed things.

Closely related to my lack of self-trust was my inability to express my feelings and knowledge by speaking them aloud. I was prohibited from saying what I thought.

"You are so angry, aren't you?" I said to my father one morning at breakfast.

"What are you talking about?" he said sternly. "I am busy reading a report for work. Just eat your cereal and don't bother me again."

Many other times I would report on what I was noticing and end up feeling ostracized, ridiculed, criticized, and punished. I was told to shut up, so I shut down inside.

More and more I borrowed others' perceptions to replace my sense of what was happening around me. It was much safer that way. I buried my feelings and my perceptions. And just as damaging, I buried my own voice. I thought my puppet-like behavior would give me the greatest possibility of being loved. *What can I say that won't cause me any more humiliation?* I thought.

In another incident from childhood I made the decision to agree with their assessment of my education, even though I wanted so much to go to a regular school. "I'll go wherever you think is best," I said, trying not to show my sadness at giving up my greatest desire – to be at a school that had boys and football and cheerleaders and, well, normal stuff.

It was okay that it was not my own perspective, my own internal wise advisor. This way, at least, I had the potential of receiving caring attention rather than punishing words. I just had to be careful about what I could safely know and say. I didn't realize it at the time, but I was being forced out of the development of my precious, flourishing self.

Unfortunately, the constant suppression of my reactions and feelings created a reservoir of unprocessed expression. I felt so sad all the time, as if I were carrying a heavy load everywhere I went. And I was. I was burdened with all those unloved parts of me. My body was numb, my heart deprived of love. I felt useless. All of these feelings were stuck deep within. I was bogged down with lots of misery, deprivation and this heavy burden.

Rather than relying on my intuition, I learned to filter the world through others' eyes. I continued to mug my soul any time my self tried to perceive things on its own.

I failed to realize that my soul was dying, deprived of the nurturing it needed for its development. I was mugging my soul to protect myself. I had to have love, even if it meant beating up my soul to get it or even just the prospect of it.

Hope eventually did me in by sealing the fortress made by my own denial. My shield of denial was impenetrable, made of creative intellectualizing and long steeled control over my spirit and emotions. Hope had made my denial bulletproof. I hoped that what I had done to get love, nurturing and approval would work. I became trapped by what I had learned and taught myself so well. Denial was my dark ally.

I was a woman with parts missing. Lacking clear eyes to see the truth and an audible voice to speak it, I entered into this incredible relationship with Jonathan – one I thought occurred only in romance novels. I certainly did not realize that I was in denial and constantly leaning on hope.

There were whole aspects of the relationship that I not only missed, but lacked a voice with which to speak about. Entrenched in denial, I did not even let myself see the major risks I had taken by saying "Yes, I'll marry you," to a man I had known for only a few months. I am not proud to say that I was desperately responsive to the great amount of attention and endearments from a man who nourished the most neglected aspects of my self. Allowing another person to meet these needs, if only occasionally and unpredictably, I now realize was digging an even deeper hole in my soul.

Snapshots of My Soul-mugging relationship

There are several incidents which illustrate the consequences of my soul mugging as it carried forward into my adult life and this relationship. My soul mugging started early in my life due to my unwillingness to claim my own perceptions and inner knowledge. I beat down my inner messages; I mugged them. I adopted the views of others as more real than my own. My inner image was formed by my sense of what others thought of me. I was totally dependent on approval from others and highly susceptible to being defined by them. I was still a victim of my own denial, denial of my perceptions and denial of my responsibility to restore my own soul.

As I recount these incidents, pay attention to what you notice about your own relationship. Ask yourself the following questions:

   • Are these experiences similar to my own?

   • How have I defiled my own soul?

   • What am I denying in my relationship?

His Public Arena, My Private Hell

"You were so humorous," someone said to Jonathan at a dinner where he was the keynote speaker.

"You gave us so much to think about," exclaimed another.

"You had me in the palm of your hand from the start. You seemed to be speaking just to me," one gushed.

Jonathan was very successful. He was engaging, brilliant, well-read, and had advanced degrees. He was also charming and witty to everyone we met.

I found it extremely difficult to imagine that a man so intelligent, so highly regarded by his audiences, could be insulting and distant when he was out of public view. The pictures didn't match, and I could not make sense of the discrepancy. Therefore, I just made up an excuse inside my head any time his behavior shifted. I overlooked the discrepancies between the public and private sides of Jonathan. This was part of my continuing denial.

Actually, I felt at Jonathan's mercy. I was totally in love with him. For the first time in my life, I had given tremendous power to a man. I had given him my whole being and certainly assumed he had given me the same.

When Jonathan and I eventually went back to our hotel room, he was sullen and quiet. All the exuberance he had exhibited moments earlier had vanished.

"What's going on?" I asked him. "You seem so silent all of a sudden."

I worked very hard to sound matter-of-fact. In truth, every muscle in my shoulders and neck was constricting as I spoke. It was like someone was turning a knob inside my upper back, tightening every part of the area simultaneously.

"Look, I'm not about to be interrogated. Don't you dare start in on me with those damn questions. You're no lawyer," he shouted as he moved to the far side of the hotel room. He gave me one of his go-to-hell looks as the bed, the two chairs and a table stood witness to this outburst between us.

The intensity of Jonathan's response startled me into complete silence. I now felt as if a knife had been thrust between my shoulder blades. I even imagined I would have to maneuver my body extremely carefully so as not to disturb that blade and cause more pain.

This was not the first time Jonathan had gone from being quite charming to rageful. One minute he was extremely cordial with his public and the next, intensely explosive with me.

What did I do? I said to myself. It must have been horrible.

I felt like crying. I felt like running. Instead, I just sat there on the side of the bed in the hotel room, still as far away from each other as he had placed us. I stared at a painting above the table in the opposite corner of the room. I was definitely trying not to think, not to feel.

"Just shut up and leave me alone. And by the way, get your fat ass out of my sight. I don't even want to look at you."

He was screaming again as he moved onto the other side of the king-size bed from me. He shut off the light and turned his back completely away from me.

My God, I thought, *could something I said to that couple who joined us before dinner have offended Jonathan?*

Tears were pouring out of my eyes now, and I could not have stopped them.

What about that woman who said something as we were leaving? I wondered silently. Did I sigh or roll my eyes? I don't remember doing anything that he could have misinterpreted.

I got up and stumbled into the bathroom, shutting the door. I wanted to lock it as a way of locking out the incident from my memory.

Instead, I reran the entire evening as if watching a movie in slow motion, thinking *I must find out what I did.*

After an hour and a half, I tiptoed back into the bedroom. I carefully climbed into "my side" of what seemed like an oversized bed. I prayed he'd wake up just enough to hold me tight. I needed the tranquilizer of his closeness so that my body could let go. He held my being already, I just wanted literal confirmation that I still existed.

Had something I didn't even realize that I did robbed me of his tenderness, his love? I never found out. He never even turned my way. I know for sure because I never could get my swollen eyes to shut. In the morning he finally spoke.

"You ruined my evening. I'll bet you're glad of that."

The words stunned me. There had been so much complete silence. Now, though, we were in an airport shuttle with eleven other people. I had no resistance left to defend myself against the piercing statement. *I must stay still and mute.* I repeated these words to myself as if they were a mantra. The closer we got to the airport, the more my body reacted as if I'd been in a car accident. I imagined as I sat beside him that I had actually been thrust out of my seat and slammed against the door of the shuttle.

I ached all over. I had no energy to respond to anything. I also knew better. *Why can't I speak up? Where is my voice?* I pondered this thought only for a second. I was in too much pain already to begin confronting myself with such ideas. *How ridiculous anyway. What do I think? I'm going to leave or even make a plan? I am in this relationship to stay. He and I are intertwined to the very depths of our existence. That's the end of that story."*

I must say I did feel acute pangs of desperation in my chest. Even then, I was barely aware of the tension from glimpsing what I had become: a vanishing soul.

Ask Yourself

Does the above scenario sound familiar to you? The person you have been involved with may not have these same qualities of charm, wit, and speaking ability. Yet, there is something about the way a particular relationship in your life intrigues you and draws you towards him or her. Contemplate what those special qualities are. Do you ever go over an incident, wondering what you have done? Do you question every behavior you have had through the day when you get a sudden burst of anger from the other person? In what specific ways do you think you give up your vision and lose your voice? Is it when you feel threatened about the relationship changing in some way? Do you review past incidents for which you got blamed and then bring those accusations back to mind to see if you might have repeated any this time? Do you ever silently agree with this person's targeting of you as the cause of his or her outbursts? Do you ever think you just may have been mugging your own soul long before this person entered your life?

From My Perspective

Jonathan's qualities placed me in a huge quandary. From my point of view at this point, I did not realize this man was defiling my soul. Rather, I wondered what I had done to make him act this way toward me. It made my heart hurt to even contemplate questions about our relationship.

I saw Jonathan primarily as a person who could move straight into my mugged soul. More often than not, he sent marvelous acclamations to this deeply wounded part of me. It was extremely important that I continue to receive this balm, this healing potion for my soul. I was willing to overlook negative tones of voice, harsh, demeaning words and looks of contempt. I was a victim of my own denial. I couldn't see that what he was doing was unacceptable and certainly never suspected that he was reinforcing what I had already been doing for many years.

I was focused on receiving the soul affirmation I had been aching to receive for so long. I played out this scenario day after day, hoping to get this nourishment. I didn't pay attention to the times that he was being demeaning. I only said to myself, *What do I need to do to keep him from becoming cruel to me?*

In my mind I was confident I could prevent his demeaning behavior toward me by changing how I acted. I didn't know any better. I was doing all that I could to keep the sought-after words and behaviors coming to me. Only now do I recognize what I was doing. I held onto this relationship any way I could, hoping that it could restore my soul, which had been beaten for so many years.

After the relationship ended, I finally realized that I had been allowing the soul mugging so that I might get what I thought I had to have. I am embarrassed to admit this because I am seen as a person who can take care of herself very well, and in fact I do. In reality, I think that was part of the problem. I was too good at hiding, even from myself, what I really needed. I had closed down that part of me very early in my life. My soul had been neglected way before Jonathan entered the picture. Eventually, my soul was far too empty to be easily satisfied. I had let too many years go by without focusing at all on what I needed in terms of love and nurturing. Finally, I got to the point that my soul rebelled and said, in a sense, I'll take anything as long as you let me have some of what I want.

In my romantic relationship I let myself be mugged. I am responsible for the time I spent in the relationship. At that point, of course, I believed that I couldn't leave it. I can say now that I built my own prison, then lived in it. He was merely repeating words I'd said to my-self many times before. That's why the impact was not penetrating me. I denied the damage to myself, and I denied the impact of his behavior on me.

I kept in mind that I was now living with this man who was continuing to pour accolades on me, saying he would stay with me, have faith in me, and give me all I could ever need emotionally. He said he would be there for me, and that we would be there for each other. It sounded so perfect to me after all the barren times I had experienced throughout my life.

For the first time, I was perfect to someone. If I was not perfect at certain times in his eyes, then I was sure I had done something wrong, and it was up to me to fix it. I had to be the perfect one. I believed I had enough power to fix any imperfection, to make things great. At least I hoped so. So I stayed in the situation, attempting to get my soul needs met by this man.

At the time, I was truly a victim of my own denial, a trap that I had structured over many years. I was mugging my own soul, and in my lover I had found a convenient agent to continue the mugging. He was just the right one because he was also the one who was putting the healing balm on the previous mugging wounds that I had inflicted upon myself. It was an intricate set-up and lethal for a soul that had been through so much, but I was caught in it and blinded to it.

It's as If I Were Invisible

Then there was the incident during our first holiday weekend together. We had been living together for three months. Jonathan and I went to a party where several women were flagrantly flirting with him. As soon as we arrived, a woman came over to him, kissed him and began hanging on to him as if she had done so before.

This feels awful, I thought. *I can't believe this woman is acting as if I'm not here.*

Though I tried to ignore how that felt, my stomach was getting tighter; my body was giving me away to myself. I attempted, without success, to distract myself by moving into a different room with another group of people.

Then Jonathan entered the room where I had just gone to escape. A second woman stepped in front of him and reached out her arms.

"You aren't going to let me kiss you? Why not? You have before. When we were on the boat, you sure were more responsive, Jonathan."

The gap between the frivolity of this dialogue and my internal turmoil was widening by the second. The pain I felt was prolonged by my unwillingness to speak. I had long ago given up that voice. Besides, I might give my anguish away to strangers, and I had much too much pride to reveal that kind of pain to anyone, even to myself most of the time.

No one seemed to notice I was even present. How ironic I thought it was that I who was radiating immense hurt from every pore was invisible.

The agony was a poignant reminder that I was witnessing one more in a series of desecrating acts to my soul. Yes, the mugging of my soul began way before this man, and I was continuing it by my denial, my silence, and my unwillingness to take in and process what I saw. I didn't want to see. I definitely didn't want to acknowledge what I might be seeing. Unacknowledged pain didn't seem at the time as agonizing as facing the pain straight on. My soul may have been crying out to be rescued from distress, but I was most aware of my huge need to make it all turn out okay. I desperately wanted this relationship. I felt I had to have this man. My self depended on it.

What did it matter that my soul once more was being negated by my allowing this scene to continue? It had certainly been mugged at my own hands numerous times before. I was not aware of how imprisoned I was by not wanting to mar the foundation I had laid to support my love. The aching now ran across my whole being. My body was betraying the denial system I had so carefully built over the years. I wanted to find something to distract me from this agonizing situation.

Instead, I saw Jonathan coming towards me.

"Jonathan, could I please speak with you in the hallway for a moment?"

"Listen, Lucy, you are a jealous, unreasonable bitch. You're embarrassing me in front of my friends. Get with it. Furthermore, I am sick and tired of your behavior around my friends. You get quiet and everyone notices. In fact, they think you're a snob. Why can't you just enjoy yourself? Get over it now, damn it. I mean it."

I felt as if I were five years old. I couldn't understand why I was being scolded. Why did everything seem to fade into the distance, to go out of focus? My sight blurred as it usually did when I didn't want to see what I saw. It cost too much to see. I'd found that out when I was very young.

I felt seasick on dry ground. All I wanted was to disappear without a trace. *Please God, let me die.*

"You are such a baby. I can't take you anywhere. You just can't have fun. I can't believe you are such an abominable asshole. I never should have invited you. You don't deserve to go with me."

My soul was being assaulted. I had negated it. He was just continuing that negation now.

This desecration was causing my soul to feel as if it were bursting. I was also desperately clinging to the notion that I must have this man, this love of my life. He was my life, my bridge to all the nourishment I had ever hoped for since I had been a small child. I did finally speak up, even though my voice was more tentative than confrontational.

"What were those women talking about when they referred to your letting them hug and kiss you more at other times, Jonathan?"

"I don't know what you're talking about. You get so paranoid around other women. I just can't take you around my friends anymore. I see that. I didn't do or say anything that borders on being unusual, so just shut up. Go to hell. In fact, I can't wait to get back so I can leave you."

I quickly began to remember a loving scene. I had to convince myself that this was not real. I went straight back into my denial so that I could keep this system in place. I said to myself over and over that he was not leaving. He couldn't leave. I felt I could not exist without him. The deepest part of me sobbed uncontrollably at the thought.

Ask Yourself

Have you ever experienced similar scenes in your relationship? Do you ever receive threats to or attacks on your soul? Do you then deny that the event had an impact on you? Does it seem familiar to ways you have mugged your own soul, even before you had a partner?

From My Perspective

I did not stay in this relationship for years. I stayed in it a day at a time. I was completely convinced that the salve for my soul was available; I only had to figure out how to behave so that the mugging would stop. Part of the healing process was to reclaim and nurture the parts of myself that were missing due to the damage I had sustained as a child. I had to begin to acknowledge what I saw, to own my own perceptions, to begin to move out of my denial. It was not easy at all. When I first began that process, I thought I was going to be extinguished. I was already negating my soul, but instead of seeing this process as a way to heal the soul, I felt the process as one of further danger.

I often trembled as I acknowledged what I saw with my own eyes. I began to quiver as I would finally start to give in to what I wanted so badly to say. Starting to own again those missing parts of myself was a painful experience. I was not going in a straight path either. I would easily slip back into the denial and begin to allow my own perceptions to take a back seat to what I preferred to see. And what I didn't want to give voice to, I didn't.

It is important to remember that the healing process takes a long time. I do not want to give the impression that once I became aware of the problem, I simply corrected it. The trap I had developed over a long time came back even though I had gained some understanding.

I thought that once I began to own my own denial, then the problem would go away and never come back. It definitely came back again – the justifications, the rationalizations, the excuses, not just about what some person was doing to me, but what I was doing to myself with my own denial.

A Desperate Grasp for Hope

"Jonathan, I just got an extremely upsetting phone call. An anonymous one. She said I had better go get a blood test because you have been sleeping with several women. Have you been with anyone else sexually?"

Three hours after receiving this message, I was still shaking. I had not been able to eat. I thought I was going to throw up. I wanted to. Maybe then I could expel all the horror, the anguish, the desperation, the disgust, and the extreme violation I felt.

I had picked up this terrifying voice mail message at noon. I immediately began paging Jonathan. I raced from public phone to public phone, attempting to find one that allowed incoming calls. I was a wild, wounded animal, barely able to execute the task. But huge doses of adrenaline spurred me on. My mind was frozen on a single thought: *He will make sense of this.* Though my body was attempting to lessen the pain it felt, I was shattered.

"What would ever give you that idea? Do you believe everything you hear?"

His inauthentic tone and unwavering calm gave him away. I panicked. This time he couldn't alter the piercing words that had reached my heart. But I didn't let myself dwell on this thought for longer than a second.

"How come you didn't tell me?"

Now I felt empty. My body was only an image to me. Fully into my denial again, I had left it. It certainly wasn't serving me to stick around at this point. My body was betraying my intricate system of denial by telling me the truth. The pain was greater than my capacity to contain it. I had lost the battle. All that I had dreamed of, hoped for, was falling to the ground in total disarray.

"I just didn't want to tell you. I thought you would not go to bed with me if I did."

Jonathan was changing his answer. I saw the phenomenon. I could not jar myself into awareness, though. I kept probing for a response I could stand to hear.

Please, I pleaded silently, *Make it all right for me. Pour that salve onto my soul. It needs you so badly.*

I heard myself beginning to speak aloud again.

"Why did you lie to me about sleeping with other women? I have a right to know; it's my body that's in jeopardy here."

I knew I was clutching at straws. I searched for reassurance that could not come.

"Those women didn't matter enough to tell you about. Only you matter. You're the only one I love. I've never loved anyone but you. And it just never seemed like the right time to mention it."

His proclamation that I was extremely important to him mended my soul enough to stop the physical pain. I was wanted. I was loved. The mugging I was so familiar with had been assuaged by his affirmation of love. I was beginning to feel safe again, my denial back in place. But the denial that I thought was saving me was actually killing me. Hope had deceived me into thinking I was now going to get the love I had been longing for.

Ask Yourself

Have you talked yourself into believing explanations that you can't reconcile rationally? Have you let certain excuses bring you back into your relationship fully? Do you recognize that by continuing this behavior you are continuing a lifelong pattern of denial? Have you made it a top priority to love this person, thinking that was what would keep your soul filled with love, safe from the mugging that began way before your partner entered the picture? Has the necessity to have the love of another person ever stopped the violation of your essence?

From My Perspective

By allowing myself to believe such excuses, I was mugging my own soul. Though I appeared to be a victim of my surroundings, I was actually the victim of my own inadequacies. I was victimizing my own soul by believing Jonathan's explanations.

I agreed with what he said because I had shut off my own perceptions and inner knowing. Through my relationship with Jonathan I continued to negate my soul. I did not understand that I was already doing this to myself. It was indescribably painful to mug my soul as I did and then to continue to have it mugged by my lover.

Even more painful, however, was facing and attempting to stop what I had been doing to myself for so long. It was familiar and therefore "safe" just to go on and wait for those wonderful moments of ecstasy while enduring the rejection, the insults and the defiling behavior. I was much more familiar with not seeing than with seeing, with not speaking than with speaking.

The first times I saw, and the first words I did speak were faltering, tentative and often taken back when they weren't well received. However, once I was awakened to the fact that I was ignoring major signals, I could no longer make the old behavior work as well as it had.

The Impossible Occurred

In the ladies' room of a church I had never been in before, someone called my name. I turned in the direction of her voice. I thought that she must be someone who recognized me from one of my weekly television shows.

"I know that you and Jonathan have been in a very serious relationship for nearly two years," she began. "Well, he and I have been intensely involved for several months now."

Oh, my God, I thought. *He and I have been talking about marriage.*

The room seemed to start spinning. This room we were in suddenly felt much too small. I was smothering, afraid even to take in air. It seemed like hours before I finally stammered:

"I think we have to talk."

As she nodded, I rushed out of the ladies' room, wishing I could run from what I knew was coming. I had had enough pain. We headed towards an empty parlor. She settled into the corner of a couch. I turned to face her, perching on the extreme edge of the same couch, but at the other end. I was cold and shaking.

"My relationship with Jonathan has gone on now for almost three months," she announced.

"Wwwwhaaat?" was all I could say. My voice would not utter any more words.

"But Jonathan and I have been talking about marriage… "

I just couldn't continue.

"Really? Jonathan has talked about marriage to me."

I could make no sense of her self-assured response. I had to divert my eyes from her to lessen the pain. I began to focus on the ficus plant in the corner of the room as she continued:

"He told me that he has never loved anyone but me."

I could feel my energy draining away. Jonathan had said these very words to me. I had comforted myself many times by saying, "At least I know I'm the only woman he's ever loved." Now she was claiming proprietorship of my relationship.

I perceived no emotion in her statements to me, a major contrast to the slash those same words created at my core. Everything about life, love, sacred trust, commitment, loyalty, vulnerability, relationship lay before me like a stack of dead bodies piled in a heap. The foundation of my beliefs in one horrible moment turned to shifting sand. My heart had just been torn out of me and thrown at the wall behind that plant I'd used to numb my pain moments earlier. I could even imagine the stains being left as a reminder of a moment I never ever wanted to remember.

I was robot-like as I sat there unable to speak, think, move, act, feel. I could no longer be in any denial. My heart may have kept on beating but I was most aware of a deep sense of death: death of my soul, death of my spirit, death of what for two years I had called my world. I didn't just give my love to this man, I gave him my whole being. I was utterly empty, an unoccupied being trying to stay upright. In this unfurnished existence, my perfectly good brain could do nothing.

20

It was a soul-destroying experience. I felt extremely nauseated. I prayed my unstable legs would carry me to the ladies' room.

Central to my pain was not his involvement with her. It was the crumbling foundation of my beliefs, my values, my denial system, my hope. Everything I had thought was my life had truly just died.

Late that night, unable to sleep, I muttered, "I must make a radical shift now. I have no choice. I've got to retrieve my soul."

I startled myself by speaking these words aloud at three o'clock that Monday morning after the previous day's death experience. I sat on the couch trembling. No one was in the house. Jonathan had left the preceding Wednesday for a business trip. There was no one whose comfort I could seek. There was nowhere to go, nowhere to run.

That one critical chance meeting at the church extinguished my life. I had so longed for this relationship. I had been faithful to it every living hour. I had hoped it could carry me through my remaining years. It was the only banner I had never lowered, no matter what had gone on between us. I never even considered I could betray the relationship by ending it as long as I was still breathing.

At that early morning moment I connected, on some deep level, with what I had come close to permitting in my life. In a flash, I saw what my life had become. I was simultaneously astonished and repulsed. I had all but killed my soul trying to get my body to be loved. I had done it before Jonathan, and I had done it with him. I had literally gotten to the point where I would do anything – beg, plead, promise things, allow continued mugging – just to have this particular person who could soothe that soul at times. At other times he would remark, yell, or shout:

"You are such a shit."

"You ugly bitch!"

"You're not worth my time."

"You'll never amount to anything."

These horrible slurs were juxtaposed with tremendously endearing statements:

"You're the only woman I've ever loved."

"I treasure you with all my heart."

"You have all the qualities a man could ever want."

"I just want you for my wife. You'll be even more beautiful when you're ninety years old."

Ask Yourself

Do any of these remarks sound like comments you've heard?

Are any of these decisions ones you've contemplated but then not acted on?

Is the person you are right now who you thought you'd be at this point in your life?

From My Perspective

The sense I make of this now, looking back at all the behaviors that I experienced, is that Jonathan was both quenching my thirsty soul's needs and mugging my soul that I had already beaten up. I was denying his mugging in order to get the soothing, comforting, treasuring part. I stayed in the relationship, hoping eventually to receive that wonderful salve for my wounded soul. In denial about what was going on, I had convinced myself I could make the ugly words go away and the appealing words stay.

It wasn't until my encounter with the woman in the ladies' room that I was forced to face the truth. I had been immobilized by a pattern of my own design which I put into place to get my needs met. It is a paradox that this juxtapositioning of terrible and great, hot and cold, lovely and putrid with Jonathan was precisely what had kept me in the relationship. The hope I had had definitely turned on me, deceiving me into becoming a believer at any price.

That early morning conversation with myself after the traumatic encounter that Sunday absolutely persuaded me that I had to make a drastic personal change. I had to stop mugging my own soul. Also, I knew I had to get this insidious, toxic behavior out in the open. I had to tell about the damage people do to their core by robbing their own souls. I felt compelled to tell others what I was going through.

The Path Ahead

I wish I could say that the way out is easy. I wish I could say it is quick. I wish I could say it is straightforward. I wish I could say it is painless once the decision is made. I cannot make any of these statements. All I can say is that it is possible.

Until the shock of that chance encounter in the ladies' room, I might have remained captive to my own denial of the mugging being done to my soul. That day, I realized my essence, my whole self, was in great jeopardy. By permitting this man to define the most essential part of me, and by allowing others to do the same thing early in my life, my self had nearly disappeared. I was facing a vast absence in my being. I had to wake up and do something. That delicate balance between living and dying was in danger of shifting. I was fighting to live. Yet, I was in a living death, hoping for someone else to save my soul. Hope had sustained me. Hope had maintained me. Hope had had immense power over me. I had relied on hope and it had deceived me. It had truly done me in.

Now hope had to be killed if I were going to rebuild my life from the ground of my *own* being. I resolved to never again let anyone define who I was at my core. I had decimated my soul by supplying myself with others' judgments of me, definitions of who I was at my center.

With the incident in the ladies' room, I was forced to rethink my whole way of being in the world. After that, I began my first small steps out of the soul negation that I had placed myself in and put myself through for more years than I cared to admit. It was terrifying and liberating to know I had begun to allow myself to see with my own eyes, speak with my own voice, and eventually to flourish. What a concept. What a challenge for me. Ultimately, what a victory!

A Bitter-Sweet Ending

Before I go into the process of how to reclaim, replenish, and, eventually, fully reclaim your soul, I want to share what happened in the relationship with Jonathan once I had gone through that journey myself.

I would like to be able to tell you that I marched up to where he was speaking one day and confronted him directly with what I felt he, with my consent of course, had done to contribute to defiling my soul. It didn't occur that way, though.

After more than a year of intense work, moving through all the steps, all the many stages that go into healing such a profound and long-standing wound, I went to a conference on Creativity. I was still nurturing my self in every way I could. I picked this event because it had wonderful speakers on the various areas I loved such as art, music, and theater. I was just leaving a session when I saw Jonathan standing by himself at the doorway.

My first reaction was to walk back into the room, avoiding any contact with him. It only took a second to realize, though, that that behavior was outdated and definitely not even close to who I was now. My soul led me straight up to him. I just let that part of me, now fully developed and in charge of who I deeply was, speak.

"Hello Jonathan."

He was as startled to see me as I was to have first spotted him across the way that morning.

"What I have to say to you I want to speak without interruption. I have no need for a response from you, in fact, I'd prefer not to have any. I have no anger towards you, but I know now, with much more clarity, the damage you did during the entire relationship we had. I have to say, you did make me aware, due to the many defiling things you did, of what I was willing to put up with, what I was willing to take, in order to have what I thought was love at the time from you. I now know that that was not love, not even close to love. I could not have been loved and yet treated the way you treated me. I see now that I could never be myself with you. I didn't even know how to do that. What I learned about myself, though, is not important to say to you. What *is* necessary to say is that I find your behavior was not only disrespectful and dishonoring to me but absolutely despicable. What you exposed me to by your yelling, your ignoring, your belittling, and your betrayal of our commitment to each other is a horrible, in fact, unimaginable way to treat another human being. Though I have forgiven you and in some ways have to be thankful that I became a completely different person because of what I went through and learned, I have never had that kind of intense and prolonged pain and will never forget the abhorrent way I was treated. No one deserves that. I certainly didn't. Good bye, Jonathan."

I walked away and never looked back. I felt greatly empowered by having done this in person and will always remember how, trusting my soul completely, I was able to let what came out be effortless and authentic in a way I would never have been able to do if I had not restored this essence to its central place in my life.

You can feel that inner strength, that resoluteness in all you do and are in your life by beginning now to build that foundational place deep within you where the source of all life resides.

Chapter Two

Bewitched, Bothered and Bewildered

Self-Discovery For Soul Mugging

For what is a person profited if he or she shall gain the whole world, and lose his or her own soul? Or what shall a person give in exchange for his or her soul?
– Matthew 16:26 (paraphrased)

"I feel as if I have been erased."

Eve spoke these words slowly, softly, plaintively on her first visit to my office. Her words raced through me. I knew well the helpless, vacant feeling of becoming invisible. As she elaborated, it became clear that she had allowed people in her life, and most recently her lover, to take over defining who she was. She had given up sovereignty over her own life long ago.

I paused, taking in Eve's wardrobe choice for the day – a bright print jacket over a fuchsia colored blouse. It was an extreme contrast to her description of having a sense that she had vanished.

I revisited a scene in a jungle from a movie I had seen years ago. A young woman was tied to a stake. As she struggled to get loose, the knots became tighter and tighter, until she became immobilized. Eve, too, was making an attempt, one of many, to fight the bonds which entrapped her. In her struggle to break free, she had only become more entangled in the mire of her feelings of nonexistence. I guessed that little by little, as her life deteriorated, she had fought harder and harder to sustain it. In the process, all that had occurred was that she had increasingly drained her spirit, her sense of self, and her soul.

I had faced the sense of the absence of being in the past. There were no adequate words for the feelings that accompany such an experience. It is truly as if there is no one existing within the body, no one valuable enough to occupy that space.

Focusing on the cheerful colors of Eve's jacket for a moment, I tried to form an image of Eve in a better time. I pictured her standing alone and strong, leaning into the wind on a high bluff above the ocean. Forming another picture, this one in an at-home setting, I saw her confidently smiling into the mirror as she readied herself for an executive meeting where she would make an important presentation. I wished there were a way to magically place Eve into those scenes.

"I've been there myself," I said, looking at Eve. "I know it is an agonizing place to be. And I can tell you that it is possible to triumph. I've worked with many others who have succeeded in recovering their sense of self. Your commitment to the process will need to be your highest priority, however long it takes and however difficult it gets." She nodded, and so we began Eve's journey back to the source of her life, her soul.

24

What Is Soul Mugging?

Soul mugging is a profound spiritual and psychic trauma to the critical life core of one's existence. ("I feel indiscernible.") Soul mugging is often a lifelong pattern which we unknowingly perpetuate through interaction. ("Why do you continue to act as if I don't exist?") Soul mugging distorts reality. Even simple actions on one's behalf become incomprehensible. ("I don't know how to act in any situation. I'm lost.") Soul mugging entraps people and holds them captive, creating devastating, ongoing suffering. ("I can't possibly go on living with this much distress.")

Soul mugging is a widespread condition that occurs internally and often continues when one gets into any relationship where you give your authority for you who are over to that person. Often it is a romantic partner, but it could be a boss, a co-worker, a parent, a child, anyone in your life that you feel you must please in order to survive psychologically and spiritually. You may not be conscious of how strong this need is, but let yourself think about who that might be and what you've done to keep that relationship, no matter what. Soul mugging may definitely be present but has never been named. I made up this term to describe a dynamic that deeply affects the personal and spiritual connection one has primarily with one's self, and with others on a secondary level.

In its extreme form, it becomes a syndrome – the soul negation syndrome. There are two things which lead to it: 1) a hole in one's soul because of some perceived deprivation, a soul hunger that was never fed; 2) one has, over time, become a victim of one's own denial of having this void. Subconscious attempts to get another to fill this place only perpetuate the mugging and can lead to the syndrome.

Soul mugging can be identified by particular characteristics, patterns, and interactions that take place over time, many times internally, but certainly with others. It is pinpointed through certain identifiable traits matched with a specific set of susceptibilities within a person.

Many people are highly vulnerable to soul mugging and its eventual outcome, the soul negation syndrome. These people are the ones most likely to be attracted to others who will continue to maintain soul mugging within the relationship setting. Sadly, some people experience soul mugging from the time they are very small without ever recognizing it.

In part, soul mugging is a phenomenon where denial is foremost in one's life. In fact, many people are victims of this denial without ever understanding they have perpetuated their own pain. A multitude of means may be used by this internal mugger, including fear, humiliation, and verbal assaults to one's own sense of self.

- What soul mugging erodes is one's experience of having a self to identify with and care about.
- What it confuses are perceptions of the most vital part of a person, the soul.
- What it leads to is tremendous doubt about the visibility of one's self to one's self.
- What it dishonors is the spirit, the very essence of one's being.
- What it dislodges is where one's grounded-ness comes from. Soul mugging often begins with reprimands one makes to one's self which barely seem worth a second thought. It can escalate, though, finally placing its full signature of ownership on

25

the soul. Eventually, these people, their inner resources diminished or depleted, don't know what hit them, or why. They are then wholly ensnared in the soul negation syndrome, and ultimately have lost the sense of their core. All of these inner wars are set up unintentionally and continue without interruption until some kind of awakening of consciousness occurs.

While the variations are countless, soul mugging has a clearly recognizable profile: A person is neglectful of the self, relying on external resources that are often unreliable and very inconsistent. Knowingly or not, they allow behaviors from themselves and the environment to add power to this inner voice. These behaviors tend to weaken and defile them. As they try harder, that very behavior further diminishes them. Eventually they feel demoralized. It is an endless cycle of pain, deprivation, denial, and more pain.

As soul mugging progresses, people inadvertently collaborate in undermining their essential self, the soul. They continue to neglect themselves, hoping unforeseen or imagined changes will somehow make the difference. They inappropriately take the blame, no matter what is occurring in their world. They often change their behavior to appease someone they barely know.

As time goes on, they further drain their spirit and energy trying to please this demanding, unnamed inner dictator. Eventually, they believe the unattractive image in the mirror which they, in fact, have created. Finally, these people completely doubt, not only their own intuition, but anything about their lives. They have lost a solid place on which to stand, a place central to their ability to identify who they are and what their predilections are.

Soul mugging slings out damaging consequences which greatly cripple people. In extreme cases, when the soul negation syndrome has set in, they become devoid of their inner resources and are almost incapacitated.

People may continue this inner strife by getting into a soul-mugging relationship, denying their plight. Obviously, if society doesn't have a name for something, it is easy not to acknowledge it. Giving the label "soul mugging" to this debilitating condition helps people recognize the effects of this state on the self so that those who think they may have it can take the steps necessary to recover from it. This book is a guide to help restore the spirit to its original state. Then people can create internal environments as well as relationships which reflect a partnership which is whole, grounded, and immensely satisfying to all involved.

Soul mugging erodes our spirit and gouges our personhood. Soul mugging took what was most precious to me and in me, my essence, and defiled it. Most of all, it greatly disillusioned me about my concept of love as a sacred connection within myself and, ultimately, with another. I could not, because I had negated my soul for so long, purposefully care for, look out for, and work toward my own greatest possibilities, as well as do the same for anyone I was in a relationship with. I had built this narrow, but predictable, context for my life.

Soul mugging systematically wore me down. I lied to, intimidated, and criticized myself. I deceived myself with hyped-up words I'd learned from books of affirmations. Soul mugging consistently tore and wore away, not only my self-confidence, but also my trust in my own perceptions and my ability to act on my own behalf.

I experienced soul mugging as spiritual and psychic violence, tearing apart my precious, fragile essence when I actually thought I was nurturing myself. No degradation has been as disastrous to me as the degradation of my soul. Enmeshed in this soul-mugging condition, I was haunted by faint but persistent voices from my soul, pleading with me to resist and rebel, voices which I pushed aside. By the time I heard them, I was too devastated to take action. I had lost the ground of my being. I had no place to stand.

I know now I lost my being through my own choices, by what I thought I needed. I had no freedom because I'd given over to others, and eventually to a man, the power to decide who, in the deepest, most sacred part of me, I was. Finally, I lost my courage to be and thus lost my own being. I did so because I feared ending up alone in an all-too-empty world.

What Does Soul Mugging Do To a Person?

- Soul mugging beats you down and leaves you feeling humiliated.
- Soul mugging diminishes your sense of self, that is, your essence, your being, your personhood.
- Soul mugging dishonors you and destroys your self-respect.
- Soul mugging tears at your core, conflicts with values and beliefs you once held, ones which form the cornerstones of your identity, and throws you off balance.
- Soul mugging affects every level of your existence. It eventually creates a profound sense of internal instability.

Is Soul Mugging Dangerous?

It slugs you where you are you, the lens through which you view the world and on which you depend to make sense of your life. YES, SOUL MUGGING IS VERY DANGEROUS!

How Do You Know If Your Soul Is Being Mugged?

Just as a storm with thunder and lightning occurs when several elements are just right, soul mugging also occurs when certain conditions are present. Just as there are many types of bad weather and many kinds of negative relationships, it is possible that soul mugging is entirely absent, even when you have a very negative attitude and are in unhappy relationships with others.

A simple and quick way to know if your soul is being mugged is to take your own temperature in terms of your soul, spirit, being, essence, and personhood within the context of your life. Is your soul flourishing? Is it damaged? Are you affected somewhat? Moderately? Seriously? Severely? Drastically?

If soul mugging unfolds within the framework of any relationship, very tangible changes are evident. You can become aware of ways to detect the negative effects of these differences. You can reflect on how your friends and loved ones are reacting to certain shifts in your behavior. You can discover whether it is heading toward the serious, even dangerous, stage.

You can be certain you have also been mugging your own soul for many years. The changes in you due to soul mugging are detected by observing and reflecting on:

- your feelings
- your actions
- your internal dialogue when you notice certain soul mugging behavior in others and the way you relate to others concerning the soul-mugging incidents in your own life.

You will find the chart on the following pages useful. It is a map of soul mugging. By finding points on the chart which seem particularly relevant to your situation, you can get a perspective on the extent to which soul mugging is affecting you.

AM I MUGGING MY SOUL

Extent of Soul Mugging	I Observe About Myself	I Feel	I Tell Myself and Others
Fortunately, none. I have a healthy, and even flourishing, soul.	Showing respect for my self; sharing ideas with others; facing issues as they arise; working with others as we resolve problems; caring by the way I speak about my soul; nurturing my self; knowing I have a strong, healthy soul; enjoying positive relationships with others.	Blessed by love and sharing; my life is rich, grounded and free; connected to others, to life; balanced and focused; true to self and values; a sense that all is right; joyous about my interests.	"I am secure within my self." "I have high regard for my self." "I am confident I will overcome challenges." "I look forward to the future." "I honor my soul's wisdom." "I am indeed fortunate." "I turn within for solutions."
Yes, possibly, or somewhat	Making derogatory comments about my self; acting rudely to myself and others at times; telling lies to make my self feel better; justifying results regardless of means	Unsettled; disquieted; perplexed; watchful; guarded.	"Am I that stupid?" "That makes me furious." "I can't get it right." "I *hope* I can ignore what happened."
Yes, moderately	Sending mixed signals; shifting moods suddenly and erratically; saying insulting things to my soul; making adjustments to please others; *hoping* that problems vanish; feeling regard for my being runs hot and cold; saying one thing and doing another; neglecting to follow through; blaming self for my problems.	Confused; unconsidered; apprehensive; disconnected; never good enough; disappointed; discouraged; wary.	"I must have said or done something wrong." "I *hope* I can get it right tomorrow." "Next time I will do better." "I *hope* they didn't mean what they said." "I have to have this love."
If you place yourself in the stages of soul mugging below this point, you have soul negation syndrome.			

Extent of Soul Mugging	I Observe About Myself	I Feel	I Tell Myself and Others
Yes, seriously	Avoiding sharing thoughts and feelings	Betrayed	"I can't figure out how to get love."
	Exhibiting increasingly unpredictable moods	Dismayed, shocked	"What am I doing wrong?"
	Wanting love regardless of cost	Devalued, put down	"This has to be temporary. It will be different when… "
	Behaving erratically	Overwhelmed	"I know I can learn how to handle my partner."
	Saying harmful things to my being daily	Powerless	"I must change."
	Changing to please others	Frightened	"I can't live without my partner's love."
	Abdicating making decisions and actions	Despised	"I hope my partner will be happy now – they got their way."
	Shaming self/partner in public	Unforgiven	"I hate who I am."
	Violating promises, commitments	Despondent	
	Hoping I can make it better		
Yes, severely	Closing my self and others out emotionally	Humiliated	"I must have my partner."
	Making desperate attempts to get love	Thrown into chaos, disarray	"I'm desperate. What am I going to do?"
	Being punishing to my self	Uprooted	"I'm lost and vacant."
	Wishing I had never been born	Ungrounded, foundationless	"I can't exist this way."
	Hating all aspects of my soul	Isolated and alone	"I'm invisible to myself as well as my partner."
	Making changes even when they are at great cost	Despicable	"How could anyone like me anyway?"
	Disconnecting from agony by numbness	Empty	
	Considering suicide to end suffering		

Extent of Soul Mugging	I Observe About Myself	I Feel	I Tell Myself and Others
Yes, drastically	Negating self on every level	Puppet-like	"I'm soulless."
	Criticizing my every behavior constantly	Silenced	"I have nothing to offer. I am nothing."
	Clinging to my partner	Despairing	"I'm the only one who's never been loved."
	Begging, pleading, demeaning self for love	Numb	"I'm lost. All I see is darkness."
	Ceasing all caring about keeping up appearance	Disconnected	"There's no where to go."
	Isolating from all of life	Incapacitated	"I pray God knows how bad it is."
	Functioning only when essential	Emotionally emaciated	"I'm nothing without someone to define me."
	Magnifying tiny traces of love	Utterly abandoned	"I'm terrified."
	Hoping for a miracle		
	Becoming actively suicidal		

Is Your Soul Flourishing in Relationship With Yourself?

If so, you're feeling free. You're grounded. You're *you*. And you are fortunate. You also feel connected to life, sympathetic to others, empathetic, receptive, alert, alive, and vital as a person. As your life continues, you find yourself awakening more and more to the possibilities of who you can be. You will choose to move toward ever new horizons.

As expressed in my journal, "When I am thriving, I know I have a life free to be lived on my own terms, from my own soul, from my own love of self."

You face life's challenges by yourself or with a partner and a network of friends who consistently support you. No matter how down and frustrated you become, you do not sling mud at yourself through put-downs, attacks, or wrongful blame.

You are there with your self through life's unpredictable times, working with, not against, your essence to find satisfying outcomes for every situation. You find joy in working through difficulties. It helps you feel stronger because you are cooperating with that internal part of you that is wise, intuitive, flowing with the source of life itself. You are focused, balanced, centered, and on-track, doing what you want or need to do. You are spiritually tuned in to the infinite possibilities of what life has to offer and what you have to offer life.

Your soul is nurtured in your relationship with yourself and permits you to experience life fully in or out of a romantic partnership. You can probably relate to an excerpt from one of my poems:

What is love anyway?
More than a feeling –
a way of being,
being close to God,
being God in form.
Love is the light
glowing in that
dark room.
All else can shrivel
But love expands
the shriveled,
the despairing.
Love is
whispering
wonder-filled phrases
into the ear, saying
ALL IS WELL
when nothing
seems right.
Love
shows there
is
no final despair necessary.
Love says "I am with You always."
Love is Presence,
a Comfort,
a Safe Womb
we climb into
to heal and protect
and save us
when
all else betrays
us.
There love is, yeah,
there God is
surrounding us,
being us
So
what is Love?
It is Me
and You
at Our fullest,
deepest,
grandest.
Love is
here.
Be still and know
It,
Me,
You.

How Damaged Are You? Stages of Soul Mugging

Somewhat Damaged

With a flourishing soul you are deeply grounded in your being. An important signal of first-stage soul mugging is the loss of that perfect symmetry. Your sense of knowing and feeling that all is right in your world disappears.

If soul mugging progresses, it will lead to behavior that is disrespectful, degrading, and dishonoring. Your first sign of a propensity for soul mugging may come from observing the manner in which you relate to others. Warning flags are abruptness or rudeness to others, inappropriately placing others' wishes above your own, and perhaps small lies which you claim you make to avoid hurting anyone's feelings.

In a relationship with Joanne, Sam reported in a therapy session that he had experienced a meaningful tip-off about himself. He showed some embarrassment as he reported it:

"Joanne asked me if I'd seen her TV show last Saturday morning. I told her that, yes, I was drooling all over my tie-you were great as usual. While Joanne was working later that day, a colleague asked her why she hadn't been on television the previous Saturday morning. She told Joanne she had gotten up to watch her on her business segment of the news and she hadn't been on. Joanne started to shake as she confronted me that day. I can't quite comprehend why I do that. I really want this relationship, but I've lied to myself for so long, it seemed natural to continue it in my romantic relationship."

If you listen to yourself and soul carefully at this early stage, you will probably experience a disquieting sense. You may be perplexed when some of your observations and feelings do not match the ideal you hold for yourself and of what you want your relationship with another to be.

This is the best time to develop a thorough understanding of soul mugging. If you are alert, you may be able to reverse a tendency for soul mugging to develop. If you have ever been aware of past soul mugging behavior, you will know that you do not wish to repeat the experience. Sam certainly didn't. The ability to admit that he lied to himself and to others was his first step out of denial. The confrontation with Joanne had awakened him early on to his tendency.

This is also an opportune time to evaluate your alternatives and your commitment to your self. How important is your relationship to your soul? It is crucial that you understand that whatever relationship you have with your self, your essence, will be reflected in any relationship you enter into. If you are mugging your soul on any level, then you will unconsciously perpetuate that mugging by the choices you make in a relationship with any important person in your life.

Moderately Damaged

Are you walking on eggshells a lot of the day? In the moderately damaged stage of soul mugging you regularly change your behavior trying to keep the good times going and to avert the bad times. When you filter your feelings and impulses by asking the question, "If I pay attention to this, is it going to help or hurt?" you neutralize your soul's power.

You have also experienced the punishing sense of not being quite good enough, of not living up to your own unrealistic ideals. This may come out in subtle ways, as it did once for Sue, a patient of mine. She and her father were hurriedly getting ready to go to dinner at a friend's home.

"I had just finished pressing my father's shirt," Sue said, "when he blurted out, 'Where did that iron come from? I brought the one I wanted used for my clothes. Now my shirt looks worse than it did before you ironed it; it has creases where there weren't any before.' This was so stupid of me. I know what my father likes, and I just didn't do it. What's wrong with me? I can't get it right. Last time I used my iron it was the right thing. This time it ruined our evening."

Sue had no doubt mugged her soul with clues from her environment long before this interaction with her father. He had now become the agent with which Sue unintentionally continued this self-defiling, self-defeating behavior which perpetuated itself.

In this stage of soul mugging you frequently insult your self. You may be hearing yourself say words such as:

"I know I'm not worth listening to."

"I am so stupid."

"I make myself sick."

"Why do I think anyone would want to spend all afternoon with me?"

Even before this level of your soul mugging experience, you will begin to note reactions of others:

"I can't stand how you talk to yourself. What you're telling me, even in casual remarks, is so demeaning. Why do you do that?"

"You are not the same person you were when I met you."

"You must stop treating yourself this way. I hurt when I see you in pain."

"Please don't ruin your relationship. You seem to be robbing yourself of any happiness."

If you are not yet fully entrenched in this soul mugging behavior, this is the time to take a hard look at the prospect of drastically changing it. If it is firmly established, and you have not yet awakened to what you have been doing to your soul, you are advised to become intentional and committed to ways which will lead you toward moving out of this deep disconnection with your essential self.

Perhaps you can begin to see that there is a hole in your soul that you have never attended to directly. At least experiment with this notion for a few days. Denial may have been so pervasive in your life that you have never taken the opportunity, until now, to contemplate just how you treat your being on a daily basis. Right now is the time to begin asking these painfully probing questions. Soul mugging leads to the soul negation syndrome. Then it is even more difficult to ascertain and certainly to move out of. My poem dramatizes the progression from soul mugging to the soul-negation syndrome. I actually wrote it to Jonathan during a part of the relationship where I felt he would understand how I was feeling if I could just express it in a way that he could grasp:

You know, I think you're blind
to what you have and
who I am:
a flower,
that delicate, killable,
gift of God's.
That moment when the
flower just opens
to grasp for breath,
for light, its life,
it's crushable,
so soft and easily broken
into scattered petals
across a stone, cold pavement.
You don't even see that that precious fragile heart
is easily wounded,
has been stomped on.
The flower must stand
for itself,
by itself,
for enjoying,
for savoring,
certainly, for light touching.
Oh yes, gentle
gently wanting to be intact
for its whole life.
Instead, it gets holes punctured in it
as if by a madman with a shotgun.
You come.
You take.
You devour.
You shoot, shout, scream
at the flower,
kick its freshness
into a stagnant pool of
sewer water
as if it were to thrive
on dirt or vulgarities.
You never notice the
dew on each petal
are actually tears,
drowning in tears of "Stop it.
Quit the savage slaughter"
a flower, pure,
expecting room to flourish,
expecting care and love

told it is beautiful.
You see my splendor
why do you tear at my soul?
Don't you know it's all
bound together,
that to beat at my outsides
is to cut at my core?

This poem captures the insidious, toxic way we can treat ourselves. We can take the precious flower at our core and beat it up, defile it, and crush its beauty with our own words, our own desecration of its uniqueness.

Seriously Damaged

You have adapted your behavior and perhaps your lifestyle to please everyone but your self. You are in complete denial, believing that another person can ever fill that void inside of you. By adapting to everyone else, you compromise your being, even sacrifice your soul, and you don't even notice. In your mind you look forward, hoping for the positives (how you were as a small child) to re-emerge, for the potential to reappear, and for you to zoom into a great future. However, at this point in the process, you are living solely on hope. Soul mugging occurs with such regularity that you find yourself coming up with myriad excuses for living in this hell. It is the only way you have been with your self for so long. If you are now in an important relationship, the way this person treats you is probably similar to what you started doing to your soul long ago.

Unfortunately, at this stage, soul mugging includes much more desecrating tactics than mere verbal stabs aimed at your essence. Now, without your conscious awareness, the soul negation syndrome has taken over. You are about to face a profound feeling of nonexistence. If you have a partner, he or she not only does not make up for what you have done to yourself, but in fact adds to the process by replicating what you have been doing to yourself internally. The damage is heavy, the lessening of your vital being, immense.

Barry, a patient, came in one day and told me about an incident with his lover, Jean. It was very clear to me by what he reported that he had reached this horrendous stage.

"Jean came home noticeably upset one day. She asked me how come I was wearing a particular ring. She thought I had disposed of it after I told her that it came from a rich woman that I used to date. She was so torn apart that she started crying. 'Don't you know how much it hurts me to see you with that ring on?' Dr. Papillon, I lost it. I did. I screamed back at her that she better not tell me what to wear and what not to wear. I told her in no uncertain terms I needed to present an image. I'm embarrassed to say that that is the most important thing to me. So I just told her to shut up."

Barry told me that he had yelled this last sentence at her, very much degrading her in the process. As he was relating the incident to me I could tell that he was genuinely appalled that his tone of voice had been so dishonoring to his lover. At this point he had been in treatment for several months. He had become more cognizant of how he mugged his own soul, but at times he noted he slipped easily into this same behavior with his lover, Jean. His response negated her feelings, her response to him. He was mortified that he had once again injured his essence by hurting her. Unfortunately, even though denial is broken through, the path out of soul mugging is still not a straight one. It takes time to transform into more loving, nurturing patterns.

At this stage of soul mugging you may keep yourself going by recalling someone's (perhaps your partner's) endearments and the caring way he or she looked at you during happy times. You are existing by focusing on the words another person says, hoping these endearing words will fill that void you have but are not yet consciously aware of. The words may express sentiments such as, "I love only you," "You are the precious treasure of my life," "I must have you," or, "I'm so glad you were born."

By this time your method of handling day-to-day living includes other compensating behavior. You may isolate yourself from everyone or seek only people who believe the way you do about your self.

As much as you dislike your bad feelings, the soul mugging, and now the complete soul negation, you are unknowingly "doing your soul in." You have done so by adapting to others, starving your soul, and searching for love in external, unsatisfying places. You have used hope and denial to lead your self astray. You are caught in an insidious cycle; your own soul negating behavior leads you to accept your partner's behavior, which in turn leads to more soul negating behavior of your own.

To those around you, your ability to function at work may seem normal. It is probably because you have artfully perpetuated denial to such an extent that you can appear happy. You are careful not to let yourself know how much pain and despair you are experiencing. It is unbearable to consider it for very long anyway, or any alternative, so you do your best just to carry on.

At this point, I advise you to begin seeing a therapist. You have to immerse yourself in effective corrective action. It is important that your plan be focused totally on your being. You need to nourish your soul and bolster your core, your divine essence.

Severely Damaged

At this stage, you are hanging on. You hurt badly. The relationship you are in is perpetuating the suffering by defiling and degrading you on a daily basis. You may have withdrawn, only risking contact occasionally. You want to continue believing that this other person will somehow fill this void and make you feel loved.

While you hope for this miracle, you are beginning to feel imprisoned. You tell your self and others that things will get better once something changes, when your partner stops demeaning you and says only endearing words. You may sincerely believe this, as it is a common mind trick that people who can't face their present situation play on themselves. Friends tell you that your beliefs about your self and the value of the relationship are major distortions. You can't process the information, though. It is too frightening to consider.

An example from my session with Sally shows how a woman can be fooled into believing that a romantic relationship is the answer to unbearable soul agony and then get further injured by her own belief. The day after Valentine's Day, Sally came in, tears streaming down her face.

"George met me for lunch on Valentine's Day; we exchanged gifts. He wrote so many tender and loving thoughts on the card he gave me. Then he said he felt a cold coming on and told me he wanted to get to bed early."

Sally could not go on for several minutes. Finally she continued. "I learned the truth, Dr. Papillon, when I tried to call him last night. He never answered. I finally called his old girl-friend's house this morning. She told me what I couldn't bear to hear. 'Yes, he was with me last night. He was with me all night long. He gave me gifts, a card, the whole thing.'"

My journal describes the consequences of soul mugging and of the soul negation syndrome. The following was actually written as I was just ending this agonizing period:

> Soul mugging is threatening my integrity. If I don't stop it, it is going to devour me, like a hungry, wild animal at prey. I am destroying myself by exposing my soul to repeated mugging. I see it as a self trivialization. I'm not willing to take my self seriously. In fact, I am misplacing my compassion. I lie to my self and I don't begin to give my soul the attention and hard work I give to others, especially my lover. I am numbed into blankness, afraid to think and terrified to feel. My soul is fading away. I can see now that my existence is only validated by others, now by this man I love. I guess I am so inculcated with self-hatred that I just allow soul negation to flourish. I have been into soul mugging so long I am like an insect against a screen, caught by the very wires that look like the way to liberation. The insidious aspect of this syndrome is that I have lost my faith, especially in my own life on any level.

If you are severely damaged, you definitely need outside professional help and much more. You must build strategies which include a strong support network. You have to develop nurturing outlets for your soul and design a multi-faceted plan which might include journaling, expressing your self through art, walking in the woods, photography, dancing, taking a class, or reading a book that might bring you out of the numbness you are so familiar with. You have to commit to specific, concrete plans that you can carry through and that can contribute to your recovery.

Drastically Damaged

You have paid a huge emotional price for many years. Your energy – physical, mental, emotional, and, most importantly, spiritual – is drained as you try to deny the severity of the soul mugging and strain to generate the hope which you need and have relied on. Remembrance of better times and your hope of returning to those times only sustain you for short periods of time now.

You may feel like Beth when she first came into therapy.

"When I saw your television show, Dr. Papillon, I thought you were talking just to me. I started answering your question, 'What do you cut yourself off from?' At that moment I realized I cut myself off from everything – my friends, my goals, my growth, my diet and exercise routine – well, just everything. I stay in bed all day long. By evening I say, 'Tomorrow I'm going to get up and exercise and ride my bike and go get a job of some kind.' And then the next day comes, and I can't get up."

Your sense of self is drastically diminished; you cannot muster the internal resources to function in the outer world. You have lost the sense that you exist on any level at all, that you have any value whatsoever, that you have anything to contribute to anyone.

You have negated your self out of life. The words that the relationship you are in used to say, the words that you fed on, are now only faint echoes to you. You can't remember when you've had a decent interaction with anyone. Other people no longer seem present to you, even when they are physically in the room. The truth, of course, is that you are ignoring your essence. You are no longer present to your self, your soul, on any level.

It is unbearable, and yet you know you have to bear it if you are going to stay in the world. You feel as if you are in solitary confinement, punished severely for something you can't quite understand. But who put you in this place? Even that question is too terrifying for you to ask yourself.

You can't mention your extreme suffering to anyone but your therapist. You don't bother talking to friends; they wouldn't know what you are talking about. Besides, you have no idea how to describe what you are experiencing internally. On your worst days, you even imagine that your therapist doesn't want you to keep your appointment. After all, you are a lost cause, you think, and who cares if you die. You don't die, because you don't think you exist anyway, not on any level that you can grasp.

When you have gotten to this drastic stage, you are deluding your soul by hoping that there is someone out there who can rescue you other than the therapist you are seeing on a regular basis; yet to envision doing it all yourself and for your own soul is beyond your comprehension. There are many options that you cannot see at this point. All you know is blackness. The darkest night of your soul is here now. It doesn't get any worse.

Believe me. You are not alone in this experience. Others have been in exactly this place. So have I. And I survived. You must be willing to seek much more help such as going for therapy sessions more than once a week, rest, rereading portions of this book, and being committed, as you've never been, to continuing the process you started by picking up this book. There are no accidents and that is an enormous first step.

How Can You Recognize Another as Capable of Mugging Your Soul?

"It works," exclaimed Bill.

In a psychotherapy session with Mary's husband, Bill, I had just asked why he used the silent treatment at home. Although surprised by the directness of his response, I instantly recognized its truth.

"It's pretty easy for me to get Mary to do what I want," he continued.

Bill simply did not realize that his silent treatment and other manipulative schemes were demeaning to his wife. He used them because they worked on her.

In many relationships soul mugging is an unwitting event for both partners. It is often perpetuated by a lack of awareness. Other times it emerges because a partner (for any number of reasons) lacks a full set of skills with which to effectively make his or her wishes known, that is, to negotiate on his or her own behalf with the partner.

Unfortunately, a person in a soul-mugging relationship may not realize how his or her be-havior affects the other. This person may have a narrow range of coping abilities. The inappropriate behavior is reinforced until it becomes habitual.

Eventually it becomes irreparably damaging to the relationship. It perpetuates the defiling you have already been doing to your soul. People who have practiced these behaviors in several relationships will unknowingly continue to seek relationships with other people who offer minimal resistance to these behaviors.

You have unintentionally entered into a relationship with the kind of person who will treat you the same way you have been treating your essence. The toxic system is set up and con-tinues until the revelation occurs.

If a person has the characteristics listed in the chart on the following page, there is a good possibility that this person is capable of perpetuating the soul mugging you have been doing for many years:

Characteristics of a Person Capable Of Mugging Your Soul

Facade person presents to the world
Over-achiever
Driven (means justify ends)
Proud
Vain
Image matters greatly
Charming
Sociable

Early warning behavior
Sends vacillating messages, hot and cold
Keeps person off-balance
Inconsistent behavior
Slights, cutting remarks
Distances self erratically
Slow to share, has secretive side

Response when explanation requested
Shifts subject away from self, blames you
Slippery, difficult to pin down
Gives unsatisfying answers to questions
Attacks when confronted
Unwilling to elaborate on feelings, emotions
Lies, gaslights (fools you)

Advanced stage behavior
Does not act in your interest
Volatile, can erupt at any moment
Intimidates, humiliates, degrades
Punishes
Repeatedly threatens to leave

Unexplored internal side
Has sense of powerlessness
Cut off from emotions
Lacks inner security
Has low self-esteem

How to Tell If You Are Susceptible to Soul Mugging

Sara seemed eager to begin our therapy session.

"I made an especially nice dinner for us last night," she said. "Baxter seemed pleased. I hope things are getting better between us!"

She has gone back into denial, I said to myself. This was our tenth session together. We were still sorting through the complexities of a roller-coaster marriage. "Sara, you say he seemed pleased?"

"Yes, well, he kind of smiled. The way he got up from the table seemed different. He appeared happy."

After all the effort she had gone to, she was satisfied with such a minuscule response from him. This small sign, magnified way out of proportion, inappropriately refueled her expectations. I asked Sara if she hoped things would get better now.

"I feel contented and centered only when things are all right between us. Even though it's hard to find just the right way to please him, it's always worth it."

It seemed that Sara defined her self in terms of Baxter's response to her. Trying extra hard to please is a typical, but invariably ineffective, remedy for soul mugging.

"Well, Dr. Papillon, I really don't think things are all that bad, now that I'm talking about it." Sara was exhibiting a tendency to glorify good times and underplay bad times, a characteristic of soul mugging. I recognized this pattern and remembered that at our previous session, Sara had seemed near despair and had serious complaints about how Baxter treated her. She had resolved to undertake several assignments we had gone over. As I attempted to ask her about these, she interrupted. "Maybe I was just imagining most of the problems. They were probably my fault."

Taking the blame is a soul-diminishing, but commonplace reaction by a person in a soul-mugging relationship. I made mental notes to point this out to her during our next session.

It seemed clear to me that Sara was imprisoned by this relationship. She definitely was reinforcing the negation of her soul. As a therapist I had often heard other people say the same words Sara had just said. Her words were warning signals; there were so many that it was impossible to devote attention to each one in a single session.

Your early home environment may have made you easily susceptible to a soul-mugging relationship. Perhaps you learned to quell the anger of a volatile, explosive father. If you have given up your perception of yourself, your intuition and your voice to speak up on your own behalf, you may have slipped into soul mugging. Your self-image was probably defined by your care-givers' approval and disapproval. You may have been denied full approval, particularly on your own merits.

Perhaps your early religious experiences emphasized hope, trust, and loyalty as values to hold no matter what. An idealistic or romantic inclination may also influence a propensity to gravitate toward a soul-mugging relationship.

It is likely that something in your early relationship with your partner was so appealing to you and fed parts of yourself which you'd been neglecting that you were willing to overlook clues which might have prevented your allowing the relationship to develop.

If you are in a soul-mugging relationship, you may be surprised to learn that it is you who, by your own reactions, "taught" your partner to be an effective soul mugger. You do this inadvertently by accepting your partner's behavior, which is similar to what you have acquiesced to in your own internal dialogues. Though you change your behavior in order to avoid more soul mugging, in doing so, you perpetuate the very actions that you despise. Given the traits of both you and your partner, you cannot help but reinforce negative tendencies. You are caught between loving and hating. It is a horrendous cycle, a room with no doors.

Do you mug your soul? If so, your background and personality probably match these characteristics.

Early Family Life, Values
Unpredictable, inconsistent parenting
Explosive home environment
Learned to repress rather than inflame
Obeyed, even when it didn't match your desires
Relied on hope as a major means of coping
Trained to have unqualified trust and loyalty
Shielded, overprotected

Role Perception
Idealized romantic visions
Place partner on a pedestal
Peacemaker
Responsive to partner's wishes
Never give up
Comforter, appeaser

Approach to the External World
Naive, gullible
Unaware of how others perceive your partner
Not street smart
Lack effective screening ability
Overly trusting in relationships
Competent in career
Use denial to handle incongruities
Rescue the wounded

Self Image
Fit image to appeal to other
Look to other to define who you are
Feel you don't quite measure up
Hungry for approval and praise
Overvalue feeling, underplay rational thought
Don't listen to own intuitions and perceptions
Experience sense of powerlessness

How Soul Mugging Leads to Soul Negation Syndrome

Soul negation syndrome (SNS) is an emotionally debilitating condition. It is the eventual outcome of soul mugging and related effects.

If Your Relationship Is New, Watch Out

You are susceptible to developing SNS if you and the other person in a relationship have the following personality traits and behavior patterns:

Person you have relationship with: The most prominent characteristic is a tendency to manipulate, usually by a lethal combination of lavish, endearing words of affection and negative, biting insults. This person may not knowingly set out to couple these two behaviors, yet for a variety of reasons the person lacks internal boundaries that would ordinarily prevent him or her from desecrating your soul. In addition, this person tends to blame you for the sudden, degrading comments he or she makes about you. The person targets you when things don't go right and expects you to cater to his or her needs and desires. There are times when this person acts as if you are invisible; you become one of the objects in a room, along with the chair, the bed, the couch. This person eventually invalidates your being on a profound level while you unknowingly give your permission and full cooperation.

You: It is typical to be overly swayed by some kind of deep attachment. After all, you hope it may culminate in the filling of that never-named hole in your soul. You tend to be extremely loyal, trusting, hopeful, and accommodating, even when it is not appropriate. You have built a strong denial system; thus you tend not to see, to hear, or to react vocally to this person's dishonoring tactics. You deny, or at least minimize and justify, the insults because there are times when this person makes you feel good about yourself. You truly believe that these words will make the difference in how you feel about your essence, that part of you which you began mugging before this person ever came into your life. You will also take more than your share of any blame and then attempt to fix whatever you must in order to receive the adoration once more. You believe that you need it, that you must have it to fill the hole in your soul.

If Your Relationship is Established, Pay Attention

If your relationship has already been in place for some time and soul mugging occurs on a regular basis, SNS is definitely present. What you will notice is:

Your relationship's incongruous, unpredictable behavior becomes habitual.

You perpetuate this way of relating by inappropriately continuing to adapt, acquiesce, and placate.

You and the other person are now more bonded than ever by the interlocking of this configuration.

The Soul Negation Syndrome in a Romantic Relationship

Soul-negation syndrome exists when a specific set of elements come together. Through the ways in which you work out individual and mutual needs in your relationship, you may permit soul mugging to develop. Soul negation takes hold when you allow another to mug your soul for an extended period of time, such as a month or longer. You may tolerate soul mugging if you are holding on too tightly to the hope that you can recapture only the good in the relationship. That illusion, coupled with an assortment of denial tactics, sets up a completely untenable basis for your relationship. And yet, the relationship continues.

You are ensnared in the soul negation syndrome when you allow another's view to define your sense of self, when you submit to another's desires out of a fear of losing him or her, when you become desperate to keep the relationship at any cost.

In order to keep the other's love, you stop functioning as a whole, complete being separate from him or her. You are imprisoned by this diminishing capacity. Your attempts to make this unviable relationship work only aggravate your situation. By doing whatever you have to do to keep the other person, you are negating your spirit and your soul.

This insidious system is self-feeding. It ultimately progresses into a profoundly debilitating situation. You may find you no longer have any internal foundation, and that your external one is built on shifting sand. Finally, due to the pattern which you unknowingly set up early in your life, you are face-to-face with your complete absence of being. It is utterly ravaging to experience and challenging to overcome. You will benefit from making a marked change in your life, and will need outside help to restore your soul from its greatest negation.

An amazing counterpart in nature to soul negation syndrome has been found in the Solomon Islands in the South Pacific. The villagers there practice a unique form of logging. If a tree is too large to be felled with an ax, the natives cut it down by yelling at it. They creep up on a tree just at dawn and suddenly scream at it at the top of their lungs. They continue this for thirty days. The tree dies and falls over. The theory is that the shouting kills the spirit of the tree. According to the villagers it always works.

Yelling at living things does tend
to kill the spirit in them.
Sticks and stones may break our bones, but
words will break our hearts.
– Robert Fulghum

Chapter Three

It Had to Be You

Hope As the Hidden Trap

And we desire that every one of you do shew the same diligence to the full assurance of hope unto the end...
– Hebrews 6:11

"I hope he brings me back. He took everything but my body with him when he left."

Jodie, a 45-year-old Canadian, uttered these words as she tearfully began her session with me. A turmoil-filled marriage had led her into therapy nine months before. Today she looked depleted – no energy in her step, no life in her face. She walked slowly toward the couch, almost falling into the pillows as she sat down. She looked rumpled, as if she had slept in her clothes. Her mismatched shoes were a clue as to how overwhelmed she actually felt.

"Sid just stormed out after our horrible fight, though he did manage to grab two suitcases filled with his belongings as he left. I'll bet he's been planning this, Dr. Papillon. He knows full well what to do to devastate me. Now he's used his biggest weapon of all. What am I going to do? For months I've begged and pleaded and hoped I could make this relationship work. It still fell apart. I just knew I could somehow make it better. Now look what's happened. I feel like such a fool. I have to have him. He is my life. He is. You know that. If he's gone, I'm gone. Hope is all I have left."

Even if you did not grow up in a religious home, you probably received plenty of messages about hope. Our culture instills in us the importance of having "hope" about the desires we voice and the achievements we dream of. We have all heard the same lines: "I hope all goes well at your interview tomorrow." "I hope you and your parents have a wonderful trip." "I hope the doctor doesn't find anything wrong in his examination." "I hope you can patch things up with him; you seem to want this relationship so much."

Hope is a part of almost every conversation you have heard or taken part in from the time you were very small. If you had a religious upbringing, the word has taken on even more meaning. It has been essential to have hope in your life, hasn't it? "And now faith, hope, and love abide, these three ..." (1 Corinthians 13:13)

The poets say that hope springs eternal in our souls. Unfortunately, if your soul has been mugged, hope stays central in your vocabulary and, more importantly, in your heart, where it can do tremendous damage.

Hope is both a verb and a noun. As a verb it means to expect or look forward to with desire and confidence. As a noun it means an expectation of something desired.

In the context of the soul negation syndrome, hope is a paradox. What you think is giving you a sense of assurance is actually entrapping you. Hope prevents you from comprehending what is happening to you. In the context of this syndrome hope can destroy your life. In a soul-mugging relationship you use hope to keep yourself absorbed in, immersed in and enmeshed in a relationship that is tearing you apart internally. The dilemma is then one of bondage to an illusion. Hope, which is usually an ally, turns on you.

If you suspect that you have soul negation syndrome, your essence has been almost annihilated over time. You feel:

- completely distrustful of your perceptions;
- totally to blame for everything wrong in your life;
- extremely degraded, disrespected, dishonored, dismissed;
- unable to define yourself;
- shriveled by another's definitions of you;
- torn by both words of tenderness and repulsive assaults from those around you and by your internal dialogue;
- often off-balance, shaken at your foundation and numbed by a profound instability concerning your being;
- disoriented about your values, your loyalty, and your central beliefs;
- invisible, no matter where you are, what you're doing, or who you're with.

There are several important characteristics that emerge from the incidents discussed in chapters one and two. It is essential that you be exceptionally aware of these. If you begin now to put together the pieces of this puzzle, you will be well on your way to understanding the complexities of the soul negation syndrome.

What I have discovered through research and clinical practice is that people who use the word hope as a way to stay frozen in their relationships no matter how bad they feel or how negative their situations have become, are extremely susceptible to the soul negation syndrome. They keep hoping they can prevent the next outburst or lie or desecrating behavior by changing their own behavior.

In fact, I have noticed hope is the word most often spoken by people who, after having mugged their own soul for many years, continue to allow their essences to be violated in relationships with others.

"I hope she won't call me a 'fat ass' again. I've pleaded with her so much now."

"I hope I can get him back. I'll do anything, anything to have him."

"I hope she won't explode tonight. I'll be on my best behavior. Maybe that'll work."

"I hope she stops ignoring me in public. I feel invisible."

"I hope I can please him now that I have changed all those things he listed that he hates about me."

"I hope she doesn't wake the neighbors by yelling at me tonight."

"I hope he will see how much he has hurt me. I have tried to tell him, but he does not seem to get it."

"I hope I can get him to quit being so angry with me today. I'm exhausted from yesterday's rampage."

"I hope she can learn to respect me. I live for that day."

"I hope I can get through to her today. When she's mad I can never reason with her. She just keeps threatening me and terrifying me. It is so awful. I feel so demeaned."

"I hope my dreams with him can still come true. I have to have him. I'm lost without him."

"I hope she finally wakes up to what I tell her I am experiencing. I feel like I'm going crazy. I cry all the time. She acts like she doesn't care. I can't stand it when she says she loves me one minute and she hates me the next."

"I hope I can stop him from screaming 'go to hell' over and over. My stomach's in knots. I feel so sick to my stomach."

"I hope he still loves me as much as I love him. He only tells me when I ask him to."

"I hope the words that are really true are how much I mean to him, not how much I bore him and that he's leaving."

"I hope that what she promises she finally produces. I want a life with her."

Just as poignant are how people minimize or make excuses for these prisons that their use of hope has built:

"I just can't see that her ignoring me and the words she calls me are faults. I shut my eyes and pray things will be different once this incident is over. I can't afford to see her as she is any more than I can imagine what I have done to my soul. Reality would shatter my hope."

"He makes me feel terrific. I put blinders on because I need that person to feed me this love. I am starving for attention and for someone to tell me I am beautiful. My favorite fairy tale as a child was Cinderella. My favorite movies are about passion, love, and romance. I want that and he sometimes wants that, too. I hope he will fit into that role. I never want to give up on him, to give up hope."

"If she gives it to me now and then, I know we can have it all the time. I just have to figure out how. I never give up hope. I am magic; I can make the difference. I can transform her."

"I can provide what he never had – love, nurturing, support, and consistent companionship. I can give him all those things. The problem is that he isn't giving me the chance. He doesn't even see me. Could it be he can't take in any of these things? I hope that changes soon. I can change whatever I have to if he'll just notice me and give me a chance to change."

Hope is toxic in the context of the soul negation syndrome. It prevents recovery. It prolongs pain. "Hope dies last" is an old Spanish proverb. Those who are vulnerable hope for someone who resembles an unrealistic ideal. Such a person gets a person who at times talks like that ideal, but at other times acts like an irrational, raging monster.

If you are currently in that kind of relationship, hope will not get you anything but more annihilation. Wouldn't it be wonderful to live a life outside of hope?

Giving up hope means turning towards your self in a way you may never have learned. You must recognize the heavy toll which hope takes. It is necessary to take that first step with conviction and intention:

"I have to stop hoping she will quit saying these awful things to me."

"I have to stop hoping he will no longer lie to me."

"I must stop hoping he will eventually notice I exist. I am only an object to him."

What if we took these sentences that people have actually said to me over the years and substituted one that took out the word hope? Notice the difference with these first few statements:

"I know she will call me a 'fat ass' again. She has done it many times."

"I know I can get him back. Do I want him back?"

"I know she will explode tonight no matter what I do. It actually has nothing to do with my behavior, although I may trigger the rage she already carries within her."

"I know I can count on her being rude to me in public at times. I am invisible to her, but I am committed to being visible to my self now. I must count on myself to honor my own life."

Power is present in these statements. What you have done is take a passive word, "hope," out of your vocabulary and substituted the word "know," which gives you a choice. You can continue to wait for this person to stop defiling you, or you can tell yourself the truth about what he or she is doing and make a decision based on the truth. When you can live outside of hope, you begin to make choices on behalf of your life, refusing to deny your own experience of the relationship. Wouldn't it be wonderful to live a life without hope? By that I mean a life filled with possibilities derived from facing the full reality of a situation. One definition of hope is postponed disappointment. When you live outside of hope, you are not faced with this delayed pain that you inevitably experience. You then look, without hope, at what exists in your life and in your relationship, not what you wish were there. You view what is occurring now, not what you hope will be present someday.

It is important for you to understand the insidious process of hope within the context of the soul negation syndrome. Then you can get to the point where you start to give up hope and take action.

Unfortunately, what you have been doing to yourself for years is less important to you than what you hope can be different. That says a lot about how you delude yourself with hope. It is an extremely inappropriate use of hope. If your soul is being constantly desecrated by you and a person you are in a relationship with, you have repeatedly called on hope. In my relationship, for example, while hope had sustained my persistence to make the relationship work, it was actually depleting my self. Hope was taking my life from me, a life I wanted back.

Hope was one of the most positive words I had heard growing up in a family where religion was central to our lives. My parents went to church every Sunday. I also attended services at least two or three times a week. While I sang the hymns, recited the liturgy, and listened to the sermons, I often thought of the encouraging promise of hope.

However, hope did not help me live a wonderful life. I had to stop saying, thinking, and believing in hope before I could recover from my own mugging. My soul had been negated, including the foundation of who I knew myself to be at my core.

Because of the way that I used hope in this relationship, it had become a trap for me, a way that I didn't have to examine the painful aspects of the relationship. I told myself that I hoped what I did today would be acceptable to him. By stating that, I was passively, though unintentionally, able to ignore what wasn't working in the relationship. More importantly, I wasn't doing anything constructive or action-oriented to strengthen the relationship by communicating my unhappiness to Jonathan. Instead, while living a life of damage to my essence, I fed on this negative use of hope. It seemed to be easier to blame myself for my partner's rampages as I internally said, "*I hope he stops yelling soon. It hurts so much.*" Typical thoughts are:

"If I placate him, I won't get put down."

"If I just stay quiet, he can't twist my words and use them against me."

"If I change my tone of voice, she won't threaten to walk out on me."

Hope is implicit in each of these statements.

The incidents offered earlier may help you identify similar degrading characteristics in your own relationship. Like me, you may have gone to extraordinary lengths to explain away clues you have already gotten from a relationship.

Are you tenaciously holding on to hope even though you have to let go of your soul to do so? Facing the truth will empower you to make decisions on your own behalf.

You may wonder how someone like me, who holds a doctorate in clinical psychology, could be so unaware, so vulnerable to being ensnared by hope. I will mention only a few reasons people, including me, are so susceptible to the damaging of their souls. I will elaborate on each of these in later chapters.

Part of the vulnerability is due to cultural influences. The intense, sudden, and dramatic way that movies often portray romance makes it look extremely inviting. These scenes often cause people to say to themselves such things as "I want that" or "I could live like that." "I want him to tell me these endearing words, then I can believe them about myself." "I'll do anything to have that. Then I can feel fulfilled."

The behavior that is modeled for a child as she is growing up is a powerful influence. I learned I was expected to give up my own voice, needs, definitions of myself, and my own desires for my life for a man who could look after me and tell me who I was. From my perspective as a child, this looked great to me. I hoped for something that emulated this type of relationship.

I realize that as a child I often intervened between my parents in order to protect my mother from any possible anger. For example, I would often search frantically for a missing article. It could be a knife for carving the pot roast which was sitting in front of my father. Or it might be the keys that were missing from their normal hook as my father was rushing to an important meeting. I remember that I raced to provide the knife, key, or whatever else it might have been, hoping that would maintain or restore peace. At the time, it seemed like a small price to pay for keeping the peace.

I can only guess that I probably averted many arguments. Maybe there wouldn't have been any. The impact of even a few scenes to a small child can be enormous. A child makes assumptions from what she experiences as she relives such scenes over and over. I somehow felt growing up that I wouldn't be loved by both parents if I didn't appease each of them. It was perhaps unfounded, who knows, I just know I lived with that assumption and acted accordingly. Later, I feared most men and especially ones who were already into their anger. Early on, I hoped whatever I did would smooth things over.

I concluded that it was essential to placate. I had to do whatever it took to please the man in a relationship. I definitely decided I must give up who I was and who I needed to be for "him."

It is relevant to point out a child's conclusions about what they perceive life to be. I had not updated my early conclusions. You may not have, either. Society, my assumptions about my parents, and other experiences taught me what I had to do to survive – mug my soul so that I would be accepted, cared for. I robbed my soul in the hope of pleasing another person.

It is very human to go towards that with which you are familiar. I know I was drawn to men, though certainly not consciously, who carried an air of "you must please me," thus ones who had to be treated carefully. They sometimes voiced an ultimatum, but often a look, a sigh, or a tone created the same internal reactions.

I was extremely attracted to this familiar feeling. I knew what to do when that feeling was present. I had to hope I could do something; and I was determined to do whatever I had to do to quell the raging waters.

Because of the culture in which I was raised and the particular family system in which I lived, I believed praise, support, and acknowledgment were hard to come by. In a soul starvation mode, I was vulnerable to a man who I hoped could give me these things, even if only intermittently. Since my soul was hungry, I would take whatever small indications of fond utterances I could get. That's how I defined my self as lovable.

Can you see how this scenario gets created? It is truly a lethal set-up. It is reinforced by the ways we view our lives in relation to others. To many, a partner not only comes first, but decides who and what you are. "That is just how it is," you say to yourself. You are not consciously aware of what you are doing or what you are deciding when you put yourself in these situations. You only hope it works.

However, hope was a nearly impenetrable barrier when I attempted to move out of these situations – like trying to walk through molasses. Hope kept me embedded.

When I look back at the dichotomy between how I expressed myself in a professional situation versus how I experienced myself in a personal one, I am astounded. I was two different people in every way I can name. The worst part was that, at the time it was happening, I could not begin to reconcile the gap that existed for so long between these two worlds.

In public, I was extremely confident, competent, and in charge of my life. In the professional realm, I was powerful, reliable, consistent, help-giving, caring, authentic, responsive, and on-top-of every situation. I successfully taught classes on relationships, which included describing the qualities necessary for a fulfilling match. In fact, I exhibited these qualities in every situation except in the presence of someone whose love I hoped I could have and keep.

Because the partner I chose was very charming, seductive, and romantic some of the time, I had fallen in love with him the first time I saw him. I viewed him as someone I had looked for to fill these, until that point, unmet needs. He went beyond fitting any description I had for a man. I put myself at his mercy by allowing him to say who I was, to decide my soul's fate. Besides, I wanted to be with him forever.

I had gathered a lot of evidence over the years to back up what I wanted to have in a relationship. The way we met, how deeply I had become attached to him, and the hope-filled stories I told myself about him added to the myth for me. Hope was claiming my life, and I did not even realize it.

It didn't matter, unfortunately, that I found out fairly early on that my lover had a great deal of rage inside of him. I minimized it by hoping I could change not only myself, but him, and even the situation to such an extent that the rage would disappear.

I did not perceive at the time it was something he had brought with him into the relationship. Furthermore, I did not see that I had given this man the power to cause me to continue to feel soul mugged and off-balance. At that point, my heart was ruling my head.

Personally, I ignored everything that didn't coincide with the fantasy I'd built about how the relationship could be when these "little" things were refined. Then, I hoped, I would be treasured and cared about in just the way I had always dreamed I would be, and even had periodically been told by him that I would be. You may say you are systematically worn down. You are not alone. You have most likely minimized the destruction to your soul for many years. Of course you mistrust your perceptions. You are entrenched in patterns and cycles that have created enormous pain over time.

I know the pain, and I know the way out because I finally triumphed over the many hidden traps and seemingly impassable obstacles. I know what kind of courage and tenacity it takes, especially when it comes to taking the word "hope" out of my vocabulary. I also know what kinds of resources are called for.

However, until you say, "My essence is being invalidated, and I am committed to stopping it in my life no matter what it takes," the information I present will not filter through your hope. What I say will not make a difference. You will stay as you are.

People have probably tried to get through to you. They certainly attempted to speak to me about my situation. It did not work.

There is a part of you that already knows, though, that what I am saying to you is true. It creates such anxiety that the tendency is to slam the book shut or say, "How interesting. She is right. She has a point there, but… " The words "but" and "hope" have kept you embedded in a pattern of soul mugging. You must be willing to go beyond the "but," to give up hope, to risk hearing distressful things, and to tolerate being excruciatingly uncomfortable for awhile. Otherwise you will not listen in a way that will awaken you or empower you to take a stand in your life *for* your self and *against* soul mugging.

51

When I say "excruciatingly uncomfortable," I mean that when I attempted to move out of my romantic relationship, I felt that I would die. I wanted to die. Giving up hope and not using the word "but" anymore left me in the bleakest, darkest place I had ever been. I had to face the complete absence of my being. I had robbed myself over time of my essence. This relationship, which I hoped would restore me, further robbed me.

You may have briefly experienced these feelings in the past. To stay in that blackness for any length of time is the worst pain that you may ever have experienced. Yet I survived, and you will too. You will not think so while you are in the midst of it, though.

I could not write this book until I had moved through the agonizing process. I kept hope going for a long time. I used "but" with every sentence people in my life brought up to me about their concern for the well-being of my soul.

I could not even grasp what they were saying. It did no good. None.

The attachment I had with my partner was deeper, stronger, and more intense than anything I had ever had. Yours is too. You already know that. It is a strange bond in that it is full of negatives as well as positives. Yet, in a weird way this contrast only serves to strengthen the bond and creates a further barrier preventing you from moving out of it.

I am asking you to do something that I personally and professionally know is the hardest request one can make of another human being. I am asking you not to avoid what is difficult for you.

It would be easy for you to put the book down now and not read it. You have done that with other books. It would feel safer for you to stay with what is familiar to you. I strongly suggest that you stay with this book and see what happens.

My favorite story is about the caterpillar. Wouldn't it have been easier for the caterpillar not to build a chrysalis, not to build a dark place that became, in a sense, his very own death spot? The caterpillar built that dark chrysalis for the purpose of changing form, developing wings and becoming free.

I suggest you stay with the first three chapters at least a couple of days before going on with the rest of the book. Make a decision about whether or not you are willing to face what you must take on to have a different life, free of hope but full of freedom and possibility. If you make the commitment to end soul savagery forever in your life, then by all means, do not put this book down.

Recommit to continuing to read this book and, more importantly, to examining your soul each time you begin to feel uncomfortable with the feelings coming up as you read. Pay close attention to those feelings. See if you can let the feelings be and let yourself be with the feelings.

Great value can come from your being willing to stay with your discomfort. It can tell you as much about you and about the ways you have refused to face your situation as anything you have ever done.

Be willing to be with yourself, your feelings, and your discomfort. You will not die from that. In fact, you may begin to sense a new life breaking through.

Do the following three tasks before continuing to read the other chapters in the book. Be willing to take the time to answer the questions thoughtfully and completely.

> Make a list of what you would like in a life that is flourishing, one that does not have the word hope in the internal conversations you have about it. Be as precise as you can. Start to imagine specifics of what you would like.

> Write a paragraph on what it feels like to be considering breaking up and leaving a whole set of beliefs about your self, your essence, and relationships in general. Do you suddenly get short of breath? Where in your body do you feel the most discomfort?

> Write a paragraph about what, until now, has stopped you from leaving the soul mugging and soul negation. Now write one about how you would feel if you could be free of obstacles which until now have kept you from moving to a new world of options and a new realm of freedom. Would you be ecstatic? Would you feel empty? Would you feel there is meaning to life? Would you suddenly feel visible for the first time in years? Keep going deeper for more feelings.

In the following chapters, I will do several things. First I will continue to provide ways for you to wake up to what is happening in your life. I will offer theories to explain why the soul negation syndrome occurs and specific ways you can be freed of it. I will also invite you to commit to never again allowing soul mugging in your life.

Included in every chapter will be the integration of spirituality and psychology which is essential for transformation. Spirituality is broadly defined as the courage to look within. What is seen and what is trusted is a deep sense of belonging, connectedness, and openness to the infinite.

Some part of you already knows that this wisdom exists inside you, although for years you have become disconnected from it and unable to join with this wise place within yourself. This voice, which guides you and holds your essential self, is whole and perfect. It always has been and always will be.

Psychological growth involves recognizing that place deep within you and living from it. That place is one you have been distracted from, pulled away by, vilified for, and have forgotten due to many experiences in your life. There are spiritual and psychological principles which together can uncover these experiences. They can facilitate reconnection with that source of life.

By interweaving psychology and spirituality, transformation can take place, awakening you to who you are now and helping you move toward who you can be. To transform literally means to move beyond the form you are presently in.

The purpose of this book is to identify those of you who have experienced profound instability at your center and to help you create for your self a life that is free of any and all desecrating situations.

You can move beyond the form you now experience to a place where you will no longer accept relationships that do not honor and deeply revere you. In transformational work, you will systematically step out of the denigration of your spirit.

> I *want my stuff back ...*
> *stealing my shit from me*
> *don't make it yours*
> *makes it stolen ...*
> *and it wasn't a spirit took my stuff*
> *was a lover*
> *I made too much room for...*
> – Ntozake Shange

Chapter Four

How Deep is the Ocean? How High is the Sky?

A Self Exploration

We must be still and still moving
Into another intensity
For a further union, a deeper communion
Through the dark cold and the empty desolation.
– T.S. Eliot

"I've Been Dying For Ten Years"

A woman came into my office for the first time, having called the previous night for help to quell her unbearable terror. Through her sobs it became apparent that her footing on the ladder of life was slipping away, and she felt an acute awareness of her loss of self. She threatened that if she stayed one more day in her relationship, she might just as well take that lethal overdose she had been tempting herself with for many months.

That next day, as we met in my office, she told me more about her emotional state. I was reminded of a line I'd once read:

> If thy soul is a stranger to thee,
> the whole world is unhomely.

Indeed, this woman's soul had become a faded image, barely traceable to her now, as it had slipped away without her conscious permission.

How are the soul violations (she had no name for her plight) that this woman described allowed to occur at all? How are they prolonged, especially for a period of years? And how are they tolerated over time? You will learn the many answers about your own self as you read and study this chapter. You will be led through a process of questioning and reflecting. As you participate in an intense and rigorous exploration of your own life, you will gradually discover the answers to these questions and many others. This process is for yourself, from your soul.

This guide is similar to a road map, beginning with where you are now. Your destination is your own understanding as you form answers to questions such as:

> How could this have happened?

> How could I have let my soul be desecrated for even one moment, much less for such a long period of my life?

This guide allows you to explore the intricate rationale you have built, especially your denial of your suffering soul, suffering which you have accepted as necessary for sustaining your relationship.

As we begin this self-examining, self-probing, self-unfolding, and certainly self-revealing process, look at it as an adventure. Remember what Henry David Thoreau stated:

The cost of a thing is the amount of what I call life which is required to be exchanged for it, immediately or in the long run.

When you tried to exchange your life for affection, unconditional love, respect, attention, soul nourishment, and a caring person, have you found the cost to be quite great?

You will find that the process of self-examination is not easy to take. It will demand unwavering honesty with yourself about your experience. You will encounter areas where you have had the most difficulty – not on the surface, but inside, as close to the depths of your feelings as you can reach.

If you choose to bypass these questions, to minimize them, or to skip over pertinent details in any of the questions, you will be cheating yourself. You will perpetuate your life experience of not getting what you need because you are unwilling to delve deeply into the center of your existence and pull from it the relevant answers that will inform you about you.

I invite you to let these questions, statements, incomplete sentences, and jarring confrontational inquiries take you so far into your own deep valleys that at times you actually may feel as if you are in the shadow of death. You will not die, but you may want to or think you might.

That is probably why you have never been willing to go there. This could truly be your own dark journey into the black night you may have heard others speak about. It is extremely important to remind yourself that if you persevere you will gain revealing insights, provided you have the courage not to deny in your dark moments what you have seen in the light.

You see, at one time you did see, you did know. You were completely aware of your soul and the delight you had in being in the world and in fully flourishing as that soul. Some, or perhaps many things happened along the way, and now it is time to find out just what those things were, to name the unnamed, to explore the unexplored and ultimately, by the end of this book, to heal the unhealed pain, grief, and hurt that you have carried with you until now.

You will be tempted quite often, maybe every two or three questions, to slam this book shut and distract yourself. This is a normal reaction to the deep work we are now initiating. However, taking only a short break, leaving the bookmark in its proper place, will serve you now. A long period away from the process will only pull you back to that familiar prison in which you have sought refuge for many years.

Keep out of that place and you will find there are many other wonderful places to know. I plead with you to continue with these structured, carefully designed exercises. They will help you gain the insights you must have for your transformation out of misery, and you will thank yourself forever.

Trust my sight, since I know it is difficult for you to see the light ahead at this point. Right now you most likely feel very disconnected from your soul and cannot imagine choosing something that would be only for your own best interest and no one else's. I will not lead you astray, but you must keep close to this road map and refer to it often.

Before you go any further, be sure to have a thick journal with you at all times as you go through the questions. Let this journal be only for this process, not the journal you may have for some other purpose. Also, have more than one pen at hand, since sometimes something as minor as not having a pen that writes well becomes an excuse to interrupt the journey. Here is the first set of questions and probings:

Finding a Frame for Yourself

Ql. How long have you been dying? How much longer are you willing to die while you hope for a change in the relationship – not an evening of bliss, but a substantial change that lasts over a period of time, a change you know you can count on?

Reflections

Throughout this chapter I will deliberately provoke your soul. Each question or statement has as its purpose to aim well and pierce through your protective deafness. You were not meant to live the life that you have been living. You are familiar with it, as perplexing as it may be to you. You also are strangely comfortable with things exactly the way they are. Do you agree? "No," you may scream. I don't believe you. However, you, as everyone else, are doing what you want at every moment since you do have a choice, even if you aren't consciously aware of that choice and when it was first made.

One day during my own journey, I looked out a window. I saw a large, corroded, rusty gate and I panicked. *I am in prison,* I thought. Then I realized that I could open the gate any time I wanted, because the lock was on my side of the gate. You must realize that your prisons are made moment by moment as you stay where you are, as you are, and who you are.

An Unanswerable Dilemma

Q2. Do you feel imprisoned and trapped? Does any decision you think of making create indescribable anxiety?

Reflections

I know those four prison walls very well. I have even written "Help, please, somebody hear my plea" on those walls. Your soul is in danger, and you do not know how this happened. All you did was love someone and believe in that person and his or her promises. That's all. Or is it?

I bring striking new vision to your relationship now. You cannot think of excuses I have not heard in my practice or used myself. If you keep reading, and I certainly am urging you to for the sake of your soul, you will discover the treacherous ways you have fooled yourself into believing that you and the other person in the relationship could be different without hard work. The revelation comes when you are transformed from a believer in magic to a knower of true possibilities.

Read the questions slowly and take five to ten minutes or longer to ponder each one before you begin answering. The part of you that first reacts to the question is not the part of you that knows your answer. Your answer comes from the core of you, from the deepest part of you.

Develop a specific kind of external and internal environment before continuing this process. Find a quiet place where you can feel a sense of reverence around you. You will most likely receive answers from a silence within you, from your sacred place of inner stillness.

Begin only after you know in both your outer and inner worlds that you have created an environment which will help you through the difficult journey ahead.

Your Early Imprints

Q3. Assuming that you reap what you sow, what is the earliest seed you planted about who you were to be in relationship to another?

Q4. What part of you did you have to suppress in your childhood in order to be accepted?

Q5. What specific phrases stand out for you as you think of ways you began to be defined in your family?

Q6. What style of relating did you use with the opposite sex in your earliest school years?

Q7. Finish this sentence: "I am most likely to be received favorably by others when I…"

Q8. Make a list of all the people you can think of, living or not, who love you. Beside each one list specific things he or she says or does to let you know you are loved.

Q9. What is your favorite activity to do alone? How would it change if the person you are in a relationship with were along?

Q10. Close your eyes and summon up the first image of pure love that you can remember. Open your eyes and write about this experience, even if some of the details are missing. How did it develop? How did you feel? How long did it remain?

Q11. When in your current relationship did you first cry or feel very upset? What was happening at the time? What led to that particular event?

Q12. Recreate the memory of the first time your soul was disturbed (even if you did not understand this concept at the time). Who was in the scene with you? What gave you that understanding?

Reflections

It has been said that those who float with the current, who do not guide themselves according to higher principles, who have no ideal and no conviction, become a thing moved instead of a living and guiding being; they become echoes, not voices. Those who have no inner life are slaves to their surroundings, just as the barometer is the obedient servant of the air at rest.

Does the above statement make sense to you when you apply it to your life as you begin to understand it? These first questions have focused on how your behavior is swept along, as if you were a thing moved instead of the guiding being who drives your own spirit. Are you an echo instead of a voice?

These first questions allowed you to expose the intricate web of denial that you built in order to live in the condition you are now examining. As you can see, the beginning questions ask you, in different ways, to relate to your life in a deeper, more introspective manner. In this way, you can discover the various patterns that you created, not consciously, but over time, little by little, step by step. Gradually it will become very clear just how you became a slave to your situation, or at least why it feels that way to you.

Let your soul inform you. It can.

Your Conflicted Inner Self

Q13. What picture, image, or phrase do you think of when you hear the word "love?"

Q14. How many times in your current relationship have you said to the other person "treat me in a different way, or I'll leave," and then not left?

Q15. Do you believe anyone would believe your claim of distress, given the absence of outward signs (such as bruises or a broken jaw) to confirm the inward violence that your essence has experienced for many years?

Q16. How often, after an interaction that you realize, upon looking back now, was injurious to your soul, have you said one or more of the following to your self:

    a.   This person has just had a bad day at work.

    b.   I must have done something to displease this person I am interacting with (if it was early in your life).

    c.   I'd better call and make things all right again; I'm afraid this other person will leave and not come back.

    d.   This other person had a rotten childhood and has not handled it fully, but I know when he or she deals with it in therapy that everything will be fine.

Q17. Is there a toll you pay for managing all that has to be managed to keep your relationship intact? Do you think it is completely up to you to keep the peace? What pursuits have you laid aside in order to devote more time and energy to making this relationship viable?

Q18. Have you ever noticed the other person's behavior, social etiquette, and the ways he or she interacts with others as being strikingly different from the way he or she treats you in private? Do you ever conclude that it is you who must be wrong, or at least confused, about the other's interactions and behaviors with you? Does the other's perception of reality override your own?

Q19. Has anything your friends or family ever said about your relationship prompted you to protect and defend the other person?

Q20. How often have you thought of leaving but didn't for any number of reasons, including your hope that things would turn around within the next few weeks? Name the reasons both for your wanting to leave and your choosing to stay. Be as specific as possible.

Q21. Which of the following warning signs that someone is desecrating your soul can you identify with?

    a.   This person is hypersensitive, easily insulted, and claims hurt feelings when he or she is actually angry. This person rants about injustices that you see as just a part of life.

    b.   This person has sudden mood swings. He or she can switch in a matter of minutes from being very loving to being explosively violent and distressing to your soul.

    c.   This person has threatened worse treatment, saying such things as "I'll break this bed apart" or "I'll choke you with my bare hands, and don't you think I can't," then immediately dismissed these comments with "Everybody talks that way," or "You are just too sensitive even to interact with" or "I didn't really mean that."

    d.   This person is often critical or even blatantly cruel to very deep, sacred aspects of your being.

Q22. Rate between 1 and 10 (with 10 representing the highest rating) your own value in the following settings: 1) by yourself; 2) with your best friend; 3) with your favorite family member; 4) with a person you dislike with whom you must interact often; 5) with the person you are currently in a relationship with.

Reflections

These questions are designed to help you begin an in-depth inquiry into your relationship. These kinds of questions are scattered throughout the chapter. You are confronted with new perspectives which may reveal to you how immobilized you have become. The outcome of any decision is probably unbearably painful for you. You may actually imagine being annihilated by any of the options you can think of. At this point in your life, in whatever direction you look toward, dying seems to you to be the best option.

If you relate to any of the above descriptions, you are exactly where you need to be to explore the ways in which this immobilization has been set up throughout your life. Then you can unravel what you have carefully woven, even though you wove it that way in order to accomplish what you wanted. Perhaps you now realize that it cannot, the way it is, bring you anything but immense pain.

Now, as you begin to discover the complex and perplexing set of circumstances that placed you here in the first place, it is important to have a conversation with your soul about your awareness of your inability to break free. It is certainly no accident that you are here. It is also not something you would knowingly have ever done to your essence.

It is extremely important to avoid judging where you are. The purpose of this chapter is to inform you, to give voice to your emerging insights and terrors about the soul mugging that has occurred in your life. You must see the need to stop beating up on your self as you have been doing for many years.

You are at the perfect place. I have faith that you will eventually arrive at a place where you can accept that statement. This truly is needed in order to free your soul for movement to a higher level of growth. I know that you certainly do not see soul mugging as something you want to admit to at this point. I believe you when you say that you do not perceive that you are at any place but a hellish one right now. I felt the same way at this point in my progression through this mire. Thus, trusting in the process of what you are doing at this moment and then the next is all the more essential as we go along. Are you willing to do that?

I realize that your trust is an act of pure faith. However, except for the feeling that you are on solid ground and that your soul is intact, what do you have to lose? You are already in so much pain that this soul restoration work is absolutely necessary for your well being. Remember that the dark night of the soul comes just before revelation and new life.

Deeper Insights

Q23. Have you ever noticed your fears keeping you away from the experiences you would most value?

Write about this statement in terms of its meaning in your life and in your relationship: "The very cave you are afraid to enter turns out to be the source of what you are looking for. That dreaded, horrid thing in the cave has become the center. It is by going down into the abyss that you recover life's treasures."

Q24. If the healing hurts more than each incident of diminution or violence to your soul, what inspiration can you provide yourself so that you will be willing to go through the pain? It is important to think about this long enough to form some plan that will inspire you.

Q25. What parts of yourself have you actually given over to another? Name each part that is missing and describe why you decided that it was necessary to give it up. These things might be your needs, self-respect, self-value, self-evaluation, and ability to feel in control of your own feelings and thoughts.

Q26. List at least five different ways in which you have completed the sentence "I hope… "

Q27. What role does confusion play in keeping you in this relationship? Describe exactly what is confusing to you.

Q28. Have you ever spoken to anyone who knew this person you are in a relationship with before you met him or her? How did this person describe the other to you? Did you let this person know what life with him or her is like for you? Why not? What are you protecting?

Q29. How have you justified what is happening to your soul? What have you said to yourself about the robbing of your essence that you have experienced? Write it out so that you can evaluate it carefully.

Q30. What do you tell your self about what may happen to this other person if you leave? How likely is that to actually occur? By staying, are you choosing to take care of him or her over your soul? Be extremely honest here.

Q31. Who have you lied to about this relationship? How come you lied at that moment? List each person you have lied to and why you felt it was necessary. What do you think would have happened if you'd told the truth? And then what? And then? Go all the way to the end of your fear here.

Q32. Are you with someone whom no one would ever guess has another side to his or her personality? Does that situation make it more difficult for you to believe your own experience? Would others believe you if you told them the truth? How large an issue is this in your decision to stay or leave?

Q33. If you are on this other person's side, blaming only yourself for the problems in your relationship, and this person is on his or her own side (also blaming you) then who is on your side?

Reflections

These questions are designed to help you gain insight into what may occur if you continue in the same direction you have been going. Continuing on that path may have enormous consequences and even cause a great imbalance in your life. Even now you can see that you are unable to consistently embrace your life with enthusiasm.

Though it may be painful to face these responses directly, you can name, examine, and then move through them, knowing that you are taking steps toward your own soul renewal.

The process cannot be rushed; it has its own time and pacing. Let your silent part inform you, not frighten you, as you continue to unfold.

Additional Insights

Q34. As a child, you most likely filtered many events using the denial tactic. It probably became so familiar to deny that eventually you did not see the repeated injury to your soul. You probably didn't think denial was disruptive to your core. Now, though, can you recognize the closely guarded perceptions you may be ignoring? Where are you hiding them and who is the one who loses the most? What secrets are you keeping from yourself? Name them.

Q35. What percentage of your staying has to do with children? Do you think they are oblivious to the tension? To the anger? To the pain to your soul? Do you honestly think the children are thriving if you are slowing killing your essence by the choices you make?

Q36. A soul naturally moves towards knowledge; for it not to know or be confused by a gesture, a look, or a certain mood is absurd. Its knowledge can move that soul into despair. When information is ambiguous or not forthcoming, a child's essence takes on blame and guilt for circumstances beyond its ability to influence. Give an incident from your childhood that exemplifies this phenomenon.

Q37. Have you ever said "I want to die?" What alarm did you want to sound at that moment? Describe in detail the message you wanted to send.

Q38. What is your excruciating pain about? What powerful and deep sorrow are you avoiding by staying in the relationship? Is this relationship keeping you from a despair that you imagine will kill you or cause you to feel as if you had died?

Q39. What do you want to do with your unique, sacred and precious life? Write at least a page on this.

Q40. Do you ever miss yourself – that feeling of belonging to yourself, of knowing that your wants count?

Q41. When was the last time you chose to overlook a robbing of your essence, even if you thought it was only a small thing? Describe the incident without judging anyone. At what point did you know you were lessened by the incident? At the time? Later? Not until now, when asked to think back with awareness?

Q42. Your mind registers the truth of a situation, even though outwardly you may deny what is and has been happening for many years. What have you denied that, deep in your mind, you know to be true? Be specific and write at least two pages about it.

Q43. In order to unmask the unnamed agony of your life, it is necessary to speak about the unsettling and unsatisfying things that keep showing up. Name, in the various forms that this disturbance appears, at least two events that stand out now as similar, though at the time you did not connect them in any way.

Q44. A woman once voiced this observation: "He took my life many years ago. He destroyed everything about me – my way of thinking, my preferred style of dressing, my views about life and about myself … " Do these words describe any thoughts you have ever had, even if for only a passing moment?

Reflections

Be patient with yourself. You'll know whether or not it's time to make a move in the relationship. For now, you are doing exactly what you need to do: exploring the internal nature of your reality to expose the thinking patterns that may have created a sense of feeling stuck, impotent, or helpless.

By reading this far in the book, you have acknowledged that something is awry. That very willingness will prompt you to change and will carry you to the next stage in the journey.

Be gentle with all that's opening up for you. Judging it will only cause it to go underground again. Note it and allow it its sacred space in which to breathe. I find it is important to be curious about all that is unsolved in your heart. Be grateful that you are allowing all you have buried to have its own unique reawakening.

The Relationship as a Mirror

Q45. List five reasons you have stayed in the relationship. Include any of the following if you have ever uttered them to yourself, even once:

a. There's something wrong with me. This does not happen to other people, so something's wrong with me.

b. I feel humiliated and betrayed by life in general.

c. I want to believe I'm with my best friend, so when this person turns on me, I just remember my first impressions and desires and forget the rest.

d. It'll get better; I sure hope it will.

e. Who'd believe why I left? Anyone would think I was crazy to leave someone with this person's standing in the community.

f. I know this person loves me, and that's really the only important thing to me.

g. I feel caught, like in a spider web; I can't move in any direction without pain.

h. I saw my parents act ugly with each other, and they stayed together. In a strange sort of way, I think closeness and devaluation of my being just kind of go together.

i. I'd rather be with this person than be alone. Who wants to be alone?

Q46. Do you ever envy this other person? Do you think it takes a lot of power and authority to diminish another person's soul? Would you like a little of that sense of assertiveness mixed with intimidation?

Q47. A line from the movie *Pretty Woman* states: "The bad stuff people say about me is easier to believe." Do you ever have that thought?

Q48. Sam, a character in the movie *Avalon,* stated: "I went to see Helena Street and it was gone. I went to find my home on 3rd street, but it wasn't there. Finally, I found the street where I went to school. For a moment, I thought I never was."

Is there ever a moment in your relationship where you have a sense of being invisible, unattended to on every level, as if you, your essence had vanished? Think about this then write about your own experience of being absent from your self. Where were you? Who was around? What was occurring in the environment? Be as specific as you can and go back to as early in your life as you can remember.

Q49. How does it serve you to play small, that is, to be quiet, compliant, unobtrusive, obedient, silent and non-confrontive about the erosion of spirit that you feel in this relationship?

Q50. Have you ever asked yourself: "How could this have happened to me? I've always been told, and I used to believe, that I was so smart?" This fallacy of the place of intelligence in the onset of soul mugging is pervasive. State on paper, in your own words, how this belief relates to you. Has someone besides you ever asked you that question?

Q51. Are you willing to trust God in the darkness? As you move deeper into the awareness of your soul's demise, is your spirituality an anchor you will grab? Or did it also disintegrate with the dark journey your soul has taken? As you respond, write out a definition of your spirituality and state what it symbolizes, if anything, for you in your life right now.

Q52. Have you ever thought about how different your life with this other person would be if your conversations were broadcast on radio? What would be the impact on others, on your relationship, and most importantly, on you? What would change?

Q53. What positive place did hope have in your early life? Give some specific instances where you either first heard this word used by others you respected or you found yourself offering it as a way to say something uplifting to a friend. What role has it played in your current relationship? Be exact in your answer here.

Reflections

These last ten questions have helped to magnify the ways you see yourself in relationship to another. In my clinical practice, I have actually heard every single one of these statements about why people stay in relationships that disrupt and degrade their souls. I have had patients feel ashamed that they were not good enough to receive the kind of love that embraced their souls. They thought they'd be protected if they could just "get it right." On the other hand, they felt they would be ostracized by the community who taught them how to act in relationships if they did not do as they were told.

Some of these same perceptions of your self may be coming to the foreground of your mind now. They are being presented to you by you in whatever form they appear (your thoughts, your judgments of yourself, your own shame, your own views of how stupid you must be, etc.) in order to be healed, not to further punish yourself or beat up on yourself. It is not a matter of right or wrong thinking, but rather a result of being inculcated with a set of beliefs that led you to understand yourself and the world of relationships in a certain light.

This world, as you are viewing it from a more informed position now, may seem less plausible than it did when you carried it around in your head as if it were the truth. It has been said that it's hard to fight an enemy with outposts in your own head. That's accurate. To take these beliefs out of your head and put them into a journal to read and re-read, plus to be able to sift through them and find yourself in them, are major steps out of denial. They represent major steps towards soul renewal.

Keep exploring. By continuing to read even when it is very challenging and painful to continue, you are progressing toward reclaiming your soul. Now is the time to take particular care of your self. Take long walks, have soothing baths, drink comforting hot liquids, lie on soft, scented pillows, and find new experiences to have with nature. When taking short breaks, start noticing things in your environment that you are drawn to but never caught your attention in the past.

Facing Your Past

Q54. "Don't grow a wishbone where your backbone needs to be." Interpret this statement in relation to your life at present.

Q55. Presume for a moment that you entered your relationship with a hole in your soul. What caused that hole and how would you describe it? What does it feel like in your body? What images emerge as you hear the words "hole in your soul" stated in terms of your own soul?

Q56. Anais Nin once wrote that we don't see things as they are, we see them as we are. Write in your journal whatever thoughts this comment brings to mind.

Q57. Who influenced you to focus your love on another, to value another's attention and nourishment over being sure that you paid attention to your own needs as well as theirs? Take time to ponder this question. It can easily be overlooked as "not applicable" to you. Somewhere, at some point, someone modeled this way of life for you or you figured out (we are very bright as children) how best to receive what you felt you needed.

Q58. Did you learn to define love as evasion, self-denial, enslavement, and/or capitulation? Elaborate on what other similar definitions you learned through the years. In any of your past or present relationships did rage accompany love? Have you recognized that, even though you may have been damaged instead of treasured by your early caretakers, you were not able to walk or even crawl away from them?

Reflections

If you feel the least bit anxious (stomach churning, head throbbing, a strong impulse to slam this book shut) take a deep breath now and let it out very slowly. Once more, take a breath saying the words "I am" as you breathe in and "peace" as you breathe out. Do this three more times deliberately and slowly. Good.

The discomfort you are experiencing stems from facing scenes and feelings you have been running from for some time. It is perfectly normal to be uncomfortable. Do not run now. Your discomfort is telling you something you need to know. If you push your unwelcome feelings away with food, drugs, alcohol, or anything that you have used in the past to pacify your discomfort, you will perpetuate a vicious cycle which will lead to even greater despair.

These feelings are present for a reason. Do not ignore them and do not be frightened of them. They will not destroy you. What will slowly destroy you is not addressing them.

It is natural to have physical reactions to these questions, and it is a positive sign. I urge you not to stop but perhaps to pause for a few minutes. This is intense work you are doing. While it is not to be postponed, neither is it to be rushed. Your body is speaking loudly to you. One part is saying "What if I have to leave this relationship? I cannot handle that; I know I can't." The other part is urging you to keep moving through this discomfort, knowing that there is a purpose to it all.

Unfolding within you now is a soul long pressed down, numbed, pushed aside, and ignored – all without your conscious endorsement. This happened over a very long period of time. Waking up to your self is a difficult process. It is painful to discover that you did not have any idea what you were doing.

Be particularly gentle with your self at this time. What do you like to do – walk on the beach, hike in the mountains, explore nature, listen to the birds, or plant seeds in your garden? Whatever your favorite activities are, do at least three of them within the next week. It is as necessary as an antibiotic for an infection to nurture your self in these ways. It counteracts some of the heaviness of these new realizations. You must spend time on you, with you, focused lovingly inward while going through this book.

Finding YOUR Self

Q59. What pulls and tugs are you experiencing from within? Whose voices are telling you. "Stop this whole process, now. Do not go on to another page in this book. It is a waste for you to delve into this area. Just quit it. It is dumb and will only bring you grief."?

The appeal to obey this voice is strong. Are you ready to get off this repetitive cycle which is going nowhere? Are you going to continue to listen to this voice? You have had, until now, a fixed role with your internal board of directors telling you how to run your life and your relationships. Are you prepared to fire any of them? First you must identify them. Name each member. Where are they sitting in the imaginary boardroom in your head? Who is the chairperson? That's as far as you need to go at this point. There can be up to twenty-five people, living or dead, in the room, so be sure you have named each of them by name. Who is actually the boss of your life?

Q60. According to a hero in a James Joyce novel, when a person's soul is born, there are nets flung at it to hold it back from flight. What nets were flung at your soul early on?

Q61. In T.S. Eliot's play *The Cocktail Party,* the author portrays a man under the influence of alcohol leaning over to a psychiatrist at the cocktail party. The man pleads with the psychiatrist to please make him feel important. Have you ever, through your behavior or words, made this same plea?

Q62. Do you know your greatest power right now is to change your mind about who you are?

Q63. How does this passage from Dan Millman's *The Way of the Peaceful Warrior* (H.J. Kramer, 1985) speak to your current situation?

"As Joy sat behind my slumped form and gave my shoulders a rub, Socrates spoke: 'It's time you began learning from your life experiences instead of complaining about them or basking in them… your upsets and your unhappiness or happiness are the product of your thoughts. They have nothing to do with the actual events… your mind, not other people or your surroundings, is the source of your moods. Your anger is proof of your stubborn illusions.' Dan began to see as he thought: I met a man in a gas station who has shown me that life is not what it seems."

The way most people live kills them. They may take thirty or forty years to kill themselves by looking in the wrong places for their sense of self.

Did you know that you do not have to do anything except stop seeing the world from the viewpoint of your own distortions? Observe the debris of your mind right now. Can you begin to say, "I've finally seen the futility of trying to live up to the conditioned expectations of others, or of my own mind. I choose when, where and how I will think and act."? If not, how come?

Q64. Do you believe life gives you a gift of knowledge about your self every day? Do you think of everybody and everything that comes into your experience as either moving you towards your enlightenment or pushing you back into your distorted perceptions again? Try to write at least three pages on this idea. Examine it from the perspective of your entire life.

Q65. Can you even imagine that you see nothing as it actually is? In other words, you view everything through filters – the beliefs you have gathered through the years about your essence, your relationship, how to act, what to do in certain situations, etc. Your perceptions are limited by a mind that is still relating to your life as you have experienced it before this day and you have brought all those memories and "truths" into this moment. Once you can process this idea then the choice is not whether to see the past or the present, but to see in a brand new way. Many of those so-called truths are merely beliefs that do not presently serve you. I realized in my own experience that my choices about what I saw in my life had cost me my vision, my ability to perceive what was in my own best interest. How about you? Write about the beliefs you have carried with you for many years. Once you become aware of something, you can change it (or not). Which beliefs might you now choose to keep and which are you willing to let go of?

Q66. Do you imagine you need this other person to take care of you and save you from your worst fears? Have you ever noticed that you grasp at hope to assuage your fears? Do your fears often increase to such an extent that giving love to get love becomes the driving force in your life? Does it frighten you to feel so out of control in this area of your life? Does it keep you feeling off-balance as you are pulled into ways to keep this love going and keep this person around?

Reflections

I must confess that these last questions were difficult ones for me to ask you. When I was exploring my own situation, I frequently struggled with these issues, and so I know they are not easy ones to answer. For as long as I can remember I was taught that I must use others' eyes, ears, and voices to find out who and what I was. As a result, I was unaware that I had even learned that view of life. To me, it was natural and normal. It certainly worked every now and then. What more was there to ask for? I look back, and the image I get is climbing a huge mountain that keeps getting taller and steeper as I attempt frantically to reach the top. The "top" was hearing the words "you are good enough the way you are."

Yes, I can only recently see that I abandoned my sense of self, my own essence, so early in life that I never thought about it until I got into trouble in my romantic relationship. It took a lot of pain and suffering for me to finally become clear about what I had been doing.

I am telling you of my reaction to these last questions because I know that it is quite likely you had a similar early experience of closing your self down to try to please. You have probably been doing this for so long that you don't even realize it.

Chances are, you have done much of what I am prompting you to consider. You just cannot remember how, when, where or with whom. That is understandable. For now, simply keep your attention focused on discovering things about yourself. That focus will help make you aware of what you have unconsciously decided to believe over your lifetime. Awareness itself is a process of uncovering. There are many thick layers which cloud the vision you need to have now.

Your Even Deeper Self

Q67. How do you think the media, commercials, and songs such as "You're Nobody Till Somebody Loves You" influence your image of your ideal relationship?

Q68. Do you have any of the following beliefs? Select the beliefs you adhere to and write a paragraph about each. Be specific concerning the ways in which the statement matches your view of relationships:

   a.   Another person can protect me better than I can protect myself.

   b.   A relationship will make me happy.

   c.   A relationship will complete me.

   d.   A relationship will bring security to my life.

   e.   If I give my partner top priority, he or she will also give me top priority. My partner will be fair. If I give a lot, I will also get a lot.

Q69. Security is not found by merging two personalities. In fact, if you have sold out your individuality to your partner, then your attraction to each other is severely jeopardized, and your soul is lessened or nearly destroyed. You cannot be attracted to your own arm; neither can you be an appendage to another person and expect them to be attracted to you. Your soul gets lost in this type of set-up, and you wonder why you feel so empty. Reread the above sentences, and then write at length about your feelings and reactions.

Q70. When you lose your sense of self, your soul, by allowing another to define who you are, have you noticed that you have also lost your creativity? Creativity cannot function without a soul that is flourishing. You lose more than your self-esteem, your confidence, your ability to make decisions, and your joy. You lose the greatest gifts given to you at birth. Does that seem similar to your own experience? You are robbed of your core, which contains essential, unique treasures that can shine only when you are fully present to your self. List several occurrences of feeling when your creativity has been blocked or stunted. Also list occurrences when your creativity flourished. Do most of your experiences of satisfying creativity occur when you are within the relationship or do most occur outside of it?

Q71. The author Anais Nin expressed this thought: "When I look at the large green iron gate from my window it takes on the air of a prison gate. An unjust feeling, since I know I can leave the place whenever I want to, and since I know that human beings place upon an object, or a person, this responsibility of being the obstacle when the obstacle lies always within one's self."

Respond to this thought. How do you react to this assertion? What feelings emerge immediately? Especially note any feelings or thoughts you have about that prison gate image.

Q72. Do you maintain a dialogue with your soul? Consider this assertion: "People can share whole worlds with each other, but first they must have access to their own." Write in your journal about how you have given up access to your soul by asking another person to speak for your being.

Q73. How much of yourself have you disowned and for whom? Make two columns. In the left column name some of your qualities, and in the right column write the name of the person you gave it over to, or gave it up for, and when.

Reflection

At this point in your journey you may feel as if you were shoveling out mud after a flood. If so, you have allowed something essential in your soul to be purged. This precious part of you needs to be touched, opened, saturated with salve and allowed to experience what it means to be honored, renewed, and restored to its perfect place. You need to prepare your soul to proudly reside at the center of your awareness.

You may have decided by now that these probings have moved to another level, a place where they have become more challenging to admit to. That is understandable and absolutely normal. Take time to give space to your feelings. These now include a mixture of disbelief, hatred of every person you know or thought you knew (including yourself), sorrow, grief, shakiness, repulsion – a jumbled-up assortment that you see as you look into this mirror. Perhaps you are seeing this for the first time and noticing that the objects in this mirror are closer than they appear. These questions are about you, aren't they?

Getting to Know YOU

Q74. Make two columns. Title the left column "My Public Self" and the right column "My Private Self." Below each heading, list characteristics and observations about yourself. Compare your entries without judgment and draw some conclusions based on what you become aware of.

Q75. In your journal, draw a straight horizontal line across the page, left to right. The far left represents no sense at all of feeling complete, enjoying life and experiencing happiness. The far right represents a full sense of these feelings. Mark an "X" to indicate where you are right now. Put a "V" where you would like to be.

Not at all   Fully and completely
0_____10

Q76. When I was in the relationship I described in chapter one, I held several deeply ingrained beliefs. Do any of the following statements ring true for you? If so, write about those.

   a. Life is a struggle.

   b. Most people are mean and cruel to those important to them.

   c. I am a victim and have no power to change anything, including myself.

   d. I must be compliant and smooth things over. That is my job in a relationship.

   e. I can't make waves so I just won't express my anger about this incident.

   f. I must not speak up or take a stand if I want a relationship.

Q77. In the context of your relationship, which of these thoughts have you had over time?

   a. I must be crazy to stay.

   b. I don't know where I would go if I left.

   c. People will say it's all my fault for not sticking it out like I'm supposed to.

   d. I'm the only one in this mess, so I must try to fix it somehow.

   e. My religious beliefs say "turn the other cheek," "pray harder," "endure and make things work out. It's your duty and obligation."

   f. The person I'm involved with says he or she's sorry each time he or she has beaten down my spirit. I'm supposed to accept someone's apology.

   g. I am committed to this relationship. I can't imagine myself leaving and not being a forgiving person. I just couldn't live with myself.

   h. I can't abandon this other person. He or she has problems and I am a caregiver by nature. I know I can make this person better by loving him or her more and understanding his or her childhood horrors.

   i. I'm afraid of what will happen to him or her and to me if I leave.

   j. Who else would love me? I'm not that young or that attractive. And, after all, I am damaged goods. Who else could want me?

   k. I believe this person's insights about me, and I'm too embarrassed to tell anyone of my dilemma. Who else would understand or care? Besides, I'm sure this person is right about me. I am all the things, good and bad, that he or she says I am.

   l. When I tell this person what a friend or relative has said about some of the issues in our relationship, he or she always says, "Why do you believe that person over me? That person will tell you anything. When are you going to start just believing me?" Then I feel bad that I have gone outside the relationship for feedback.

   m. I understand that this relationship I'm in has a sense of entitlement and control. I feel I must adhere to this.

   n. I believe this person's promises to change. I really do. It just takes time.

o. Actually, I'm as terrified to leave as I am to stay. There is so much at stake here.

p. This person is under a lot of stress at work (or because of the loss of a job). I know he or she is not really like this.

q. I have no money of my own. What would I do for shelter, food, resources if I left? I can't just leave.

r. I am so ashamed and embarrassed that I am in such a predicament.

s. I have such guilt. I must take full responsibility for being here and not being able to make it better.

t. I've withstood so much in my life, I can withstand this too. I know I can.

Reflections

Sometimes a soul does not know what it needs until it gets it. As you may have noticed from this last set of questions, you may have been looking for affirmation of who you are for many years now. Perhaps you have looked for affirmation that you are loveable. It is important now for you, even if only in an intellectual way, to see that for soul renewal, you must give up the hope that another person will ever fill your emptiness. When you choose to stop, you will begin to hear a voice deep within you saying, "I've been waiting for you. Can you listen to *me* now? I will provide you with love. Trust *me* for a change."

It may help to repeat the following words to yourself as you continue unraveling the knotted and tangled pieces of your life: "This moment is the right time. Fulfillment is possible. It is available to me whenever I choose to look inward rather than outward for solutions to my dilemma."

Further Self-Discovery

Q78. Consider the possibility that you are not as afraid of your darkness (un-lovability) as you are of your light (your own internal power, your uniqueness). If you decided to own that light, you might be more alone than ever because you would then be a threat to others. Assume that these statements are true. Respond by writing down your reactions to them.

Q79. What does living outside of hope mean to you? What would it mean for *you* to live outside of hope?

Q80. Have you noticed that you have a high tolerance for pain? Throughout your life, have you minimized injuries to your body and/or to your essence?

Q81. A person whose soul has been repeatedly mugged often exhibits the following symptoms. Circle and write down in your journal any of these conditions if you have experienced them even once during your relationship:

Helplessness; powerlessness; increased heart rate; hyperventilation; nausea; trembling or shaking; excessive sweating; dizziness; feeling faint; blurred vision; tingling sensations in the arms or hands; diarrhea; nervousness; outbursts of anger; headaches; restlessness; hypersensitivity to sudden or rapidly changing stimuli (noise or light); fear of an incident recurring; difficulty falling asleep or staying asleep; recurring dreams about negative experiences; being jumpy, edgy, and easily startled; numbness or lacking emotion about anything; difficulty concentrating.

Q82. What are you avoiding by staying in a relationship where you are starving for love, but getting nothing but garbage for your soul? Usually pain will force you to pay attention. This is an indication of just how powerfully you have been held. You now need a new vision to propel you into a new place. That can happen when you allow your pain to become a sacred wound which can tell you a great deal about yourself. Are one or both of the following factors present in this desolate relationship and influencing your decision to stay? a) You isolate each negative interaction between you and your partner. Therefore you see no pattern or long-term detrimental effects. b) The other possibility is that your experience from early in your life was very negative. Then when this person entered the picture, and your relationship had its own negative aspects, you were not alarmed.

Reflections

It is extremely important that you notice what is going on within you as you examine your experience and your feelings.

How is this process affecting you? How do you feel about that? Do you gravitate towards things you know will be soothing to your soul? Are you taking breaks that allow you to gradually take in what you are discovering without overwhelming yourself? Are you altering your typical pattern of life, even if only slightly?

Are you still judging yourself as you answer these questions? Just notice it and let it be okay. Are there particular questions that you respond to with self-judgment? That's important information for you. Remember to say to yourself "What is, is" instead of those other harsh words.

Acceptance and approval are not interchangeable. Your acceptance of yourself is crucial, but your approval of your reactions to the questions is not. Your answers result from aspects of your life that perhaps you do not like now. There is a problem in your life because of that. What perpetuates these negative elements? The answer to that question is found by focusing on what you are doing to produce the same negative consequences over and over.

When you answer these questions thoughtfully and completely, as well as purposefully and with authenticity, you may say: "I don't want to change what I do, but I want the results to be different." If so, you must expect magic.

Free individuals are those who live as they choose. How free do you feel? The purpose of this chapter is to open some windows in that stuffy, tiny cubicle you've been existing in so that you can begin to experience freedom. Have you sensed that freedom yet? You will.

Envision a grander view of life where you have real choices, a life in which you will flourish. This grander perspective must include the realization of a soul, an essence that exists within you, which is beyond any relationship you are in. It will be beyond any role you now play or image you have of who you are. It will certainly be beyond any other person's definition of you. It will be that you who lives, steers your life, and nurtures your being.

Finding YOUR Truth

Q83. Have you ever stopped to think that feelings are not always a reliable indicator on which to base your decisions, especially if they are filtered through distorted perceptions? In other words, just because you feel strongly about this person and feel you would die without him or her, you are not "sentenced" to stay with that person. Your feelings do not necessarily indicate intense love. Instead, your feelings could indicate a need, a need which likely sprang from your past before you met this person. It may be important for you to explore, through your writing, the source of your needs and hurts. Turning from this task or numbing yourself psychologically are not productive choices. You would be no better off than a prisoner, resigned to loss of freedom and saying, "Maybe tomorrow things will be different." It is dangerous to your soul to avoid examining unresolved issues.

Q84. Just before you experienced what you feel with this important person, which of the following were true about your life?

    a.   I was unhappy with my life in many ways.

    b.   I was extremely lonely.

    c.   I was unsatisfied with where I had gotten in my job.

    d.   I was angry with my family.

    e.   I was lost.

    f.   I had an idealized fantasy about someone I would meet. It was a little too perfect and unreal, but I just knew I could find him or her somewhere, sometime.

    g.   The person I met had something I felt I lacked, for example, talent, looks, money, power, self-confidence, assertiveness, ability to make decisions, direction.

Q85. React thoughtfully to the following statement: "The thing I thought would solve my problem has actually become my problem."

Q86. Stand back from your relationship. Get an enlarged perspective of it for one week. Pay attention to motivation, interactions, how often you swallow your words, how often you experience a diminished sense of your essence, what contributions each person makes either towards uplifting the relationship or bringing it down. Especially take note of how often joy and lightheartedness appear. Write a page each day about what you notice. Wait until the end of the week before reading what you wrote. Then read all the pages at once

Reflections

You may be tempted at this point to avoid any more questions. You may be experiencing an even larger "dis"-ease in your body than before the last set of questions. You may be tempted to put this book down and not continue. You do have that choice.

However, my professional and personal observation for you is: You can run, but you cannot hide, from the truth about your soul and its mistreatment. Once you can say "no" to hiding, then that damaging process, which began many years ago inside of you and which has continued through this relationship, will be arrested. You hold the keys to that cubicle in which you have been stuck and in which you have felt so cramped. It is up to you whether you want to soar to heights you may have only read about, or to stay where you are.

One definition of hope is postponed disappointment. How long are you going to hope and thus postpone making a decision that affects your soul? If you don't make that decision now, when will you? If not ever, will you be saying: "I've been dying for 10 years? 20 years? 30? 40?"

I implore you to stay with this process *no matter what*. Of course you may take breaks; I have already encouraged it. Take even a day or two, but come back to it before you lose the momentum and determination you have gained. Because you have this book in your hand and you have had the strength and tenacity to make it to this point, you are already a survivor, one with great courage.

Imagine a life free from any of the experiences that slowly but surely rob you of your essence. You have the strength to carry on. Your wholeness and the perfection of your being are already imprinted deep within you. You have only to remove the debris you have accumulated over the years.

You are now engaged in a clearing process. First, you must recognize that something is awry. Then you must begin removing the disguises and layers of denial. As you answer these questions and carry out these exercises you will advance toward reclaiming your soul. It is not easy, but it is possible.

Many of my patients come in saying:

"I hurt terribly, but I'll never be rid of this situation. I don't even think I could ever not be in pain, no matter which way I decide. I am lost, and I am in despair. It is futile and yet something brought me into your office. I don't know, Dr. Papillon. I can't even say why I came through the door."

What do I say?

"You came because there is a part of you that is very wise. It knows what you need, even when you don't. It is faint now, but at some point it will be loud and clear. The process has begun. Are you committed to seeing it through, no matter what?"

I must ask you that now. Are you committed to making your life different from the way it is? If you can trust the process, then you will not only continue, but you will come through with freedom and a flourishing soul.

Temptations to Stay Stuck

Q87. There's one thing you fear more than death, and that is life. Some people are attracted to lying down and never waking up. If you are one of these people, write about what attracts you to never wanting to wake up.

Q88. You are carrying around unresolved issues. Part of your vulnerability to soul negation is the fact that you have unnamed, unhealed issues. Get them out and expose them to the light. What are they? List them.

Q89. It may seem that if you do not name the emptiness, the terrible feelings deep inside of you, the sleepless nights, the despair, the powerlessness and the awful ways you describe yourself, then you do not have to do anything different. You can say "If I don't name it, it doesn't exist." Has that worked for you? Can you avoid negating your soul if you do not name it as such? Are you experiencing the lessening of your spirit within the context of your relationship? Answer these questions one by one and then discuss them in your journal.

Q90. Rank these phrases from "least" to "most" according to how you experience life with this person.

> Inner death, clipped wings, spirit snatcher, compromised life, lifeless life, surrendered sovereignty, stolen property, imprisoned splendor, profound abduction, unjust imprisonment, mistaken love, heart wrencher, relinquished self, unlived life, uncommon bond, disquieted soul, homeless soul

Q91. When with this other person, are you really present to his or her behaviors and words, or are you living on memories of the good times you have had? Are you living on hope for better times?

Reflections

Throughout the chapter, I have pressed the issue of choosing to stay stuck in the painful aspects of your relationship and failing to take a stand for your soul. I do not imply that you must leave, ask this person to leave, or separate permanently from them in order to have a flourishing soul once more. However, I do say that you must begin to assess your situation. What is it, really? How long has the situation been going on as it is now? Is the rug of your relationship bumpy from all the debris you have swept under it? That will only cause you to stumble over it more often, and each time you do, it becomes more difficult to get up.

Now is the time to be more truthful than you have ever been with yourself. No one except the most important person, the one living your life, has to know. Continue answering these questions so that you can get a crystal-clear picture of the life you lead daily. Take breaks as you need them and devise ways to be even gentler with yourself as you go.

Assessing Your Damage

Q92. Regardless of whether this person changes, when are you going to change? Set a specific date for when you want your life to be different and commit to work for one month towards making that change.

Q93. In what ways does the following quote by Abraham Lincoln relate to your journey out of soul mugging: "To believe in things you can see and touch is no belief at all, but to believe in the unseen and know is a triumph and a blessing"?

Q94. To search for a definition of yourself from your relationship implies that you lack one. You only seek that which is missing. Is there any part of you that believes it is an illusion to seek that definition outside yourself? Try writing at least two pages of on this.

Reflections

As you work through these questions and exercises, you will begin to understand that you are psychologically diminished by soul mugging and that you have entered a web of inner darkness filled with confusion, grief, rage and despair. I also imagine you feel like a home-less wanderer, since you deserted your essence and allowed another person (or many others over time) to define who you are at your core.

You can start to restore your wholeness by remembering the fragmented pieces of you, gathering them one by one, and carefully fitting them back into place. As you continue your self-exploration, focus less on intellectual knowledge and become more aware of yourself in the context of your relationship. Instead of leading with your mind, lead with the wisdom of your wholeness and intuition. Listen to that voice that never really stopped speaking to you.

You have discovered a deep wound within yourself. There is no deeper wound than one in which the soul is violated. Inner work is in process, and it involves grieving for the initial separation from that soul.

It is vital that you rebuild and strengthen your connection with your spirit. As the severed bonds between you and your soul are gradually restored, you will feel a sense of intercon-nectedness to all things, especially with nature. The divine is embodied in all things, so if you can find it in any one thing, you can find it in all things. Look for it in your essence.

Rising from Ashes

Q95. There are times when you have gotten so caught up in your relationship that you were literally "dying to please." Think about that phrase.

Q96. Respond to the following: Defenses (like denial) are not completely unintentional, nor are they made totally without awareness. They appear as you wave your magic wand when the truth appears to threaten what you believe. Defenses and denial allow you to quickly forget the part you play in making your reality. Who but yourself, though, evaluates a threat, decides escape is necessary and calls forth a series of de-fenses to reduce the threat? You forget you created this defense, and so it seems external to your own intent. These defenses stand because you replace what is real with what you decide should be real. Respond to this paragraph in writing when you are sure you clearly understand its meaning. React based on your internal dynamics rather than the preceding intellectualized rationale.

Q97. Do you realize that soul negation extinguishes your definition of self to such a degree that you become unable to feel whole? Have you become totally dependent on another person for your identity? Somewhat dependent?

Reflections

God's deepest mystery, wrote Parzival, concerns how life springs from death and decay. These last several questions reveal how soul mugging and the darkness from which it springs can become the midwife for a very great rebirth. Can you sense that yet?

Once you have realized that you are an active participant in your own soul desecration, you can begin to form avenues out of this dark pattern. This chapter is designed to help you find you way out of this painful but familiar place. At the end of this painful journey is a miraculous treasure. Are you willing to make the journey? If you wander off or decide to go back before it is over, you will circumvent the process and will prevent the possibilities that can come from it.

This chapter and the entire book are designed to help you find your way out of the pain. You have suffered long enough. You have attempted to figure out what to do on your own for far too long. This book is your guide through a journey that at times demands extremely arduous work. Patients who have stayed with the process, coming to session after session even when their pain seemed unbearable, are now out in a "new world," not only surviving, but thriving.

Not everyone, though, is willing to tolerate the pain necessary for the journey. Recently I had a patient who had just recovered from emergency open-heart surgery. His wife of many years did not appreciate the physical suffering he was enduring and walked out on him while he was recuperating. She stated: "You are too difficult to deal with. I'm gone." In his first session, he related his goals and expectations:

"Dr. Papillon, I just want to get back to seeing life from a happy place. I've blown bits of things off before – like when my only daughter was raped and murdered. I just left the area and worked in another state. I can't seem to shake this wife thing, though. I want an answer today or I'm not bothering with this therapy stuff anymore."

"You aren't going to like what I have to offer you," I replied. "However, I can say with certainty that if you don't take my advice, you will either be in a medical facility with another major illness or you will be in a therapist's office later. You must go through the pain of losing two members of your immediate family. Where is your grief? It is buried inside you. You can't run from it."

I never heard from him again. Fortunately, that sad case is the exception. Some of you will be tempted to stop, perhaps several times, before reaching the end of this book.

Postponing your confrontation with your pain will only lead to more days, months, and years of suffering. Go through the pain and you can live again without it. It is possible. Even though you see no purpose for suffering now, believe me when I tell you that you must go through it.

I keep emphasizing this point because I know the agony you are enduring as you stay and I know how easy it is to go back to hope and to that place inside you that seems safe, no matter how fragile that safety is. Although there may be a mansion available to you, my guess is you're living in one room thinking this is all of life there is for you. You have never even walked from your window to the door to see if it goes to greater, more expanded life. It does.

Faith is daring to go farther than you can see. Proceed on that kind of faith at this time. This is a crucial period in the process. This is a period of inner struggle and conflict. You are more aware than ever of the challenge facing you and the pain your soul has been through.

If you stop now, you will be even less content to live as you have. Once you wake up, it is not possible to completely go back into your less aware abyss. Something will gnaw at you. You will feel haunted as you go through your days.

So, here you are in the midst of the sea. Your boat has left the shore and you cannot see land in any direction. You are too far away now. You are unanchored from the past that you left and certainly have no sense of what the other side looks like. You must keep rowing. Make this your mantra as you move through the rest of this chapter and the subsequent ones: Keep rowing.

I promise you that the map to navigate you to the other side is in the boat with you. Do not lose it or drop it overboard, or you may get lost and end up where you do not want to go.

If you are willing to explore the shadowy depths of soul deprivation, you can renew your soul and place it in its original home. There is wisdom hidden in each of the questions presented. To lighten the task of journeying home, be certain to tap that source.

Know YOUR Trap

Q98. How has your selective deafness served you? Define what you think that term means and how it relates to your situation now and in the past. How has selective deafness harmed you?

Q99. Do you feel as if you are no longer grounded? Do you wake up many mornings thinking you are living with a stranger – not that other person, but rather yourself? Has that happened?

Q100. Respond to the following: "If I do not stand for something, I will stand for anything."

Q101. If you choose at some point to give up on, or at least to separate yourself from this relationship for a time, what images come to mind in response to the phrase "No pain, no gain"? Answer this question before continuing to read. I compare the process to giving birth. Giving birth does not feel at the moment as if life is being born. It feels like excruciating pain that you wish would hurry up and go away. How do your images compare with mine? Write about how they are similar and how they are different.

Q102. When you yearn for and need the "fix" of another's attention, what do you notice? Can you ever get enough of what you want? In other words, you think you want it, but when you get it, it never seems to fill that yearning inside you. Once you get an understanding of this, then you can begin to get out of this never-ending circle. If you deplore feeling so needy and dependent on this person, you will be less likely to go toward what has not fulfilled you. It can never be satisfying because it comes from much earlier in your life. In fact, that part of you can never be satiated by any other person. Write about this concept and how you relate it to the experiences you have had in your current relationship.

Reflections

The most insidious crimes do not end up in the criminal court buildings. The perpetrators are never tried and most offenses are repeated violations. They are crimes of the heart. As you suffer from these terrors, yours is the soul being violated. No one can see it, as nobody shows any bruises from it. The bruises are internal. You imagine no one will believe you, so you have not bothered talking about it.

That is why the questions in this chapter are so important. Perhaps for the first time you have been able to speak through your journal about these crimes, crimes you first committed against your self without realizing that you were mugging your own soul. Then you got into a relationship where the very words you had been saying to your soul were repeated through this person's verbal and non-verbal interactions with you. What an insidious set-up this has been, and you most likely have been oblivious to all but the intense pain of it.

This crime has systematically worn away at your self-assurance, self-confidence, self-worth, your trust in your own perceptions and your sense of competence and wholeness. The crime is covert and corrosive; often it cannot even be directly confronted, as you have seen by the questions. It is devastating to your soul and tears away at your spirit, but you continue to hope there is a magical cure just around the next bend.

Your journey has taken you far away from home. You left your internal home base so many years ago you cannot even pinpoint the moment. It was subtle but it nonetheless occurred. So many have come into my office that I have lost count of the numbers. They never say: "My soul has been beaten. I can't breathe as easily because I let someone pass unlawfully within the boundaries of my home, my private land inside, and invade my sacred rights. My essence has been trespassed upon."

No, no one has ever come in saying that, but that is exactly what has happened. All these patients have experienced similar patterns within themselves and then with their relationship. Each one says it started very early in life and continued upon finding this other person. Each person was extremely happy in the beginning period of the relationship. Then each one describes the confusion and unexpected, unpredictable, degrading outbursts that came later. Eventually each one decides that it's impossible to live either with or without that person. Each one came to my office, not understanding what happened, feeling unjustly wronged.

In therapy they grasp at one last chance for rescue. They report that for many years they had used hope as a way to continue in the relationship. Everything they said could have come from a textbook entitled *How to Use Hope to Stay in a Soul Desecrating Experience.*

These people had phrases that exactly matched each other's statements: "I hope this is the last time this person threatens to leave," "I hope I don't have to go through this again," "I hope I can maintain myself better the next time he or she yells at me," "I hope I can last through this tirade without making it worse," "I hope I can be forgiven for whatever I did to create this anger today," "I hope this person still loves me. Then I can bear this degradation."

These patients said they wanted to believe in hope because it helped minimize the other's behavior and their own pain. All of them were emphatic about never seeing their situations as part of a cycle. Each incident was seen as close-ended, one-of-a-kind, never to be repeated again. They never saw a pattern. Each time their souls were bombarded with insults, they were completely surprised and startled.

In truth, the patients ignored everything that did not match up with the fantasies they'd built about how their relationships could be when only this "one thing" was resolved. Eventually they all admitted to wearing blinders because they used the relationship to give them the nourishment needed. They also saw how they had been starving for this kind of positive attention. When they received that kind of attention, they quickly and almost completely forgot about the negative kind.

These patients reported feeling panic when they thought their relationships might end. They said they had been willing to do anything and endure anything to sustain them. Besides, they said, every now and then they got exactly what they felt they needed. These crumbs were enough for them, or had been, until the point when they came to me. These people owned up to a lot of shame over their need to have this affection at such a great cost to their being, their essence.

The people in these relationships stated that the other people reminded them daily that they were the cause of their unhappiness. Yet they endured the soul damaging remarks and desecrating interactions, hoping to figure out their own wrong-doing, remedy the wrongs, and regain the relationship they desired.

The primary reason I am discussing this group of patients is because now you have a new perspective and can begin to see your own patterns. You have met and examined the ways you persist with your own soul mugging and the various means you rely on to negate much of what you have experienced.

What these patients grew to understand as we worked together was that the severe desecration to their spirits had also corrupted their connection with their own internal source of power. In their depleted state they had no inner resources left to draw on. Devastated, they no longer felt they had any worth at all. They even said they felt they should not be breathing the air that surrounded them. They felt they had experienced an internal death. Worse yet, they wavered in their conviction that they could return to life.

You need to know about these patients and the difficulties they experienced as they looked inward, discovered themselves and committed to their own recovery. You, too, are experiencing something you thought only you were involved in. But many people are having exactly the same intense struggles that you are. They have walked into this dark tunnel that seems boarded up at the other end, just as you have. They did not search for possibilities, but instead resigned themselves to bleakness. Now that you have walked through a portion of this tunnel, you may wonder why you ever chose to start walking.

Why didn't I just stay where I was, you may ask? This is a reasonable question. You may recall asking that question when you first picked up this book. Your discomfort was most likely less bearable than it is now, though. So, just keep walking one step at a time and you will gain the insights which will tell you why you began to take that first step.

Getting Fooled

Q103. List several alternative activities, projects, and goals you could pursue if your energy were not tied up in the cycle of wanting, getting, and wanting again, which is an endless cycle of disappointment and unfulfilled hope. Write these down and put your list in a place where you will see it daily. When you begin to doubt that you can follow through with your commitment to your essence, decide to take at least three steps related to alternatives on the list before reverting back to the cycle.

Q104. Allow the following words of Robbie Gass to speak to your soul, as violated as it may seem at this point: "Like an ability or muscle, hearing your inner wisdom is strengthened by doing it." What does your injured soul say in response? Give it its own time to speak.

Q105. Have you considered that the word "despite," like the word "hope," could be a trap? For example: "Despite this person's demoralizing, violating actions, I love … " And so you move deeper and deeper into this relationship that may be robbing you of your indispensable essence.

Reflections

At this point in the process of uncovering, it is important to remember that we can *all* be fooled. The person you are attached to in so many ways is most likely a master at manipulation (and you have to admit that you are easily manipulated). Whether this person is a salesperson, a lawyer, or a welder, he or she is able to move you into his or her reality.

The only thing that matters in a soul-mugging relationship is who that person is in relation to who you are. The combination of you and that other person developed into a system that does not work for you; it blocks your grandest vision of yourself. You and others like you are susceptible to falling into thwarting and diminishing relationships because of the way you were raised and because of your willingness to keep peace at great cost to your soul. Culture plays a part, as does the media and songs with lyrics like "can't live, if living is without you." Songs, commercials, movies, and religious tenets all reinforce how one person should be in relation to another in the context of a relationship.

It is crucial for you to understand that nothing is wrong with you for being where you are. You are not a fool, nor a silly, crazy, mixed-up or stupid person. You are just not as strong as you need to be about discerning your own needs and what is best for you … yet.

Starting Out

Q106. There is a spirit-snatching malady walking around in literally millions of people today. It is silently, slowing killing the spirit of people everywhere. Yet professional journals, research studies, newspapers, magazines, and books paint a completely different picture. Portrayed on the newsstands and everywhere we look is an expectation that in the next ten years everyone can finally realize a full sense of themselves. Splashed in ink and broadcast pervasively is the message that everyone's spirits will be unharnessed, breathing freely, allowing expression of their creativity and personal power. By the millennium, they say, people will lead lives which are more gratifying than ever before. What do you think about this discrepancy in your situation, this juxtaposition of spiritual wasteland and potential for a full, vital life?

Q107. What would it mean to you to "live-in-the-leap?" What would you have to surrender to and let go of to experience that phenomenon?

Q108. Do you feel that the time for you to make a challenging decision has arrived? There is nothing more powerful than an idea whose time has come. What is preventing right now from being the right time? How do you plan to bring about your desire to have a flourishing soul? Mark off several pages in your journal and write your responses to these crucial questions over a period of a week. Write about each of your reactions and emotions, as well as the physical impact and implications.

Q109. A spider spins its web from the center of its being, then stands on it. Can you comprehend standing on who you truly are? Do you understand that this is different from standing on the image which others have told you that you are for many years? In answering this question, it is necessary to write first about who told you what and when. Then, write a rebuttal. An example would be: Told – "Aunt Mary said I was extremely stubborn, so I always felt that if I crossed her, I would merely confirm her way of seeing me." Rebuttal – "Actually, I just had a spirited way about me, especially when I was seven years old. Now I reclaim that spirited part of me. I want it back. It is an aspect of my essence."

Q110. Try to see your own life from the perspective of your creator. Can you see your life as a wondrous and valuable learning experience? If you could, what would change in you and with your relationship? What would you want to stay the same?

Q111. Here is an old tale that puts a new spin on romantic relationships:

> A woman dreamed one night that Life stood before her and held in each hand a gift – in one hand, love; in the other, freedom. And Life said to the woman, "Choose." And the woman paused a long time, then said, "Freedom." And Life said, "You have chosen well. If you had said 'Love' I would have given what you asked for, and I would have gone and returned no more. Now, the day will come when I will return. On that day, I will bear both gifts in one hand."

Does this story relate to the way you see your relationship? Do you think it is possible to feel both within one relationship? If so, when? If not, why not?

Reflections

After completing these questions, the issue foremost in your mind may not be how long you are going to perpetuate the way you have been living, but to what extent? If you stay with things as they are, do you imagine that they will not deteriorate further, or will you be even farther from fully living what you are capable of?

I emphasize that you have the power to decide about yourself. Only you know how limited or unlimited your possibilities are. Stop right now and imagine what it would mean to live at 100 percent of what you are capable of.

What if you were to allow your soul to flourish on its own 100 percent of the time? Imagine your energy flowing from your most noble and compassionate self 100 percent of the time. What if you were to honor your essence 100 percent? What if you were thinking and acting from your own integrity 100 percent of the time? What if, and this may be difficult, you were willing to allow your heart to break 100 percent, if necessary?

What would the quality of your life be like if you were living at 100 percent of your capacity? I assure you that when you have used this guidebook until it is rumpled, torn and marked up, and your journal or journals are blackened with writing, you will be much closer to living life on your own terms, with your brilliance readily apparent to you. My gift to you is a road map and encouragement to embrace all that is inside of you. Your gift to your self is your inner joy as you rise to become your own choreographer in the dance of life.

Chapter Five

Looking for Love in All the Wrong Places

Hidden Forces Behind Soul Mugging

The pattern of the carpet is a surface. When we look closely or when we become weavers, we learn of the tiny multiple threads unseen in the overall pattern, the knots on the underside of the carpet.
– Adrienne Rich

"I was so angry, I just wanted to kill her. I stole a gun she had. I planned to shoot her with it. I really did."

This patient, who was seeing me for his first session, wore a blue oxford shirt, khaki pants and a pair of stylish black loafers. He surprised me with his story, which was in great contrast to his Ivy League appearance:

"I was completely enraged at my wife. She told me if I came near her she'd use the handgun she'd bought, so while she was at work, I stole it. I decided I'd get her first before she could kill me."

Here was a gentle, soft-spoken man with a young, innocent-looking face telling me not just about thoughts he'd had, but about actions he'd conceived to accomplish his plan.

"I was put in jail once she heard my intention. I was stealing in jail so they placed me in solitary confinement. Dr. Papillon, it was only then that I had to be still long enough to face myself. I'd never had to do that. I realized that my anger at her was actually anger with myself. I totally despised myself. But now that I couldn't run from myself anymore I fell to my knees and began my inner search. It wasn't easy, but I've learned who I am and what I'd done to myself. I never would have learned this if I hadn't been forced to examine who I had become."

Bob's situation had degenerated to horrible extremes before he stopped to face himself. When he did, he finally realized that he would find his answers only by uncovering his inner self.

Understanding: The Cornerstone to Restoring Your Self

When I resolved to take my first steps out of my own emotional prison, I had to start by making sense of the dark terrain of my inner self. The terror of realizing I had nearly lost my soul was only slightly subdued by the possibilities I began to see. Numbed by years of pain, beaten down emotionally, and bereft of resources, I searched for possible answers.

Several psychological theories on the development and dynamics of the self did prove to be a useful starting point. It was far easier to work with my painful feelings and conflicting experiences when I could place them within a framework. Over time, I found six relevant theories from established research. These provided at least partial explanations.

Bob's description of falling to his knees felt similar to my early steps. Yet each step expanded my perspective, giving me a clearer view of my inner self.

I gained additional clarity as I saw patients struggling with soul mugging. Once stuck, they could find few clues to navigate their way out. Through this process, often stalled by my wrenching agony, evolved ten original theories. These groundbreaking theories were formulated by unraveling the mysteries of soul mugging. I gained even greater understanding as I moved farther along in the process of restoring my soul. Because your soul has been mugged, it has ceased to be a dependable source to inform you about what is best for you. You, too, can reunite with the splintered part of you, your spirit, by exploring yourself deeply while examining each theory. Most of the root causes, symptoms, and dynamics can be found in these original theories.

One necessary condition for restoring your soul is to understand the purpose your extreme discomfort has served. The clarity these theories provide can lessen the grip of agony. Its purpose will lose significance and you will feel freer to pursue new paths.

Even though your view is confined to your own perspective, objectively scrutinizing your issues and unhealed pain can be done. The Buddha advised that one should be a lamp unto one's self; a person's innate purity of heart is his or her sole refuge. You can become that light, illuminating your way from within by utilizing these theories.

I, too, had to do some very intense personal reflection. I had to shine that light into places where doing so was extremely uncomfortable. I questioned every belief I had held to be sacred and every understanding of myself I had ever had. Spirituality was my sole anchor as I labored through this excavation. You may want to find a spiritual anchor also.

> Search now for a memory or an image that you can use for a grounding point as you go through this chapter. Perhaps it is a memory of someone who responded lovingly to you at a young age, or held you when you were hurt, even if only for a short time.

Ways to Benefit from New Insights

The theories form parts of your puzzle. When pieced together, they show how soul mugging developed, as well as what is holding it in place. Consider each one a template for viewing your situation. I have stayed close to the surface in discussing the theories, especially those published in psychology textbooks and research journals. I have provided just enough information to assist you in assembling this template.

Over time you built a particular set of beliefs, structures, behaviors, and interactions which helped you function. Various theories reveal how these protective systems operate and eventually even feel authentic to you. They answer the question, "What have I been ignoring to keep my relationship exactly as it is?"

It then becomes clear that your sense of who you are was constructed from a distorted perception of reality. Overriding these built-in mechanisms will result in disquieting feelings. You may feel panicked, conflicted, or even quite angry. If you do, then it is important to handle the emotional responses when they arise. If you choose not to, they will resurface. Your pain is the breaking of the shell that encloses your understanding. So, view it as a sacred opportunity to remove the blinders which have blocked your inner vision.

After all, you are thinking beyond the boundaries of your usual perspective of both yourself and your relationship. Part of you knows that it is possible for you to be another kind of person. Once you have these new insights you no longer have to choose a compromised life. As Meister Eckhart said, "Truly, it is in the darkness that one finds the light, so when we are in sorrow, then this light is nearest of all to us."

You Were Too Young to Know: Childhood Developmental Theory

As a very young child, you could not yet distinguish between a broad intention and the literal meaning of negative words, such as, "You spilled your milk – you're bad!" Also, at a young age you may not have received a sense that you were a precious being. Most likely you interpreted this lack of validation as true, rather than a problem of the person who was caring for you. Your negative perceptions persisted into later life, inflicting havoc on your important relationships in the fundamental areas of trust and security. Most importantly, it became difficult for you to develop a strong, positive sense of self.

Root causes may be:

- absence or interrupted availability of your mother or mother substitute;
- primary caregivers being overwhelmed with their own issues and crises;
- caregivers who lacked the insight and sensitivity necessary to avoid labeling you or calling you names.

Barbara, an attractive and intelligent 35-year-old Caucasian woman, had been my patient for several months. She worked as a checkout clerk in a supermarket near her home. She began therapy with me because she was dissatisfied with her romantic relationship and her despair was also affecting her at work. One day she approached the session in deep thought and then began speaking in a monotone voice, "I can barely make it to work each day. All I can think of is how despicable people who come through my checkout line must think I am. I can't even look them in the eye. I just pray for the day to be over so I can go home and eat my way into sleep. I never want to wake up again. I mean it. I've just had it with this awful way I feel deep, deep down. I am worthless. Who could touch me, much less want me?

"Today I felt like a small child. I am so needy for approval and attention it makes me sick. This ten-year-old kid stuck his tongue out at me, and even that made me cry. I really am no good, just like they said when I was little."

Although she was a functioning adult, Barbara was stuck in an early childhood issue. As we worked together, it became clear that her original childhood needs for affirmation had not been met and, worse, she experienced damaging insults which remained with her, although submerged beneath her conscious awareness.

After returning from a family reunion, Barbara related times when her spirit had been assaulted. She concluded her spirit was too much for her parents to handle. They tried to beat it down and snuff it out so that she would be more compliant to their wishes.

"Once, when I was six years old, my father had me stand on a table, with my four brothers and sisters around me, and say 'I am a cheat and a liar.' I wouldn't do it. He threatened me and humiliated me so much that I finally said it and jumped off the table. Dr. Papillon, that makes me nauseous. I am despicable."

It was not easy for Barbara to see how her current situation stemmed from her early developmental history. She and I uncovered many incidents where she had been denied a positive sense of self. She thought if she did not verbalize those early childhood experiences, she could ignore their significance. Thus she tried to live without grieving over her maltreatment.

However, once she explored those early years, she saw how destructive she had been to her essence. She had not acknowledged that her needs were not being met, and she paid for this at great expense to her soul. It was both sad and freeing for Barbara to discover these painful things. However, now she could begin to make decisions for herself based on her new understanding. She no longer needed to affirm her sense of self through the opinions of others.

Highlights of the Early Childhood Development Theory

Until they reach the age of five, children are limited to literal interpretations of what they hear. For example, if a five-year-old child hears, "You are such a mean child," he or she absorbs it as truth.

Many adults get figuratively stuck in their early years due to these negative influences. Therefore, if a four-year-old girl concludes that she is inadequate, as an adult she will enter into a romantic relationship believing the same thing. Because she is unaware of the messages about her essence she took in when she was young, she never even considered updating them to a more positive perception of her being.

In *The Drama of the Gifted Child* (Basic Books, 1981; originally published as *Prisoners of Childhood),* psychoanalyst Alice Miller states that people cannot love themselves if from the start they have had no chance to experience their genuine feelings or learn to know themselves. How can you love something you do not know? How could anyone else even think of loving you when you are mysterious and unlovable to yourself?

Miller discusses many cases in which the primary caretaker was not available to help the child to develop self-esteem. Instead, the child depended on others to learn how to behave, or acted in ways that he or she believed would have the best chance of succeeding in meeting the child's needs for love and approval.

If you were a child who missed receiving positive feedback, you developed an amazing ability to perceive the needs of your parent or caregiver. You concluded that you must behave in a certain way in order to have any chance of getting what you needed. You sacrificed much to meet the requirements of those on whom you depended. As an adult you have also convinced yourself that you need to practice these same behaviors in order to get love, especially romantic love.

If you had been raised in a more positive environment, you would have felt your spirit flourish and you would have developed a groundedness that prevented your automatically absorbing what anyone said to you. At four or five years old, the positive environment you needed would have included hearing statements such as these:

I'm glad you were born. You are very valuable to us.

I'm not afraid of your anger. It's okay to be angry.

You don't have to do tricks (be cute, sick, sad, mad, scared, quiet) to get approval. It's okay to take risks (try things, initiate things, be curious); we will give you our support and protection at the same time.

These are very affirming statements for your soul to soak up. These statements nurture your essence. After reading these examples, you can understand what may have been lacking in your early childhood. It is very important for you not to feel you are blaming anyone – yourself or those who raised you. They did the best they could, given their own circumstances and their system of beliefs at that time.

Recycled Emotions: Childhood Attachment Theory

This theory explains the great difficulty you may have had in leaving a significant relationship. In your early life your primary need to bond with your parents was not met on a regular basis. This left you with an insecure inner foundation. With an important person, you may manifest your unmet needs by controlling or by easily becoming distant.

As you look back, do the following root causes or symptoms fit?

Your caregiver was either literally or emotionally absent for much of your first four years.

You feared that your parent or caregiver would leave.

As an adult you yearned for someone to be with you constantly.

You only feel a strong sense of self when you are able to bond with a significant other.

One day Janet, a 42-year-old woman, came into my office looking very disheveled. Her blouse was hanging out over her tailored skirt, and even though she had on dressy heels, she was not wearing stockings. Her hair had not been combed and she had streaks of make-up on her tear-stained face.

"Dr. Papillon, I know we've talked about my attachment to Jack before, but I can't take this. Look at me. I can't function at my job. Today my boss gave me some things to type, but I was too overwhelmed to even look at them. I can't lose this job. You know how long it took me to find it after that last fiasco?

"Help me. I'm a mess. I get so close to Jack over the weekend that I feel lost on Mondays. I lose myself as a functioning person. 'Where am I?' I say, and I have no answer. Today I realized that there are really two people in me, that small one who never could feel secure about being cared for and that adult who really can go to work. Right now I've lost any sense of the second one. This happens to me almost every Monday. I've go to do something but what?"

I had been seeing Janet as a patient for almost a year. Her complaints and sense of being unanchored were not unusual for someone whose soul mugging was rooted in unmet attachment needs.

Highlights of the Childhood Attachment Theory

Theorists such as D.W. Winnicott and Lloyd Silverman have shown that in early childhood it is vitally important for children to bond with their caregivers. Caregivers provide emotional closeness, attentiveness, and emotional security. This bonding helps children to develop the self-confidence they need to explore their new world. When these attachment needs are sufficiently met, the person can form relationships that do not have distorted forms of attachment.

Three behavioral distortions are traceable to unmet attachment needs:

Anxious attachment occurs when children receive only small bits and pieces of love and attention rather than consistent nurturing. As adults they tend to become controlling because they are always looking for a safe base. Of course, they can never find it through their efforts to control. Their early experience represents a form of trauma. Remembering times when they were afraid of being abandoned can retrigger the anxiety.

Avoidant attachment is rooted in a parent's being either too protective and intrusive or extremely distant. As adults, children of these types of parents may become skittish and mistrustful. They may pull away from any danger they perceive, even if it is not apparent to anyone else.

Attachment hunger manifests at a very basic level because it happens so early in infancy. Being deep and basic, it can be damaging and almost always emerges later in life. It has been described by several patients when their partners were away from them: "I feel a yearning in my stomach. I am nauseous and my heart aches as if I am going to die. I have no control over this experience. I am at its mercy. I cry, have no appetite, and certainly can't sleep. I have to escape and there is no way out. If there is a hell, this is definitely it."

There is no doubt that a significant person can seem to fill a longing you have. By deeply bonding, connecting, and in a sense merging with the other, you continue to try to meet your attachment need. This will not work, but you keep on trying. It can't work because you can't be an adult with these childhood attachment needs and attempt to reenact them at this point. You try to find someone who will not cause you anxiety or a sense of danger or certainly hunger. However, these experiences happened when you were small. The "adult you" can't ever meet the "child you's" needs by picking a relationship you think will resolve these early traumas.

In addition, your oversized attachment needs make it even more excruciatingly painful for you to end a relationship than it is for most people. You are willing to hold out for the possibility of eventual fulfillment. You believe your relationship is your lifeline to stay intact, that is, alive. It feels that critical for you to hold on to a relationship, no matter what is going on in it, than to let it go.

When you, without your being aware you are doing so, ask another person to play the role of a parent with whom you did not bond, you immediately return to the past. Simultaneously, you are implicitly asking this person to correct all the wrongs, to undo the past, which is also futile.

As with many of the dynamics of soul mugging and the soul negation syndrome, your unmet attachment needs leave you extremely vulnerable and unfulfilled.

Didn't I See This Somewhere Before? Childhood Modeling Theory

Your first view of the world was acquired by the perspectives and responses your caregivers showed you about the dynamics of relationships. Particularly important were cues in your emotional environment, the way they shared their feelings and their demonstrations of affection and closeness.

What do you remember about:

- sharing and showing feelings in your family?
- your need to compete for attention? Was there more strife than cooperation?
- the emotional distance between your mother and father?
- your caregivers' level of respect toward each other?

Joseph, a 58-year resident of the U.S., had come to this country from Ecuador. He had been married for ten years to someone who demoralized him in numerous ways. He could not imagine why he stayed in the relationship, except for one thing: he could not imagine leaving.

As usual at our sessions, Joseph was impeccably dressed. He held a politically visible job in municipal government. He had reluctantly come into therapy at the urging of a friend who had accompanied him to his first session.

I asked Joseph on this particular day to elaborate on his relationship with his mother. We had touched on this during his previous session.

"Dr. Papillon, please, let's not get into this any further. I am not up to it today. I have had my third conflict in two days with Sharon. Everything I say or do brings on her attacks. How can I keep Sharon off my back? Please, can't we just talk about this Sharon stuff?"

As much as I feel it is important to honor a patient's immediate requests for help, in this case, I knew Joseph, and I needed to get into the modeling his mother had provided when he was a child. This would reveal much about how he allowed women to treat him and, ultimately, how he treated his soul.

Joseph began, after some coaxing, to describe the following scene: "I was five. I was laying face-down on my bed when my mother walked into my room unannounced. When she spoke, I was quite startled. But when she said what she said next, I was dumbfounded: 'You rotten kid. Get your ass up. Don't you know anything? Your dad's out cold from drinking, and I got no help around here but you, and you know that. Get out of that bed, you lazy bum. You are no good. I don't know why I ever had you. You ain't nothin' but trouble to me. Nothin', and of no use.'"

91

At that moment, Joseph started sobbing, something he dared not do at five, for fear of worse consequences than he was already experiencing. It was as if this little boy were finally able to express the pain he had held inside for all these years: he was no good, nothing but a bother and he was not living up to the expectations which the primary person in his life held for him. He truly seemed as devastated now as he most certainly had been at five.

What this man experienced with his mother he was reenacting (as most of us do) in his relationship. He felt that every small, critical remark from Sharon reflected how much this man was of no value. The modeling that his mother had shown to him by her verbal defiling was all he knew of who he was. He'd never updated his view of himself so when his wife spoke to him, he took it in as his mother's voice.

Highlights of the Childhood Modeling Theory

From your parents and family members you learned whether the world around you was a safe or a fearful place to be. You have incorporated your perceptions of early interactions with your family. You have also internalized your parents' treatment of you and accepted much of their modeling, which is now reflected in the way you treat your being.

You learned to love, hate, or ignore your soul, to value your essence or to find it abhorrent. You have had this blueprint from childhood. All of your relationships are influenced by it.

When you are as dependent on a parent as Joseph was, your inclination is to justify that person's actions and treatment of you. You distort, you blame yourself, and you do whatever it takes to bring about a generally positive image of this person. Are there any similarities between Joseph's case and your experience with major figures in your childhood?

Think back about what modeling you received about who you are and how valuable (or not) you are. How does that influence you today? Does your choice and Joseph's choices in relationships bear witness to this modeling? Most likely so, unless you have healed these early wounds.

Fitting in and Getting Accepted: Socialization Theory

Outside your immediate family, your image of who you are, want to be, and need to be to gain acceptance was based on role models you acquired from television, movies, and books, as well as from school, your neighborhood, religious institutions, and peers. Your self development may have been curtailed by over-reliance on these models. Based on many cultural messages about who and how you were to be, you may have decided what kind of important relationships you would have. If you leaned too heavily on your heroes and heroines to decide how to be, you may have ended up with a fragile sense of self, a likely set-up for soul mugging.

Did you fall into the pattern of:

- completely conforming to others' expectations?

- always trying to gain acceptance by pleasing others?

- being influenced by others more than by your own inclinations?

Vivian, a 20-year-old junior at a local university, was in her second semester of therapy with me. She came in one day looking very perplexed:

"My date for the spring dinner dance was this fabulous guy. As usual my sorority sisters were so envious. Everyone wanted her picture taken with him. He looked like he was right out of the movies. And, Dr. Papillon, he was so polite ... at least, at first. I just can't figure it out. I always start out this way – great guy: terrific looks, really outgoing, athletic, perfect body. After two dates he doesn't call when he says he will, and then I hear he has taken out one of my friends. I am beginning to feel that my friends hang around me just to meet the best-looking guys on campus. In some ways it's exciting to be with somebody that everyone else wants. But then it hurts. Why am I so attracted to these guys? I can't stand being thrown away like trash."

As time went on Vivian began to get insight into her reasons for choosing this kind of man. Her awareness about the cause of this strong attraction was critically important to her moving away from this painful, degrading cycle. Until she came to therapy, she acted on beliefs which she wasn't aware she had. She eventually realized she had been influenced very early by television shows, fairy tales and favorite songs she listened to repeatedly.

Highlights of the Socialization Theory

Like Vivian, in your formative years you were barraged by media images about how you must look and act, who would be a desirable partner, and indeed how that partner was to treat you. You also probably learned that certain situations brought you more positive attention than others. You no doubt got swept up by these glamorous and enticing images. Ultimately, you followed those cultural messages rather than developing a sense of self from within.

> In your journal you may want to write down some especially significant influences outside your family, including heroes, models, movies, or books. State specifically how they inspired you and helped you form your aspirations. You may find it very enlightening to see who, when, and what caught your imagination and influenced you.

Once you become aware of what impact culture had on how you are choosing and living your life with your relationship, you can begin to unravel all the complexities that have emerged as you have played out the script that culture gave you. In other words, once you are consciously noticing what you expect on a daily basis from another, you can either give that expectation up or at least own that you have had it since childhood and now want to keep it as a standard for your current relationships. Either way, wake up to what the social milieu around you has been saying all of your life, but especially when you were growing up, about what relationships were supposed to look like and how you were to act within them. Then you can update your understanding and make a more informed choice.

It Seemed ... But Maybe Not

Defenses of Denial, Minimalization, and Rationalization

> Your defenses prevent you from accurately perceiving a reality which threatens the picture you want to see. The principal defenses prevalent in soul mugging are denial,

minimalization, and rationalization. Their specific function is to keep your relationship in place, just as it is now. This is done without conscious awareness. Defenses conceal reality by several means: they change it, render it inept, distort it, twist it, keep it completely from consciousness or take pieces out of it so that the whole of the situation defies recognition. In other words, defenses are similar to magic wands you wave when reality appears to threaten your beliefs.

In the past have you tended to:

- ignore what was unacceptable to you?
- make excuses to family members and friends?
- play down objectionable incidents, circumstances, and behaviors?
- tolerate compromising situations, thinking they would improve?

Denial: Don't Make Me Face the Facts

Through denial you distort the picture, avoid recognizing all the pieces necessary to put the picture into a cohesive, understandable whole, or keep it from rising to full consciousness. As a child you may have denied that your parents were inept, alcoholic, mean, neglectful, harsh, or punitive to the point of being detrimental to you. You denied any one of these by saying to yourself and to others that it was not true. Your survival depended on denying reality.

Jennifer, a 33-year-old African-American woman, contacted me after being referred by her physician. He was concerned because of her recurring complaints for which he could find no physical basis. She had been in therapy for two years when one morning, as I checked my telephone messages, I heard in her voice anger and disgust mixed with fear:

"I should have been an architect, building castles of illusion, instead of a salesclerk. I have suddenly, and I mean just last night, seen clearly how I have been blinded by my well-constructed illusions. I have held on so tightly, as if my life depended on them. I saw the truth as I was watching a movie. It was about a love affair filled with betrayal.

"I realize now that my survival depends upon my letting go of my stupid illusions. They just gave me a place to hide. I know what I have to do now. Of course it terrifies me, Dr. Papillon, and that's why I called you early this morning. I didn't sleep all night, but I know I will be holding on to nothing if I hold on to the set of beliefs I've constructed.

"My friends, oh, my gosh, so many of them have tried to tell me that he's not been faithful to me. No way did I listen, though. I am stubborn. I just knew I could make this relationship work. I really did. I wanted to believe everything he said. Well, it is, at least for the moment, crystal clear to me that I have only strung out my misery by refusing to see the truth."

You may still be using denial to avoid facing truths about your important relationships, because to allow your soul to know the truth would be as frightening to you as it was to Jennifer. Also, admitting that you have been in denial may pressure you to initiate a change which you may not want to make, or to conclude that you have to write off your investment of time and energy as having been futile.

There are many reasons why you may use denial in your life. It is possible that you were told directly that what you saw was not what you saw, what you heard was not what you heard, and what you perceived had no real basis. This technique is a way for parents and other caregivers to do whatever they do without your being able to call them on it. After all, you were just a child. What could you know? You no doubt began to question your own perceptions and intuition when you were forced to deny the obvious and accept far less probable reasoning.

Minimalization: The Peril of "Playing Down"

In minimalization you conclude that the reality which threatens your picture is not really so important. Minimizing is when you say to yourself, "This isn't as bad as I think it is."

Julie, a 42-year-old administrative assistant for an insurance firm, had entered therapy because of the pain she was experiencing in her romantic relationship. She had been in therapy for six months when she came into the office the day after attending her family reunion.

"Dr. Papillon, while at my family gathering I noticed something that I had never noticed before. I was standing next to my mother and overheard some of my young nieces and nephews talking to an uncle of mine. I told her how much I disliked his behavior towards me when I was eleven. He was now behaving the same way with these children. I was appalled at how my mother responded.

"She said, 'Uncle Mac just spoke a little too harshly with the children now. When he has had a few too many beers, he tends to do that. But he's a hard-working, God-fearing man who provides for his family and who loves you. Pretend nothing happened because you are fine now. Just ignore it. It isn't that big a deal. Now don't go making out like it is.'"

After that conversation with her mother, Julie realized she had been willing to push aside many negative interactions between her and her partner. Julie had been caught in a contradiction I had heard from many patients. All had erroneously concluded that if they played down certain unacceptable behaviors and just loved their partner more, they would be able to receive what they so longed to have for their soul: emotional support, abiding love, and a safe place to express their essence. When have you used minimalization in your life? Did it help you get through the experience? Do you benefit from continuing to use it?

Rationalization: Don't Look at It That Way – Look at It This Way

In rationalization you make up excuses for your actions or for another person's behavior. That is how you justify seeing the picture as you want to see it. Then you have no need to take action or to change your thinking. Rationalization is expressed by saying things such as:

> He's had a horrible week. I can see why he'd yell at me and say I'm a pig. I'm just a target; I don't have to be concerned.

> She is about to have her menstrual period, and she is always crazy at this time of the month. I can imagine that those raging hormones would make anyone speak to her partner that way.

He is very upset with me. He must be. He hasn't spoken to me for three days, won't eat what I cook for him, and won't answer my questions ... yet, somehow I can love him through it. I understand him and how he is. He is just this way and I can handle it.

When you use rationalization, you make up your own reality instead of facing reality as it truly is. By using this and other defenses, you hide from, instead of walk toward, the solution. Through your use of defenses, you construct a vision of something that is not true or not accurately represented.

The danger of rationalization is that you create an even bigger threat by not facing the truth of the situation. You only postpone the pain that you anticipate will result if you initiate discussion on an issue or make a change in your relationship. This may sound like an understandable reason for wanting to avoid dealing with the truth. Yet, what is it costing you?

Perhaps the initial step in letting go of this and the other two defenses is simply to answer the following questions:

- How have you used denial, minimalization, and rationalization in your partnership?

- How much suffering have you avoided by building and keeping these defenses?

- How much suffering could you have avoided by facing the truth of your situation earlier?

- If you continue to avoid your discomfort by using your defenses, how will your life change?

Now allow new possibilities to emerge and record your reactions to them in your journal.

You Mean There's Another Way? Conditioning Theory

You may have learned that it is normal to be highly anxious and to have your needs met on a random basis. This can happen if you spent your early years in a household which had a chronically high anxiety level, where you became frantic due to the erratic way you were taken care of. As an adult, you tolerate anguishing negativity mixed with intermittent uplifting euphoria in your important relationships. You have great difficulty in leaving these relationships because you truly believe your needs will be met at any moment.

Did you experience:

- unpredictable, inconsistent responses to having your basic needs met?

- fear that your caregiver would stop meeting your needs?

- panicky feelings because you thought you might miss your chance to get taken care of?

Sally, a 51-year-old woman of Irish descent, worked as a department store detective. She had been with her partner for fifteen years. They lived together but had never married, although Sally wished to. That was the original reason for her coming to see me. Jim, her lover, had presented over the years a series of excuses for postponing their marriage.

I had been seeing Sally for more than six months when she arrived one day in a bright red suit, high heels to match, and a brand new blouse. She seemed elated. I was curious to learn about the new development. As I welcomed her, I heard her beeper go off.

"Could I use the phone, Dr. Papillon? I rarely get beeped by Jim so it must be important."

I watched her face as she became pale from the interaction. She was so torn with emotion that she found it difficult to continue her conversation on the phone. I could not help but overhear her side of the dialogue.

"But… Yes, but this time you … I know, but you're always saying that something …

Her sentences were left dangling as Jim interrupted her repeatedly. Evidently, she had heard these words before.

"Dr. Papillon, I can't do this anymore. Yet I can't not do it. I'm miserable. I hate this place Jim puts me in. I make plans for an evening with Jim and then he cancels.

"Every now and then we go out and it is sheer heaven. Then the next six or seven times, he cancels at the last minute. Once again, here I am, emotionally as well as physically all dressed up with nowhere to go. It's so unfair. I feel completely powerless. I have no power to make him different and no power to leave him or cancel on him. I have no idea how to stop this whole cycle or even whether I can.

"This is the worst place I have ever gotten myself into in my whole life. I have no life jacket, and I'm drowning in despair and disgust with myself. God, what is there for me to do? I hate my life, I hate Jim; most of all I hate my inability to do anything differently."

Highlights of the Conditioning Theory

Sally perceived herself as weak because the process she was caught in was extremely difficult for her to make sense of or to change. However, it actually had nothing to do with her weakness. It had to do with the intermittent reinforcement between her and Jim that had gone on for a period of time.

Intermittent reinforcement is devastating to the individual whose soul has been mugged. It means that every now and then you get exactly what you want. At times in your relationship, but without any particular pattern, you are filled with joyful, positive experiences from your partner. These ecstatic moments have been referred to by patients as exhilarating, natural highs. They are followed by an emotional drought and punctuated by disconcerting negative interactions and disappointments.

Experiments done with mice show that if the mice do not receive any food, they stop pushing on the device that feeds them. However, if the mice are given food at inconsistent times throughout the day, they will never stop pushing on the handle that is to hand them the morsel of food. Continuing to pursue their reward, these mice often die at that device, still anticipating the food that is not forthcoming.

After repeatedly experiencing unpredictable behavior as a young child, you viewed your family environment and interactions as normal. You became habituated to these emotional aberrations and to the adrenaline rush you associated with particular events and social interactions. Now that you are an adult, you find that a calmer environment or pattern of interactions actually leaves you feeling as if something is missing.

Since you were subjected to this chaotic behavior, it is almost impossible for you to stop expecting that at any moment you will receive what you have been waiting for. Conditioned patterns are difficult to discover and modify until you understand how they were formed and how they work.

When you think of ending a relationship which provides the patterns to which you were conditioned, you panic. You imagine you will feel dead, certainly numb; you may feel that if life is this dull it isn't worth living. You may have become an expert in crisis management. You only feel alive and vital in the midst of upheaval and emotional turbulence.

This conditioned response unfortunately includes a willingness to sacrifice everything, including your soul, your friends, and your future, to the anticipation of having your needs completely satisfied.

Holding out for the occasional, random fulfillment of your needs in your relationship is a high-stakes game to play with your soul. Although you may be very strong, your strength will not get you unstuck from this ingrained pattern. However, your willingness to gain new understanding and insight will.

Chapter Six

What I Did for Love

Groundbreaking Theories by the Author

Not "Revelation" – 'tis – that waits,
But our unfurnished eyes
– Emily Dickinson

"Oh, so that's it. That's how it works."

With a mixed sense of joy, tragedy, and relief, I finally knew that I understood enough about my internal topography to give names to the soul mugging condition and the soul negation syndrome. Additionally, I developed ten new theories to explain the dynamics which are present when soul mugging occurs in relationships. I evolved these original explanations over time. During that period, as I watched my own soul mugging disappear in the distance, I welcomed my soul back to its place at the center of my self.

These new theories added substantial understanding, because, in some cases, the traditional theories simply did not reach far enough to explain the soul mugging phenomenon. In other cases nothing was available to specifically explain the negative interactions linked to soul mugging in relationships. I developed these ten theories to complete my understanding, filling in gaps where no other explanation was available.

This kaleidoscope of understanding came into being one by one as I was ready. Sometimes I struggled to find the meaning in my feelings, and finally something would make complete sense. In a few cases, a clear explanation presented itself at just the time I was searching for it. Often a patient would express a feeling or a reaction, or report a partner's behavior that would alert me in a way I knew I should pay special attention to it. Each new theory helped me find a missing piece of the puzzle or brought in a new dimension I had not thought of, and sometimes I would see completely new connecting paths.

It is so much easier to understand the complexity of soul mugging and the soul negation syndrome when you see the full picture rather than a sketchy outline. Once you get very clear about your inner self, you can make decisions that will bring you great satisfaction.

As I introduce the theories I have developed to explain the inner workings of soul mugging, I want to begin with one that is the most potent of all for keeping soul mugging intact. I believe the vast majority of people stay in their soul-mugging situation because of one word: hope. The prickly edges of your thorny relationship are softened, if not totally blunted, by this one word, and you are able to tolerate your situation much longer than is beneficial for your soul.

The Deceiver: Continual Hope Theory

Though hope is most often used in a positive context, you may be using hope in a soul-devastating way. This behavior can occur when you fall back on hope to prolong the status quo in a relationship that is mugging your soul. In addition to delaying the need to take action, over-reliance on hope focuses your attention on inappropriate tactics which desecrate your soul.

Have you used hope to:

- strengthen your resolve to persist?
- postpone making decisions and taking action?
- neutralize objectionable situations?
- extend warped leniency to your partner in expectation that things will turn out better?

Judy's Efficient Soul-Devastation Tool

Judy, a 39-year-old Canadian, was a sociology instructor at a nearby community college. She had been a patient for nearly a year. Judy originally came in because of her continuing anguish over her ten-year marriage to Dick. One day, though, Judy came into the office with a lilt in her voice I had not heard for some time. She started by telling me of a new awareness she had discovered when she was writing in her journal the previous weekend.

"I've finally pieced together what creates such a powerful contradiction in my relationship with Dick. I have loved him unceasingly for many years. Yet, what I think of as an optimistic move on my part puts me deeper into the hole I have been digging with my shovel. I see this shovel as my hope. I hoped that my love would make the difference in the way Dick and I behave with each other. But it hasn't made any lasting difference.

"The only thing that has changed is that I am now deeper in the hole than I ever was. The more I loved him and hoped for a change, the more imprisoned I became. That habit of hoping is the most enslaving aspect of this whole relationship. If I am to survive, I must relinquish hope. I don't know how to do it, but I am committed to giving it up. I think I'll go buy a shovel and put the word *hope* on it in big red letters. It should be an instant reminder to stop that kind of thinking on my part.

"Don't you think that's the most powerful contradiction there is – to think of a positive word like hope creating such a prison for me?"

Highlights of the Continual Hope Theory

One of the definitions of hope as it applies to soul mugging is "postponed disappointment." Hope refers to "unfounded anticipation" of a better tomorrow. Those of you whose souls have been mugged live in the future rather than participating in the present. You hope that by some means, never explained nor understood, things will get better and life will become worth living once more. Hope is a power which you may feel is unshakably strong, eternal, and infallible. You are willing to place your relationship in the hands of hope. You may feel a sense of safety and pride in your ability to call forth hope, a word you grew up thinking was the most positive word in the English language.

In the soul mugging context, hope is lethal because it causes those who rely on it to live on false, baseless assumptions Feeding your own illusions about life, the word hope prevents you from making an objective assessment about the destructive nature of your present relationship. You only live on past memories and future promises because the present is too un-bearable.

The inappropriate use of hope in a soul-mugging relationship can permeate your entire life. In this context, hope undermines and thwarts the formation of your sense of integrity and worth as a human being.

Those of you caught in soul mugging completely live on the hope you create over and over again, just as Judy did. You believe that some day soon your relationship will be free of pain and problems. Then together you and another person will have the time, energy, and desire to have a loving, positive relationship.

Actually, if you are caught in soul mugging, you are also hoping that another will miracu-lously see the light, and that the negative aspects of your relationship will then just disappear. Too, you hope your soul will not be further damaged by your own hands or by the other's desecrating behaviors. Your hope has sustained you through this process, and you draw on hope for the strength to continue.

Among the many styles of distorted thinking that have arisen in psychological literature since the early 1980's, Dr. Veronica Thomas, a psychologist and writer, described two which complement the theory of continual hope. She describes a need some people have to change others. Your motive, if this applies to you, is that your hope for happiness seems to depend entirely on these others. She calls this the "fallacy of change," where you expect others to change to suit you if you just pressure, cajole, beg, or hope long enough.

The other style of distorted thinking is called the "heaven's reward fallacy." Here you jus-tify sacrificing your own interests and postpone seeking your own rewards with the mistaken expectation that you will eventually be rewarded.

An insidious part of using hope in the soul-mugging relationship is your dependence on a "magic helper." When you feel helpless to exert your own power in your relationship, your dependence on this magic helper called hope provides a solution which shifts your attention away from your misery, at least for the moment. You then have a false sense that some out-side force will take care of everything. Hope has an ethereal quality which banishes anxiety in a soul-mugging relationship. But for the temporary relief hope brings, you have made an insidious trade for the further desecration of your soul.

Heroes and Idols: Idealized Fantasy Theory

You fall into a likely set-up for soul mugging when you attempt to force into reality a preconceived vision based on an image you have fantasized.

Have you ever:

- looked for someone who matched the main character of a romantic novel?

- wished your parents were like parents you saw in television shows?

- had a crush on a movie star and built a fantasy relationship?

- looked for a romantic partner who was a perfect match for your idealized fantasy?

A theory closely related to the theory of hope is the theory of idealized fantasy of the partner. Rather than just elaborating on your partner's positive attributes, you virtually infuse into your relationship a fantasy individual that you have created over time.

Jason's Flawed Fantasy Woman

Jason, a 40-year-old man from a small coastal village in England, was a journalist for the entertainment section of the daily newspaper. He called me after he had read an article I had written for a health newsletter. Jason had been in therapy for more than two months before he admitted to having a long-time fantasy of the woman he had been with now for two years.

"I have a very difficult time admitting that I truly suffer over the grievous violations I have experienced from Gretchen. You see, she fits the picture of my ideal fantasy in every other way. I kept thinking that her ranting was only a temporary phase of our relationship. I really anticipated that she would become all I hoped she would be.

"I can't quit thinking about my first time with her. She was not just my fantasy – I imagine she would be a lot of men's fantasy. She just has this one horrible side to her. I can't give up on her, though. I know she is the one for me. I dreamed her into existence in my life."

Highlights of the Idealized Fantasy Theory

Just as Jason had, you, too, may have had the frame for a picture for many years. You placed this frame into your hope chest, and when a likely partner appeared, you mounted that person into the picture frame, thinking that person could function in the idealized fantasy that you had created. Your present partner is not as important to you as the fantasy you have assigned him or her.

No matter how degrading your partner is to you or how defiling the interactions are to your essence, you continue to see your partner as your ideal. You consistently attempt to mold your partner into the mate you have been longing to find. This partner is your ideal, the one who belongs in your pre-fabricated frame, regardless of the grief this causes you.

The breaking apart of this fantasy is your self's way of signaling that a more realistic perspective is overdue. The unfinished pain and unresolved issues of living on hope and fantasy will no longer serve you as expected. Placing anyone on a pedestal is dangerous to your essence, and the disillusionment that inevitably follows is deeply painful and can be disorienting.

It is necessary to proceed through your fantasies to a firm reality. If you take action to stop permitting your fantasy to live through you at your expense, it is possible for your soul to flourish.

Name That Tune: Repetitive Cycles Theory

If you are in a soul-mugging relationship, you may not be stepping back far enough to see a cycle. You simply may not be stringing together related events so that they form a pattern which you can recognize. If you are too caught up in immediate and consuming issues, you may be missing this pattern.

You are most likely to miss this pattern when you are:

- distracted from the big picture by immediate concerns;
- consumed with the demands of coping with the situation;
- experiencing blocked perception because of pain that would emerge if the pattern were acknowledged.

In the same way that you can drive by an intersection every day and not notice obvious features of it, you may also be missing a lot that is happening in your life. Are you bypassing important markers in your soul and in your relationship?

Jessie's Emotional Merry-Go-Round

Jessie, a 32-year-old Caucasian woman, had been coming to therapy for five months. Each week she had faithfully taken time off from her sales job at a local discount store to uncover what had gone wrong in her relationship with Tim. She had never missed a session until the week after we spoke about cycles of soul mugging. I called Jessie to ask what had kept her from coming to her appointment. She could barely talk because she was so hoarse. Thinking she was sick, I asked if she had seen a physician.

"I am ashamed to tell you that my voice is gone because I was yelling at Tim last night. Dr. Papillon, I am exhausted from these debilitating yelling matches with him. I can't take it. I am coming apart, especially inside, like my stomach is being ripped out of me. It is so painful that I can't even work. Now I am really worried because in these two years with Tim I've always been able to make myself go to my job. I don't care anymore. I really don't. And that scares me.

"Each time I think he really means it when he says he is sorry for what he says. I have forgiven and forgiven, and I have run out of forgiveness. I remember experiencing my mother's unpredictable outbursts of cruelty, even when they were just horrible looks she gave me. I began to feel crazy at an early age when she would direct fits of meanness towards me then suddenly disappear into her bedroom.

"She would then come out later as though nothing had happened, offering to read me a bedtime story. Do you see what madness that is? I can see it better now, especially telling you. I've never really talked about it. You know, Tim is like that. He will leave me in a heap on the floor emotionally and then come back over to me in a little while, asking if we can make love. I feel a mixture of both outrage and relief when he does that. I felt that way as a kid, too, so glad my mom was out of her so-called mad mood, but still stinging from it. Does this just sound too weird for words, Doctor?"

Highlights of the Repetitive Cycles Theory

You can see from Jessie's description how easily you can be caught up in a cycle without realizing it.

Of course, once you see the cycle, you can either permit it to repeat again or stop it. One thing to note as you read about the repetitive cycles theory is that once you see the pattern you will never again be automatically trapped in this cycle. However, you may wish to note your own part in recreating this same set of circumstances. No doubt you have been unaware until now that you were involved in creating and repeating it.

As you can see from Jessie's response, the cycle began so early in her life that it took a long time for her to decipher just what was occurring between her and Tim. The repeating cycle doesn't seem like a repetition when it is happening to you. You experience it as an incident that, once over, you are glad to have behind you. You don't dwell on each part of the interaction, nor do you notice that it is similar to the one you had with your partner only a few days earlier.

The repeating cycle can become apparent in several ways. One signal may be the pressure that begins to build within your partner. You can sense it if you don't tune it out or deny your intuitive messages. The pressure may be about something outside of the relationship, or within it. Eventually, there is an explosion between the two of you over a trivial matter.

Your soul is re-wounded as another mugging takes place. Then your partner apologizes (or blames you for the outburst or both). After a lull the rage within your partner begins to gather force again and you become the target for another dehumanizing, demoralizing assault. In a soul-mugging relationship, this cycle continues no matter what plans you form to counteract it.

Have you noticed that once a boundary (such as your view of respectable behavior toward your essence) is violated, it is almost impossible to go back to the more honorable way you want your partner to treat you? The experience of repeating cycles may seem familiar to you due to the mugging you have done to your own soul. Remember that long ago you began to treat your essence in that same disrespectful way, so you are receiving that treatment recycled now. Since you yourself initiated that violation against your soul, it hurts especially deeply. It is like being beaten down twice, and once is too many times, as I am sure you will agree.

You may actually be cooperating in these cycles. One way you may participate is by denying your partner's defiling and demeaning ways of relating to you. Covering up what your partner does when others are around is a way of colluding with your partner's treatment of you. Still another tactic of cooperation involves rationalizing and minimizing your partner's desecrations. For example, you may use the excuse that your partner has had childhood difficulties or that you are being unreasonable in your demands on the relationship.

One of the worst parts of this cycle is that it is exhausting. For example, you may want to believe your partner's apology. But look at the effort. You may be compelled to undertake a highly complex inner emotional/intellectual sorting out so that you can make peace within yourself and get on with your life. That consumes a lot more energy than you realize. And after you do it, you have to keep doing it – over and over, for the cycle will continue as long as you allow it. You and your partner are caught in an ever-tightening trap that neither of you knows how to get out of. Neither of you enjoy it, yet it fulfills some unspecified need in each of you. Your task is to uncover the need in you, name it, and see how you can fill it in ways that are preferable to the ways you have chosen until now.

From the Bottom of Your Partner's Heart: Incessant Longing of the Soul

The theory of incessant longing of the soul is about wanting to be seen as a one-of-a-kind, precious soul by those you care most about. You long to be extremely important to another and foremost in his or her mind. You yearn to be completely enveloped by the other's eyes and his or her heart. You become acutely sensitive to another person's regard for you since you derive your self-affirmation and self-validation from him or her. Giving your self's home base to another, though, has placed you in a position of extreme vulnerability.

Were you set up for having to have reassurance from another by:

- your caregiver neglecting you in a pervasive manner?
- feeling you were of absolutely no value to anyone from very early in your life?
- feeling totally unappreciated for any uniqueness you displayed until you met this person?

Anna's Rainbow Chase

Anna was 44 years old when she came into my office for her first visit. She was petite, young-looking for her age, and quite shy in her manner. Anna had recently moved to Southern California from a small town in Montana to take a promotion as an agricultural inspector.

"Doctor, I've never been in an office for psychological help before, but I can't endure this pain any longer. I am either going to take a gun to my stomach or I've got to find out why I hurt in that area so much and so often. There is an incessant aching – I also feel like there is nothing that can penetrate it far enough to comfort me. I notice it most acutely when Mike withdraws from me.

"I get this feeling of hunger, like a yearning for something I can't describe exactly. It is a sense that I must be fed, and Mike has all the food. What a mess. I used to think I'd never let a man have any kind of control over me. This is beyond control. It is as if he carries my soul in his pocket. It disgusts me to hear myself say that. Doctor, what can I do? I am embarrassed to be here but even more so to tell you this. I am so ashamed.

"Mike is a wonderful husband, I mean the best... most of the time. When he is cruel, though, he is very damaging to me. At those times I feel he wipes me out. I no longer am. Really, I have to go look in the mirror to see if I'm still a person. I feel like a building that has been bombed, whose foundation is so damaged that everyone had to be evacuated.

"Nothing remains, no being, no essence, certainly nothing I can hold on to that says, 'This defines Anna.' Doctor, I'm scared. I've never felt so caught by anything. I am only able to see the answer to the question of 'Who is Anna?' by looking into Mike's eyes. When he gets into one of his moods, then I am totally at a loss to bring myself into existence. I disappear. I don't know where I go, but I'm no longer anywhere as far as I'm concerned."

Anna ended her session in sobs. She felt she would never be able to gain a sense of her essence. She had no idea when or if she had ever had one. She was both horrified and frightened at this prospect. She knew, though, that she must have Mike in her life. Soul longing is a very devastating experience, partly because it encompasses so many different aspects of your life, especially in your relationship.

Highlights of the Incessant Longing of the Soul Theory

Another person's initial defining of you awakens a part of you which makes you feel treasured and whole. When your soul longing is finally met, you relish all of life. Nature seems more alive, colors more brilliant; people and situations, even difficult ones, seem easier to handle. In your work you are more creative, expressive, and adventurous.

You may have experienced your invisible soul being made visible and, more importantly, adored by another's loving glances and long, inviting silences. This is your language of soul affirmation. This person's rapt, endearing attention is your lifeline. His or her acknowledgement fills a place in you that can be filled in no other way.

Yet when this person no longer wishes to interact with you in this way, you experience more than loss of his or her companionship and physical presence. You feel your soul has been wiped out.

The morning after an evening's confrontation with another, complete with defiling, degrading interactions, have you ever noticed that you had no energy? That your day was pointless? That your life was meaningless?

Your existence has rested on your perception that another person completely valued your essence. Relief from the agony of incessant longing of the soul is based on your willingness to understand where it originated and how it is perpetuated. Ultimately, you must be willing to give to your own soul that one-of-a-kind adoration, the sense that your soul is a precious treasure.

Fear and Safety: Paradoxical Joining Theory

Your soul-mugging relationship is in balance only when two extremes, fear and safety, are in equilibrium. This is a result of your early impressions of what love is.

You may recognize your need to balance fear and safety if:

- you came from a volatile family environment that persisted over time;
- you are continually apprehensive that emotional satisfaction will not last.

Almost every patient who has worked with me to triumph over soul mugging has eventually reported the paradox that fear and safety exist simultaneously in the relationship.

Stanley's Juggling Act

Stanley, a 39-year-old Caucasian man, had been coming to therapy for eleven months. He worked in the maintenance department of a utility company and had been referred by his supervisor due to his excessive absences. Stanley had scheduled an extra therapy session due to the overwhelming stress he was feeling.

"Doctor, I am having such a strange mixture of feelings and I think at times that I'm going nuts. I have just, as you know, returned from a trip with Liz, and being around her non-stop for ten days began to get to me big-time.

"I see her as the biggest gift and the worst nightmare of my life all rolled into one. She is dynamite and keeps me off-guard. Yet I crave the feeling of just lying next to her, not so much sexually, just being together.

"What bother me are the feelings that got stirred up in me on this trip. I felt that I could lie in her arms and feel her heart beating next to mine forever. Yet, I got scared of her at the same time. I would be calm, but my stomach would hurt. I couldn't explain this to myself, nor could I get rid of it. I felt like I was being drawn into her and we were merging, and then I felt repelled by the panic. It's something I just can't explain.

"Now she's upset because I tried to describe my feelings to her and she just... Well, anyway, it's a mess."

Highlights of the Paradoxical Joining Theory

Many patients I have seen are, just as Stanley was, startled and perplexed by the paradox of feeling both fear and safety in interactions with their romantic partner.

This paradox is created when two unlikely feelings intertwine between partners in a soul-mugging relationship. Ask yourself: Do I feel safe when I am with my lover? Do I also experience fear that almost perfectly matches the intensity of the safety?

Safety is the sense of supreme comfort you feel in your partner's arms. It is a soothing feeling, as if being lulled into a deep sleep, while being embraced by a bliss that can only come from your partner's touching you physically. You experience peace beyond any spoken words. You find reassurance in being very important to your partner while in his or her presence, as you are enfolded in love and appreciation that completes your deepest desires. Life is perfect at those moments.

Your positive feelings are accompanied by the same exact amount of fear. This is most appropriately summarized as a low-grade panic. Your fear may manifest itself as a distinct but undefined "dis"-ease in your stomach and chest areas. The identifying characteristic, however, occurs during the blissful times with your partner where, even then, you are alert to any change in your partner's mood. You perpetually maintain an anxious hyper-vigilance concerning small changes in your partner, looking for any signal that the relationship is shifting.

In soul-mugging relationships this fear and safety paradox is always reported by one if not both partners. These two emotions are calibrated to an amazingly constant equilibrium. If there is more fear than safety, in a short period of time the relationship adjusts back into balance by moving towards safety.

The romantic partnership virtually depends on both fear and safety as ingredients for intimacy, and even for its "normal" day-to-day functioning. The intricate, unconscious juggling that occurs within a day slips by unnoticed because it has been present from the beginning of the relationship.

Perhaps one explanation of the fear and safety paradox is that some "receiving" mechanism triggers feelings from earlier times in your life. These feelings relate to your thresholds for absorbing pleasure and pain. At some point, you developed a sense that love looked this paradoxical way. You began to know love only if it were felt with this juxtapositioning of fear and safety, experienced in uniquely specified proportions.

You were drawn into your romantic partnership and ultimately bonded intensely with your partner precisely because you had to have an uncertain and unpredictable feeling. Only then did the relationship seem right to you.

By its emphasis on certainty and being civilized, broad societal conditioning may contribute to this unsettling paradox. Even the media is loaded with news coverage and features which seem obsessed with safety. In *The Dangerous Edge: The Psychology of Excitement,* Dr. Michael Aptor states, "The safer we try to make life, the more people may take on risks."

There may be nothing more empowering and connecting for the two of you than living on the edge, that is, being permeated with fear, while at the same time enjoying a "safe harbor" as you comfort each other.

Risk may have become a part of your life in a significant way. A relationship that does not have the forces of fear and safety, calibrated to just the right balance, may feel too lifeless and boring.

Built-in Limits to Love: Measured Love Theory

Your sense of the right amount of love for you is governed by pre-set limits. These have been imprinted through long-past conditioning which continues without your awareness or permission. The dynamics which call forth this imprint were triggered in you from the time you entered your relationship.

> You grew up with a type and amount of love which you adapted to at that time. As an adult you have gravitated toward a relationship which provides a nearly identical configuration of this love.

> Some clues about your capacity to love may be found by examining your early recollections of the love that you and your siblings received, as well as the giving and receiving of love among relatives outside your immediate family, including your grandparents.

Sue's Miniature Container

Sue, a 40-year-old Chinese woman, had been in the United States for fifteen years. When she contacted me, she seemed very embarrassed to ask for my help. She was a court reporter who had not missed a day of work in six years, although she had not reported to her job for two weeks. At her first session she was horrified at not being able to pull herself together.

"Doctor, I am so sorry to bother you with this. I am at my wit's end. This relationship with Phil is going to be the death of me. I feel it. He's supposedly my boyfriend. We started seeing each other three years ago. But Doctor, it is not working. I stay so mad that I think I can't make it through another day.

"When I think of breaking it off, though, I am down and out. I can't go to work, I don't eat, and I certainly don't sleep. Forget it. One day I find I can be extremely close to him. He calls me his precious angel. I melt. He will say, 'Why would I ever want to be anywhere but here with you?' I become like a little girl; I take in those words and savor them.

"Then I get very scared because I say to myself, 'Why would I ever leave this? I'll do anything, literally anything, to have it.' I think I will. But when he starts telling me the same thing the next day, I freak out. It's too much. I want the love, but I can't absorb it. I try, but I can't.

"I can't control him, and yet I know I try to. I feel like I have to. I must get him to back off until I can reach a point where I can take in more of his love. He doesn't get it, though, and I'm going crazy. Once he even said I was like an animal that only wants to get fed once a day, if that. Doctor, I'm all mixed up. Am *I* weird to push him back, or is *he* weird to want to love me so much? What is it? I'm desperate."

Highlights of the Measured Love Theory

Sue was actually repeating a pattern that was familiar to her, although she was unaware she was doing it. She was able to take in only a limited amount of love, and having received that she focused on assimilating it, even as her partner was attempting to give her more. Although she thought she wanted more love, she had provided herself with only the amount she could handle.

The theory of measured love explains why people who find themselves in soul-mugging relationships must have the exact amount of "love" they were accustomed to having as they grew up. The term "love" as used in this context refers to attention, approval, respect, honoring, caring, and support.

The partner you chose for your romantic relationship gives you what you have always received. You find this appealing but frustrating at the same time. It is quite probable that you never did like the kind or amount of love you received. Yet to imagine that you can handle more love than you have now, or a love with a different set of qualities, is questionable.

If you received only a portion of the love you wanted during that time, your tendency is to keep trying to change your behavior, your relationship, and your partner so that you can get more. Yet without knowing it you have gravitated toward the profile of love which resembles the love you had in your distant past.

If you aspired to experience a greater amount of love than you received, you may have concluded that now you can manage yourself much more skillfully than you were able to when you were a child, and certainly in a way that is superior to the examples provided by your caregivers. You may be convinced that you have the tools and general wherewithal to make your relationship turn out better.

If you have not succeeded in reaching these aspirations, you may tend to place the blame on your partner. But this dynamic is not about your partner. It is about you, and it is about restricting yourself to some predetermined level of love in your relationship. However, you may not wish to continue to be bound by these constraints.

Unfortunately, the measured love phenomenon carries an additional problematic twist. It is highly probable that you linked up with your partner because your capacity to be open to the sort of love you received actually closed you to other kinds of nurturing. Now you are only responsive to a partner who can show love in the same way that your early caretakers did. No one but the partner you have could begin to connect with you in that profound place. Because of this close match you have become tightly tied to your partner.

Seconds and Irregulars: Defective Self Theory

The defective self theory centers on the contempt you carry with you about who you are at your core. You feel somehow ineffective, incomplete, and insufficient. Through early experiences in your life you decided that you were not like others. Your sense of inadequacy makes you a prime candidate for soul mugging.

Do you recall:

- feeling that others had something which was missing within you as you were growing up?
- looking for a partner who would overlook your defects?

You may be relieved that you found a partner to whom you could hand over your self, which you perceive as somehow defective or incomplete. If you had become aware that you felt defective in some way, you could have addressed that issue directly and perhaps prevented soul diminishing consequences.

Irene's Abandoned Treasure

Irene, a 28-year-old Caucasian woman who worked in an office, was usually very subdued. She had been seeing me for about two months when she arrived one day with a small, tattered red bag full of papers which she ceremoniously dumped all over a nearby coffee table.

"Dr. Papillon, do you see this bunch of papers? This is me. It really is. I spent all weekend writing out what John has been saying about who I am. Well, here I am, tied up in these scraps. Look at these. I am all tattered and worn, thrown around, summarized on crumpled papers with words that are not even original. The words are John's words. He's no help. I don't feel a bit better. In fact, I feel worse."

I had never seen Irene as disgusted and enraged as she was at that moment. I was seeing someone who had never revealed much about herself. Actually, it was reassuring to see.

"I can't do this anymore, and I can't not do it. I'm a cracked vase, without any sense of wholeness except whatever John gives me. It is so upsetting that I can barely look at myself in the mirror these days. Do you know I haven't the slightest idea why, either?"

"It would be easier if I had had a wreck in my car. At least I'd have a good excuse for this tattered and torn feeling. Can you imagine my ever being able to admit, 'Oh, a man took my stuff and made it over into this stuff.' Please, that's pathetic."

Highlights of the Defective Self Theory

You start your relationship with a self you somehow feel is fundamentally lacking, unappealing, and perhaps repulsive. With this other, you find instant caring, security, and someone who seems to know you very well. You are exhilarated by tantalizing promises of things to come, words that you savor and a feeling that you have found a secure foundation for your soul. Your partner offers the path to happiness, and you enthusiastically give your soul over. You willingly trade your sense of self for your vision of a new life and the abundance that this relationship will bring. You are grateful that your deficiencies are accepted, or even better, unnoticed.

You then launch into the relationship which you believe has repaired the unnamed, uncomfortable, and unwanted aspects of yourself. Because of the intensity, persistence, duration, and scope of your relationship, you become increasingly vulnerable to what your partner tells you. You have given over what you consider an inadequate self to your partner, trusting that he or she will remedy your defects.

Over time, you absorb your partner's perceptions and definitions of your essence so completely that you now see your self only from your partner's perspective. At times it may seem as if you have been brainwashed, because you truly don't know where your partner's ideas and beliefs about you end and where you begin. Your sense of self apart from your partner and apart from his or her understanding of you has become indistinguishable.

It is not surprising that your partner moves into a place where you have not healed. Your partner can seem to fill and repair those defects in you by the kind of adoration he or she heaps on you. Then, at unexpected times, you are startled when your partner only deepens the tender wounds already present. How could you have permitted anything like this? Then you get furious and decide that your partner is just cruel.

Your interaction with your partner becomes mystifying to you. It contradicts your beliefs about how relationships work, at least in an ideal world. Also, you just can't understand how this could have occurred. It may feel as if you have been captured in a net you have not yet realized you helped to weave.

You may have assumed that if you gave your deficient self to your partner, he or she would treat you with respect. But your handing over your sense of self resulted from the seduction of surrender that Joel Kramer and Diana Alstad mention in their book, *The Guru Papers* (North Atlantic Books/Frog Ltd., 1993). It is the giving up of questioning.

Because you have never felt you had the power to make a difference in your life, you have basically said by your behavior and acquiescence, "I will follow you. You know the way and will make certain that I get there." The real danger lies in the deception that by compromising your soul, you will have a better life. You also imperil your essence by mindless devotion to another. You become trapped in expending energy to fend off negative interactions. You exhaust your reservoir of energy in preserving the relationship because that is where you look for your sense of wholeness.

No other individual is going to be more respectful of you than you are of your soul. Without realizing it, you thought that by giving your soul to your partner to make you feel complete, your partner would give you back what you had never had. It just does not work that way, which is a very painful truth to discover. It can never work to take a passive role in guiding what is happening to you. Being adrift, with no rudder for your being, can lead you far astray. When you stop making decisions about who you are and what you need *for* yourself, you unknowingly begin to make these kinds of decisions *against* yourself.

Getting Back What You Give: Mirroring Theory

As you and your partner interact, he or she will invariably reflect back some part of you. If you have a strong dislike for what you hear, you may be responding to a reflection of how you treat your soul. You can confirm this by paying attention to your internal dialogue. In addition, your protestations invite further degrading mirroring.

This may apply if:

-    from early in life you look outside, rather than inward, to get your image of your being;

-    you look solely to another as the all-important reference point;

-    you have a strong reaction to something another person says and you don't know why.

Another person's demeaning treatment of your self sets into motion a downward spiral. This diverts your focus on isolating the cause of this treatment from you onto the other. You neglect to recognize that this other person's objectionable treatment of you started with your own early soul mugging. This person is now actually a mirror. Thus, no remedy can be initiated until you look inward.

Shelly's Echo

Shelly, a 41-year-old Caucasian woman, came in for the first time after she lost her job as a secretary at a construction company, where she had been working for a year. She had gotten into a yelling match with one of the workers.

"I tried to stop myself from getting into it with this man. He just reminded me so much of what I receive at home, Doctor, I lost my head! I started yelling at him to stop him from being so ugly to me.

"He spoke to me as if I were a construction worker out in the field, with no respect for me as a woman. At home, my husband will do the same thing. He is so demanding. I feel like I have to be perfect all the time. Clean this, do that, open the door, close the cabinet. It is endless. I feel like I'm his slave. I can't take it one more minute, from any of them. They can all just go to hell.

"I'm through with the whole bunch of them. I get enough of that kind of talk as I drive around or clean the house when no one is around … what am I saying? Oh my God, *I* do it too, but not to them, to me."

Highlights of the Mirroring Theory

Admittedly, it is not an easy task to examine the unexamined when it has to do with parts of you that you are not proud of. You probably see the demanding and negative verbiage you receive as despicable and unacceptable. An insidious and repeating pattern is set up through another's mirroring back to you the negative ways in which you treat your own soul.

If you notice that another person is degrading you on a profound level, then there is no doubt that you have been treating your essence in a degrading way. You may not realize, though, that this behavior is a reflection of the way you handle your self. You make the doubly damaging error of taking another's deriding comments as literal indications that you need to change your own behavior.

A downward spiral begins, deteriorating into greater feelings of un-lovability. In your attempt to feel better about your being, you begin to plead with this other person to tell you that you are lovable, worthy of respect, etc. If your demands fail to produce the desired response, you have only piled on more evidence for yourself that you are entirely valueless.

Your objections and requests that another person reconsider his or her view of you will not benefit you. Even if he or she suddenly speaks only glowing words about you, you now "know" better. Their positive words cannot reach you with any healing power.

Turning inward to examine your self is the only effective alternative. By doing this you can do something about how you assess your worth. Another person can never love you more than you love your soul, as this other person mirrors back exactly what you see inside of you.

The usefulness of understanding this mirroring dynamic is to alert you to shift your attention from another to yourself. It also shows the futility of trying to persuade another person to act differently toward you. When you project an image that is radically different from your usual self, you will then notice a change in the response you receive.

Mirroring, as do many other soul-mugging dynamics, operates completely out of your awareness. The best way for you to discover that another person is merely a mirror for your negatively perceived image is for you to see the way you already view your essence.

Just Can't Get It: Perceived Helplessness Theory

You have lost the sense that you have power in your relationship. The drastic consequences of soul mugging are a feeling of helplessness and loss of self-efficacy. You lack the inspiration to think of new approaches, and you have no energy to try new strategies. Furthermore, you have lost all motivation to change your relationship or yourself.

This may apply if:

- the relationship has gone on for some time in a toxic environment;
- you feel helpless to institute measures that will produce a positive change;
- you have given up and feel you cannot make an impact in your situation.

You imagine you are powerless and this other person is all-powerful. Over time, you have given up talking about your disappointments and your sense of loss. You have lost the motivation to talk with this other person about your relationship.

Amber's Resignation to Despair

Amber, a 51-year-old Caucasian woman, had been employed in the accounting department of an electronics firm for fifteen years. She prided herself on being more than ninety-nine percent accurate in her operating projections. A colleague of hers had called to schedule her appointment with me. He was concerned about a change in Amber that had become more evident in the past six months. He described Amber as being lethargic in her work performance. She had missed more days in the past year than she ever had since she worked there. During her first visit, Amber exclaimed:

"I'm extremely embarrassed that someone else called you about me. I just can't seem to get it together to do anything for myself these days. I almost feel as if I'm in a trance. I go to work but I'm not there.

I go home to my husband, and I tune him out. I sit in front of the television, but I couldn't tell you one show I've watched all week. It is pathetic. I feel rotten when I start to think about what I've become.

"I've been married for three years now. Wayne's a wonderful man, full of enough talent, enthusiasm, and motivation to go to the top in his field. I have never been able to get through to him, though, about things that are very important to me. Every time I make an attempt, he turns on me – either verbally attacking me or walking away. I guess I've given up. It feels useless to me to try any more.

"I might as well be an armchair, the kitchen table or even the carpet. That's how blah I feel these days, just there.

"I can't stand being silent, but I just don't have the energy to try to think up another strategy to use with Wayne. Nothing helps. I've run out of everything – especially the feeling I can make a difference in anything about Wayne. I know I'm miserable. I want to leave. And I can't. I have no idea where I'd go. That's so pitiful, and yet it's so true."

Highlights of the Perceived Helplessness Theory

Over time you have attempted many ploys to reverse the negativity that has built up in your relationship. You think now, though, as Amber did, that you have done all you know to do. You feel completely helpless to make any difference in this situation. So you are resigned to your relationship staying just the way it is. You have decided you might as well put up with what you have to, to get what you think you need.

Since your approach to life seems so different from your partner's, you are finally filled with despair. You realize his or her way is so ingrained that no amount of effort on your part will matter. Eventually, it is even difficult to continue going about other aspects of your life. Your soul-mugging relationship has completely depleted you.

You have stopped trying to get out of it for several reasons. You are emotionally drained and you feel overwhelmed. You believe your partner's claims that everything negative in your relationship occurs because of you. You have tried leaving, but that ends up not working for you, either. So, you come back to the relationship more depleted and demoralized than before you left. You are no longer able to objectively assess what is real, and you are too exhausted to think about it anymore.

Your partner alternates between acting wonderfully and then terribly towards you. Your partner blames you for any relationship mishap which occurs and seems unreachable and unresponsive when you attempt to talk about your anguish. You are at an impasse with no options that you can even fathom. Life may look very barren from this perspective.

Is Anybody Home? Inner Emptiness

You have an extreme sense of inner emptiness, a bleak internal condition described as a "void" or "internally lacking something that is foundational." You have looked exclusively to your partner to provide that grounding foundation.

If you have reached this extreme situation:

- your void can be traced to childhood;
- for a long time you have attempted to assuage this emptiness by relying on your relationship;
- you have isolated yourself in the relationship, thinking that eventually this inner emptiness will be filled solely by your partner;
- your body aches daily from this internal yearning.

Inner emptiness came well before you got into your romantic relationship and could linger long after it is gone unless you directly address its root cause. In retrospect, you may recognize that it was part of the reason you were attracted to your partner.

Tommy's Nagging Nothingness

Tommy, a 37-year-old Caucasian man, looked much older than his years when he came in for his first session. He was now in his ninth month of therapy. Tommy was a successful stock broker in a large financial services firm. During our conversations he avoided his pain by focusing on the misery he had had for the last four years with Shirley. He had labeled their relationship "an act of endurance."

"I have tried to get my wife to stop babying me, yet I keep wanting her to do what she would do with a baby. I continue to think that if she can just feed me the right foods, hold me the right way, and be nice to me long enough, I will snap out of this black hole I'm in.

"I guess I need to explain what happened last night because I finally saw what I was doing to her by demanding that she do what she can't possibly do. She has tried, she really has. It is just that... well, this is hard to say, I am not able to feel satisfied by anything she does. I am always wanting more – more of her undivided attention, more of her unwavering love, more of her telling me I am wanted, needed, and approved of.

"She is tired of this role. I know she is. I thought it was helping, but it really isn't. In fact, I think it is making things worse. She is now about to scream from the frustration of giving and giving, and I still have this deep longing to be filled up. Is it strange to never ever get a satisfied feeling, no matter what she does? I'm beginning to sense that this is not right.

"I thought she wasn't doing something she should, but now I think there's something wrong with me. I can't take it in, or I won't. I don't know. I just know the emptiness is deep, maybe too deep for anyone to reach. I can't bear to think that, though. Then there's no chance for me. I'll be a bottomless pit with no one to help me. Oh, my God, no..."

Highlights of the Inner Emptiness Theory

Just as Tommy was expressing, eventually there is a desperation that accompanies inner emptiness. You feel unfulfilled in so many dimensions of your life that you enter a relationship, attempting to relieve that aching emptiness. Your attempts may have provided you with temporary relief, but they will not lead to fulfillment of your profound emptiness. That is where it stays, perched just out of your reach. Now that you have reached adulthood no one can penetrate, much less fill, those empty places that were carved early in your life.

Failure piles on failure, despite your attempts. This only compounds the problem. Your nerves become raw. You try to turn off your feelings. Yet that does not work either, because you cannot get rid of that gnawing pain in the pit of your being.

Nothing stops your emptiness. It continues to distract you. It intrudes on your job, on your relationship, and ultimately on every area of your life. It is with you wherever you are. This experience of inner emptiness at times may loom so forebodingly that you fear you are a nobody. Finally, this inner emptiness causes you to sense that you have become absent even to yourself.

Nowhere have you found the answer to this persisting pain. It is not addressed by anything outside of you. Your partner may have done a monumental job of attempting to get rid of it for you, but those efforts have failed.

You were attracted to the possibility that this person could be the one to magically fill this enormous void. The pressure of this inner emptiness may have left you especially susceptible to the seduction of a romantic partner who, it seemed, could stop the pain.

However, as you continue to be wounded over and over, you start to shut everything out. Now, your disappointment is doubled. You not only have the pain, you also have the misery of knowing that no one, not even this partner, can replenish your spirit.

The "void within" is an expression I often hear from patients who are in soul-mugging relationships. Most view the world from a core of emptiness. They never feel full and complete. Their dissatisfaction leaves them chronically suffering – emotionally, psychologically, spiritually, and physically.

Steps beyond Understanding

The remainder of the book provides approaches, techniques, and building blocks to strengthen your inner resolve, and ultimately to restore your soul to its flourishing wholeness. Only when you complete the process, using this book as a guide, will you be fully prepared to make decisions about your soul, your relationship, and any related issues in your life.

Much is more mysterious than known, more mystical than scientific. As Robert Frost said: "Something we were withholding made us weaker until we learned it was our Selves we were withholding from this living ..."

Chapter Seven

My Heart Belongs to Me

Restoring Your Soul

Souls are God's jewels, every one of which is worth many worlds.
– Thomas Traherne

Build thee more stately mansions, O my soul.
– Oliver Wendell Holmes

A Beginning Step to My Own Soul Restoration

I wish I could tell you it was easy to dial Jonathan's number after five months of very intense inner work and that I was rather nonchalant about it. But, in truth, I was trembling as I spoke to his machine.

"Jonathan, I would like to have a conversation with you, please call me when you get this message."

After I hung up, I realized I had no idea how he would receive it or whether he would even call back. It was unnerving not to know what would happen next. I still felt vulnerable to him and his unpredictable behavior. I was surprised that it was such a big deal to make contact after having walked through all I had worked on with myself – journaling, answering all of those questions that I had asked, deciding which theories fit our relationship. I found, as I searched within, that I wasn't even sure I could name all the different emotions I felt at this point. I did think that restoration of my soul was my most important next step in healing, though. And I did know that making the call was not a sudden move on my part. I had contemplated it for several days before I dared pick up the phone.

Within two hours, I received a call from him. He began in a gentle way:

"Hi, I had decided I'd never hear from you again. What a nice surprise."

"Well, I wasn't sure I'd ever want to contact you. I thought about it for a long time. I do want to know how you are doing, and if you are still speaking around the country."

"I guess I'm doing okay, most of the time. I speak quite a bit. How about you?"

"I am being quite diligent about my personal work, the internal changes I am making. I am very committed to it even though it is difficult. You know, I am finding I feel uncomfortable continuing to talk to you. Perhaps at a different time I can stay on the phone longer. Bye."

I was very relieved to be off. I started to cry realizing that just hearing his voice had brought up strong memories of what I had put my soul through. Calling him reinforced that I must consciously, deliberately, and immediately take the next step. I was now at the point where strategies, experiential exercises, really anything I could come up with, were critical so that I could nourish, really replenish my core being. This call confirmed for me not only my readiness but the absolute necessity of this next step.

I know I have to keep reminding myself as I keep moving on this path what Pavel Florensky said: "Butterfly is the Soul of the caterpillar."

Also I must remember this wonderful statement from Rainier Maria Rilke: "The future enters into us long before it happens."

Opening to Discovery

This chapter helps you venture through the tapestry of your inner self. That venture prompts new discoveries and insights where you previously had found only impenetrable barriers. As you proceed it is also important to examine any solutions you have clung to tightly in the past, for these will not work and will only delay your soul restoration. You are just committing now to letting go of old ways, at least for a period of time, to see whether new ones will benefit you more.

Soul Discovery

Take an imaginary tour through your home. Notice everything in it as you go – pictures, pieces of furniture, objects you have gathered over time. Now pick one item that best captures what you are feeling about your soul at this very moment. Do not edit. What did you select? Describe in detail what it is with all of its varied features. Can you see ways in which this object relates to your experience with your soul now?

Regardless of the object you focused on, there is meaning in your choice. One of my patients chose a book she had on her coffee table but had not yet read. Through her exploration she discovered that having bought the book and having placed it in a prominent place represented several dimensions of ways she related to her soul. Your object, too, has invariably revealed surprising aspects about your soul restoration.

As you progress, you will identify certain turning points. At these moments you will clearly see what you have been doing to your soul. Although transformational moments may seem to come out of nowhere, you have actually been preparing for them in many different ways. Even finding this book was one of the turning points in your transformation.

"I'm not his anymore. I'm mine."

This forty-one year old Hispanic woman, an executive for a marketing firm, was ecstatic over the bold action she had taken the previous evening. She was triumphantly expressing the realization that she was beginning to reclaim her soul.

Jose and Faye had been together for ten years. Seven months before, Faye had first sought my help because she wanted to feel closer to Jose. He had unexpectedly moved out after she entered therapy, giving no explanation for his departure. She had not spoken to him since the day he left.

The night before this therapy session she had received a call from him. She told me that, even though he had sounded distraught, she was able to hang up the phone:

"I was shocked at how easy it was to take a stand with him. I mean, I was astounded. And especially that I could hold to it. You know how new this is for me.

119

"When Jose eliminated me from our relationship, I was sure I couldn't go on without him. I thought he was absolutely crucial to my happiness, and I know he knew that. But instead of speaking at length to him and hearing his litany of excuses for his desecrating actions toward me, I just told him I wasn't interested in having a conversation with him. I was tired of it all.

"I did shake afterwards, but I wrote pages and pages in my journal. I realized that the relationship had been based on my staying the same – in my job, in the marriage, in every way. I'm no longer willing to do that. I'm so excited to imagine a life without him, lived from my own inclinations instead of his. He can't define me or my happiness. Not any more. That's over – for good."

As Faye talked I was reminded of a phrase I had heard some months before, that when it gets dark enough you can see the stars. There is a part of you, your core, that is more accessible to you in the darkest times than at any other. With nowhere else to turn, you are forced to face your essence as never before. In such bleak, black periods, you can more easily recognize your soul's call for renewal.

Did you note new insights as you went through the earlier chapters? If so, you may be breaking old patterns. In addition, you have no doubt noticed that resolve and courage are needed to respond from your heart to the demands that soul renewal requires.

Restoring your soul is giving it back its rightful place. It has been lost through many years of being neglected, closed off, and shut out of its valuable power to guide and direct your life.

Taking Charge of Your Soul Restoration

By focusing on your soul restoration you are leaving behind your previous willingness to participate in soul mugging.

> To believe what has not occurred in history will not occur at all, is to argue disbelief in the dignity of humankind.
> – Mahatma Gandhi

As you turn toward reclaiming your soul, you are honoring your ability to believe that profound change is possible. An early step in this soul work is to recognize any remaining focus you have on conditions, people, and authorities external to you. It is necessary to turn your attention to a place deep within you: your inner self. Moving away from external reference points toward this inner realm is the only opportunity you have to affect fundamental change. Once you build that kind of solid foundation, you will carry it within you forever. You will know a centeredness from which no one can move you.

As you restore your soul, it is important to take responsibility for yourself and to tend to any unhealed areas that appear in your relationship. If you blame or use your partner as a target, you will inevitably give up your power to make any significant or lasting change. Transforming yourself, not your partner, needs to be your vital concern at this point. Keep your focus where you have the ability to make a lasting impact – within you.

The human soul is a tiny lamp kindled from the Divine torch; it is the vital spark of heavenly flame.
– Talmud

That vital spark is the knower within you, the soul. What you don't yet know is that *you* are the knower. When you discover that, you will notice how ironic it is that you have been focusing everywhere but within yourself for your answers.

Once you decide to leap into that as yet unknown part of you, whatever suffering you have experienced will lessen. You cannot know that it will ease up, though, until you actually leap. Are you ready to jump? It is not easy, but it is possible. It means letting go of your tendency to blame, to control, to focus outside yourself, to try even harder, or to hang on to something that is painful, yet familiar.

Faith is a decision, a judgment that is fully and deliberately taken in the light of a truth that cannot be proven.
– Thomas Merton

It requires faith to leap when there is no proof of what will be there when you land. What you have not yet realized is that you don't know what you don't know. What you don't know represents both your unknowable future and all that is beyond your experience. Intuition has been available to guide you, but you were not open to its guidance. Therefore, until now, you could not have known what was necessary for your soul's growth and well-being.

I invite you now to consider a bit of advice given to a young Native American at the time of his initiation:

As you go the way of life,
You will see a great chasm.
Jump.
It is not as wide as you think.
– Native American Wisdom

To assist you in restoring your soul, this book includes a collage of ideas, gathered as I was restoring my soul. Since this is my collection, it naturally reflects those ideas which have had particular meaning for me. I invite you to add your own treasury of resources and to draw from them as you become increasingly attuned to your spirit.

Vignettes of patients are presented to bring you into the inner dialogue of people who are progressing toward their full restoration. These stories are glimpses into others' triumphs out of soul mugging.

Several "soul discovery" experiments are interjected throughout this chapter. Perhaps they will capture your imagination, prompt your visualization of images, or even suggest imaginary dialogues. Whatever emerges as you carry out these experiments will definitely represent new ways for you to experience your soul. Each will reconnect you in some startling way to your authentic, essential self. Move at your own pace through this chapter, as you actively participate in and carry out as many of the experiments as you can. You may find it valuable to repeat your favorites as you experience new dimensions of your soul.

A Moment of Insight

A woman I saw in therapy for over a year initially came in with quite a bit of anguish. She felt as if she were damaged goods. In fact, she felt no one could possibly stand to be with her. She claimed that everything about her was wrong – her body, her face, her awkwardness, her ugly voice, just everything. One evening, alone and relaxed, she put on some music and spontaneously began to move to it. As she began to dance around the room, she allowed the music to move through her. Without meaning to, she caught a glimpse of herself in the mirror as she was making an especially freeing movement. She was startled to find that she liked what she saw.

This woman did not immediately shed of all her feelings of self-hatred in one evening, but that glimpse of a different dimension of herself showed her that she wasn't as unacceptable as she had once thought. Soon she began to initiate even bolder, more courageous actions so that she could re-experience herself in new, expanded ways.

... and then the day came when the risk to remain tight in a bud was more painful than the risk it took to blossom.
– Anais Nin

Becoming Present to Yourself

You are now poised to retrieve your soul. You understand that you had a part in mugging your soul and that this prevented you from experiencing the depth of your core. Until now you have been held prisoner by your denial, illusions and rationalized actions. This no doubt left its indelible mark. Possibly for the first time you are fully facing the truth about yourself and your relationship.

Soul Discovery

See if you can come up with an image which describes how it feels to have been robbed of your essence. In other words, conjure up a picture that fits the struggle you have had, the dismay you have felt and the helplessness you have known so well and for so long. Don't leave this assignment until you have visualized your image. Let the first image be the one you stay with even if you have no idea why you selected it. You actually weren't choosing it. It emerged from that wise place deep within you – your soul. More and more you are going to let that part bring you into a full experience of yourself.

I was amazed at the accuracy of the image that emerged as I visualized how it felt for my own soul to be robbed. I saw an insect against a screen caught by the very wires that seemed to be the way to liberation. Looking back, I can see that I never imagined as I stepped into my relationship I would get stuck in ways that further deprecated my soul. I thought I would get free of the aspects I despised about myself.

Is the image I had similar to the one you selected? How does yours match mine? How is it different? Did you also believe at the time that the actions you took would make you feel precious, treasured, wonderful, whole, secure, and safe instead of despicable? Explain your image by writing two or three sentences about it or by sketching it into your journal.

Each discovery you make places you directly on the path toward restoring your soul. Transformation of your soul occurs when you move out of the realm of feeling imprisoned long enough to permit yourself to envision the possibilities now available to you. By transformation I mean moving beyond the form in which you currently find yourself. This encompasses ways you think, beliefs you hold, feelings you have, and truths you value.

You may have remained in your soul-mugging relationship because you did not recognize that you were viewing your situation from a very lopsided perspective, a highly skewed memory system. This phenomenon, which I frequently encounter with patients, can be lethal to your soul restoration. What I have found is that you store the wonderful times in your relationship into your memory very easily, but you immediately focus your attention elsewhere when you encounter negative interactions with your partner. Can you remember being totally present to the times of great bliss and joy in your relationship? Yet what sort of memories do you have about the moments (or days) when things went horribly? Do you have any at all? Or are they mostly blocked out, excused, gone?

You can only have memories about an event that you are present to when it is happening. You probably have not been present to most of the negative experiences which have occurred between you and another person.

It will be very valuable for you to be vigilant from now on about all of your reactions and feelings, both internally and externally as they unfold. Only if you stay alert to all that you experience will you have the choice to decide if, when, and how to deal with each situation.

You've heard numerous variations of the following short story which can graphically depict what you may have experienced in the past. A person walks down a sidewalk and trips over a crack. The next day, the person walks down the same sidewalk and pretends not to see the crack. He or she trips again. Then this person walks down the same sidewalk, sees the crack and still trips. It is a habit. Then the person walks down that same sidewalk and walks around the crack. Eventually, he or she walks down a different sidewalk. To walk down a different sidewalk requires paying conscious attention to what you are doing.

When you find the way to go beyond what is familiar, known, habitual, and perhaps "safe," you are freed of the suffering that has accompanied you in that old pattern.

Stop and look at your life, really look at it. Is there a "crack" you have repeatedly tripped on? The intellect can convincingly construct rigidly held beliefs which have imprisoned your spirit. When you are not conscious of these beliefs, you will trip over them.

Grasping the Power to Change

When you have shut down, put under cover, or pushed underground those aspects of yourself that are the most essential in you – your aliveness, your light, your alignment with who you are here to be – you now realize that you have been cutting off your soul.

You can see now that by the time you had entered into an important relationship, you yourself had already jeopardized your own soul. You had extinguished definitions of your essence that did not fit with the ways you wanted others to see you. And you let go of those aspects of your being that displeased others. In this relationship you merely continued this process.

It is important for you to acknowledge and accept that you had a part in causing these unintentional affronts to your soul. For if you, and no one else, decided on some level to give up these necessary parts of your self, then you, and no one else, have the power to reclaim them. This point is crucial to your soul restoration. Recognize now that you chose to turn over your power to others. You can take back all of this power at any moment you choose to do so.

Right now I invite you to take a break from reading to do an experiment, no matter how embarrassed you may be or how self-conscious you may feel.

Soul Discovery

Start singing a song about your soul that you make up as you go. Don't think about it. Let it make itself up as it comes out of your mouth. Just do it, no matter what you are saying to talk yourself out of doing it. Sing your song, and sing it out loud. Make it as loud as you can. No judging or criticizing. Just sing it.

How are you feeling about your creative expression? Foolish? Unwilling to perform even if it is only for yourself? Jubilant to have thought of some words? Proud to have allowed a song to sing itself from deep within you? Surprised that anything emerged? Whatever your responses are, focus only on those which encourage you to keep experimenting. You will gradually find your own voice, as well as other dimensions of your essence which are vital to your reconnection with the authentic part of you.

You may find you have formed a habit of self-trivializing. This would become evident during your singing. You would have struggled with whether you had anything worthwhile to sing, for example, especially if you were your only audience.

I imagine you learned long ago not to take your self seriously. After all, did anyone else? I urge you now to not only honor your self, but to dedicate your self to give your being the attention and time you deserve. Over time you will become more at ease with this and the other changes that you will incorporate.

You now realize how precarious your existence was at every level of your being – cognitive, spiritual, emotional, and physical. This new awareness can provide a solid foundation for reclaiming your own soul. Never again will you want to use anyone else's vision of you to define who you are.

I encourage you, even if it seems silly, to continue your singing at least once a day. You can easily do it in the car, in the shower, or in any other place you choose. I would love to know that you are doing it on the front porch or in front of a friend or two. As you sing, listen to your self, but also interpret your new lyrics. The insights you receive may be startling. Listen to your self as carefully and kindly as you would listen to someone you had wanted to meet for a long time.

Since you are singing your own original creation, you are validating your essence in a way you have never done before. Let your singing be one way to let yourself know that your soul is of great value, even if external circumstances fail to honor your authentic self.

Numbed by a long period of soul mugging, first by you and then by another person, you may be struggling with the idea of placing such focused attention on your own creativity, your own internal inklings and cravings. You will find they have always been there. They have just been dormant for many years.

Taking Back Your Self

Billy, a 25-year-old African-American man, had been in therapy for several months. He told me he thought of himself as a very religious person. He remembered his mother taking him to church every Sunday, where he sat on the front row while she sang in the choir. Yet he had never set foot in a church again after he left home when he was seventeen. He told himself that he didn't need that "stuff" anymore. On this particular day, he started the session by telling me about an incident that had greatly upset him:

"I was walking along the street yesterday, going to lunch with a colleague, and I saw a cross. I'm sure it had been there for many years, but it had never caught my attention. I got tears in my eyes as a flood of memories came back to me.

"The one thing in my life that had kept me going when my father left, taking two of my sisters with him, was the church I grew up in. Now, with my wife saying she is going to take our baby away from me if I keep acting in ways she hates, I am reminded of my mother and the church.

"I knew how to pray then, Doctor; I knew that I could hold on to something sustaining. It is weird that I left it. I just left everything, including the most important part of me. I want it back. I have to have that solid place inside where I can go when things around me are breaking apart. But how do I get it back? I feel I've lost it forever.

"I stopped paying attention to myself. I even used to mumble to myself, 'What do I know, anyway?' It hurts to talk this way. In fact, right now it is really painful to feel again. It is as if I've been frozen and now that I'm thawing out, I'm bombarded with hundreds of different feelings. My chest is so tight I think I'm going to explode. It's all too much."

Billy is adjusting to many new insights. He is flooded with myriad feelings which he unknowingly closed out of his awareness for years. He is beginning to understand that his own foundation is essential and that he can become devastated when this powerful inner resource is not available to him. He realizes now that he needs it to stabilize himself.

Handling the feelings that will surface as you start to open up can be unsettling. Billy, and you, must take it one minute at a time. As you noticed, Billy was nearly overwhelmed by trying to assimilate more than he could absorb in a short time.

Your fears can also get in the way of restoring your soul. If you notice they are interfering significantly, it may be helpful for you to say, "I can do this." You may need to reassure yourself by stating these words over and over. At the same time urge yourself to keep moving toward restoring your soul. One morning you will truly feel the light has broken through that dark night which seemed endless.

Soul Discovery

Visualize a plant that seems as if it has been trampled by too many people walking on it. Its branches are lying on the ground, almost detached. Yet, upon inspection, you notice that its roots are firmly embedded in the soil, its flowering foliage still reaching toward the sun. Just to see this plant in your imagination can remind you that life has a tendency to move steadily toward growth, even under the direst circumstances. Notice how you are feeling once you have clearly envisioned this scene.

Welcoming the New You

Every process involves breaking something up.
The earth must be broken to bring forth life.
If the seed does not die, there is no plant.
Bread results from the death of wheat.
– Joseph Campbell

Once you break familiar patterns, it will take a while to become acquainted with the new aspects of your self and to find a commitment that encompasses the new you. After this breaking up of the old, you will notice a vacuum. The old way is over, but the new has not yet had time to blossom. Be patient until you fill this space. You may even feel unsure about how to act in certain situations.

You have been accustomed to manipulating and controlling yourself and your relationship so that you could seize the chance to get your needs met, even if only minimally. As you stop using that approach, you may feel that you have no idea what is appropriate. That is normal. Although you may find this frustrating, you are actually becoming stronger than you realize by stopping your familiar patterns.

You have certainly been buffeted by challenges, many of them aggravated by dialogues you have had with your self. Yet you reached for this book. That should tell you that you are eager to expand your life, perhaps wider than you ever thought possible. You can count on a silent but essential part of yourself to help pull you out of any circumstance and spur you into experiences beyond anything you had ever imagined. That place in you can do its task fully and efficiently when it is recognized and nurtured.

Healing the wounds of soul mugging is best understood as a process. However, your healing will not occur at an even pace. You will encounter days where you think nothing is working for you even as you read and reread portions of this guidebook. Sometimes you will feel that your progress has been placed on hold. At other times you may feel as stuck in the morass as you have ever been.

I tried something which may be helpful to you, too. I began to be extremely gentle with myself at those times when I felt stuck. I consciously tried to ease my frustration when my movement stopped. I saw each pause as only a temporary loss of momentum; although there were a few times I was certain I would never get any further than I was at that instant.

It is best to keep taking one step at a time. You are building a stronger foundation for your being. Besides patience, you need a lot of love for your soul. You can turn the love you have been sending out to another toward your self instead. This may seem awkward, but it will enrich that inner place that knows what is best for you. Even if you can't seem to endorse showering love on your soul, place notes on your mirror to remind yourself to at least state out loud that you are loved and lovable. They can be simply: "I am worthy of love." "I am a flowing fountain of rich wisdom." "I want my soul to be nourished. It deserves that."

Trusting your soul is essential. Then you will be guided through every step. As you can depend on its knowing exactly what to do next, you may be surprised to realize that, at times, doing absolutely nothing makes the most sense. Fully trusting your soul now can make all the difference in your restoration.

126

Moving Your Self into the Spotlight

It has been said, "A prophet is not without honour, save in his own country" (Matthew 13:57). Your "country" has been your self. Unfortunately, you were not able to make an impact on yourself because you stopped listening to and paying attention to your soul long ago. You realize now that your soul might have been telling you things that could have benefited you enormously, but in order to survive those early years, you turned it off.

At this point, however, you can be that prophet in your own country. This can be done by carefully tuning in to that wise inner self. It is full of inspiring wisdom, creative ideas, and answers to questions which you may not even have known to ask until now.

Use the following vignette as a window through which you can glance at your life. Perhaps you will notice parts of conversations you have had with yourself as well as with another important person in your life.

Jo Lynn was a 45-year-old Caucasian woman who had been in therapy for ten months. She had a thriving career as an artist, with showings at several galleries. Originally she came to see me because she was not able to communicate with her husband about issues she felt were crucial to their ten-year relationship. She began to describe what had occurred three days before this therapy session.

"As I pulled into our driveway, I found my stomach felt strange, my shoulders tight, and my mouth quite dry. I mumbled to myself, 'What is going on? I am so glad to be getting away, so excited to finally have Steve to myself without the phones ringing, his computer humming. What is this?'

"As I stopped the car I saw him coming toward me. He did not look happy. I asked him quite innocently what was wrong.

"He began yelling, 'What do you mean what's wrong? You're ten minutes late. The traffic's going to be terrible. I thought you wanted us to relax together for a few days.'

"He went on and on, saying I had obviously sabotaged the whole weekend because I wasn't even smart enough to manage my time. Finally he screamed, 'Let's just forget it. I have plenty to do here. I knew I shouldn't have counted on you for anything important, like planning a trip. You screwed up everything, Jo Lynn. What is it with you?'

"I pleaded with him that we could still go, that we had plenty of time to get to our hotel, relax in the Jacuzzi and enjoy a nice dinner.

"He said, 'Who'd want to go with you now, anyway?' Then he just walked away. I jumped out of the car, hoping to try one more time to change his mind.

"I again begged and told him how sorry I was. I said that I really didn't mean to mess anything up. I told him I had just stopped to get us a snack for the drive. I asked him if we could please go ahead and do what we'd planned. I used every ounce of energy left in me to try to persuade Steve to go. But he turned, looked at me with a scowl on his face and continued on into the house.

"At that moment, I flashed on a scene where I was in the Jacuzzi by myself, not rushing and not having to go back to the room wondering what mood Steve was going to be in. I thought about how nice it would be to go to the hotel gift shop and select any book I wanted, take it back to the room and settle down with it. I felt such a sense of peace at the thought of not having to accommodate him one more time.

"I expanded that vision into going back home and taking over the whole house, infusing it with my art, my things, my energy. It was heaven.

"Dr. Papillon, I decided right then that my relationship with Steve was history. I'm not losing my soul ever again for anybody. Goodbye, old life. I welcome the new."

What do you notice going on inside of you as you read this? What feelings are most prominent? Which specific aspects create the most havoc inside of you? How does your stomach feel? What are you experiencing in your chest area? Regardless of whether you are a man or a woman, is Jo Lynn like you at all? Do you see how imprisoned you and she have been by your willingness to place your fate in the hands of hope?

Do you think your over-reliance on hope has been completely eradicated, never again to be used in the context of a relationship? Are you willing to kill hope before it kills the life inside of you?

How strong is your vision of a new life? Is this vision completely free of hope? Is it strong enough to pull you into a future that does not include hope fueling the excruciating, unending misery you have been enduring?

Soul Discovery

Think of a scene in which you experienced an uncomfortable exchange with another person, one that had a lot of dialogue and some uncomfortable behaviors, too. Think of things you said and statements or gestures that the other person made.

Now replay your scene, but this time act differently than you have ever acted before with this person. Exaggerate your statements and the particular behaviors that you have newly adopted. Be what you have never been willing to be, but not in a punitive or retaliatory way. Rather, be that part of you who acts from a sense of self and is not willing to have another person desecrate that essence again.

Notice that when you speak differently, from the foundation of truth within yourself, you create an opening for further truths to come forward. In the past, your fear may have blocked your perceptions and prevented you from listening to the voice inside of you. Now as you begin to feel empowered to open your mouth and allow your soul to emerge, you can put into words all that you are noticing inside. Soon you can never be silenced again.

After having been given this soul discovery assignment, Stella came in for her session. She and her husband had been having marital difficulties for over a year. When she came in this particular day, she stated immediately how astonished she was at what she observed:

"Dr. Papillon, that part of me just erupted into words, ones I had never used before, especially out loud. In my imagination I saw that I did have substance, that I had a right to say what was valid for me. Of course, the harder step will be to do this with Jim.

"In the meantime, though, I have noticed some important changes physically just by going over the experiment in my mind. My stomach felt calmer than it's been in weeks. My chest, well, it seemed to expand the longer I imagined what I was going to say and how I was going to be with Jim. It even felt as if I'd gotten taller by the end of my experiment. I had been feeling so tiny and insignificant before. Today, I noticed I even walked across your office differently.

"It is amazing how silence has changed my soul over the years. I mean, not just being quiet when I was spoken to, but I realize now I had silenced everything I could inside, except of course the incessant self-degradation.

"Anyway, I sense now that I am a new being. I will never stoop, acquiesce, give in, or allow everyone but me to speak ever again. It frightens me to consider it, but it scares me even more to think of not speaking out. I may feel acute pain at some point again, but already I sense that a wave of relief has washed over me, freeing the part of me that sealed my soul off so tightly, so completely."

Unlocking the Passageways to Your Soul

When experience is viewed in a certain way, it presents nothing but doorways into the domain of the soul...
– Jon Kabat-Zinn

Can you live in this moment fully? Can you make it an opportunity for new growth? Remember, this book is your road map out of suffering. You may have resigned yourself to thinking your life was going to be a perpetually painful existence. As you travel further on this road you have chosen, staying present to the present, you are continuing to put into action the process that can restore your soul.

Living in the present moment includes honoring the pain and the grief you may still feel. These, too, are doorways to your soul. When your experience becomes nothing but doorways into the domain of the soul, then you are definitely staying in the present moment. If, on the other hand, you are not holding your experience in your awareness, its power is not available to you. In restoring your soul, you are re-interpreting your life, re-examining your beliefs, and re-establishing a solid place within for your soul to abide. In truth, your self has immense power. You will notice that you have infinite capacity to know because listening to your inner self brings an unlimited stream of messages to you every instant. It is not as if your soul speaks only every now and then. It is just that you have not been listening to what it is always saying.

When you fully embrace this inner life without any more doubts, you will find an eternal, perfect, and complete part of yourself. It is birthless, deathless, and fearless. It is your best ally and it is forever unfolding. It is a treasure to discover and become intimately acquainted with. Possibly for the first time you will know that you can accept full responsibility for directing your life.

You are entering into your deepest, most spiritual self when you choose this eternal aspect of you. Within that realm is an inexhaustible reservoir. The most expedient way to discover the many facets of this profound place is to ask over and over, "What is the integrity of my soul at this moment?" With this important question, you are breaking established systems of thought which have caused you so much distress.

O strong soul, by what shore
Tarriest thou now?
– Matthew Arnold

A question inherently related to soul restoration is, "What is keeping you from the richness of life you could be experiencing?" For such a long time your answer would have been that you have lived in fear of what would happen next, or in regret over disappointing outcomes. It will probably feel very strange to you to feel any feelings other than fear or pain. That is understandable. You may need to consciously realign with your feelings of satisfaction and joy. If you practice doing this, these feelings will gradually become more frequent and spontaneous without your having to spend effort to create them.

It is entirely within your domain to envision possibilities and decide how you will live. No one can say you must act this way or that way. Your life is your choice at every instant, as you make your decisions either intentionally or out of your inaction.

Seeing the Promise of a New You

Phyllis, a 51-year-old Caucasian woman, had been in therapy for over a year. She had originally come in after she lost her job as an accountant in a large firm. Because her boyfriend of eight years was unsupportive, she did not know where to turn for solace. During this session, Phyllis said:

"Last night I said something to myself that made an amazing difference in how I see life now. I don't know where it came from, although I do know we have been working on my listening to my self more carefully and allowing that essence to have its way with me. Anyway, Doctor, the words that emerged were: 'Act as if the light has come.'

"You have no idea what impact that one sentence had on how I viewed everything. I began to imagine that I knew how to make sense of my situation. My head wasn't pounding as it has been for months now, and my heart almost soared out of me. It just seemed like my whole body was lighter somehow, and I knew at that moment everything was going to be all right. I have no answers, but, you know, in a sense, I do now."

What is absolutely necessary to recover your soul from its having been robbed of its voice and its full radiance is to hold to your commitment to a new relationship with your essence.

A Talk with Your Self

Conduct a conversation between your magnificent soul and your soul-mugged self. I will help you begin your dialogue by telling you about a talk I had with my soul during my soul restoration. However, as you conduct your talk, be sure that it comes from the depths of your own being, without censoring, prompting from others, or attempting to resemble my dialogue. This needs to be your interaction, and it is important to continue it every day, many times a day.

A Sample Dialogue

Soul-mugged self: Tell me more. It must hurt that I have ignored you, actually abandoned you years ago. How has it felt to have no voice?

Innate wise self: It has felt awful and terrifying. I have thought I might as well die. In fact, I wanted to if there was not going to be a way I could exist as I was meant to, within you.

Soul-mugged self: I never intended for you to die. In fact, I never consciously decided not to listen to you. It was just that, well, you were wise and intuitive, and I was getting into more and more trouble by listening to you and then acting on what I was hearing.

Innate wise self: I know. I saw that you gave me up to survive some pretty awful stuff. But, then you kept it going. And now you have a partner who treats me the way you have been treating me. Did you have to choose that kind of partner?

Soul-mugged self: Believe me, it didn't seem that I was choosing anyone who would continue to mash you down as that person has. I was just so hungry for love, for affection, for someone who would treat me as if I were important. I mean, I never felt I was visible until this person cherished me. Of course, I had no idea that he would also terrorize me with his desecrating ways. He was the one who set up the terms of the relationship I had with him and with you. After that I never felt I was a free, spontaneous person. You know, I kept hoping that I could get my needs met, that you could be a part of my life, a significant part. As you so well know, it didn't turn out that way at all. And I felt caught. It was as if I were in this maze and I couldn't find my way out. I had almost given up the idea there was a way out.

Innate wise self: I'm here to let you know that there is definitely a way out. It is by doing what you are doing now – letting me speak. You are now allowing me to give you insight about what has happened in your life which has gotten you to this point. I'm able now to point out to you that you did a lot of things merely to survive and to feel that you counted. I know that. Now, though, I can be your greatest ally. Can I really have your ear? Can I speak the truth to you? You don't think you know, but I do, so lean on me. All sorts of miraculous things can show up in your life in innumerable ways through your letting me guide you. When you give me a voice, your life will flow more freely and with less conscious effort. I can promise you that. I know you can't trust me yet. I definitely know this is a slow process. Yet, inspiration, guidance, and wisdom are what I'm about. I am here to reveal them to you.

Soul-mugged self: But you frighten me. When I was young, I got into so much trouble. I can hardly stop shaking now as I talk to you. I'm starting to cry because I know you are right, but I've been so punished by using my own eyes, ears, and voice in the distant and not so distant past. To think that it might be different now is almost too good to be true. I don't know. It's all so new to me and I'm terrified. To say I'm fearful of a part of me sounds strange, but I am. You are not familiar to me anymore. You are my soul and yet you are a stranger to me.

Innate wise self: I know, I know. I have always been with you but you didn't know it. I see your struggle. I know the pain you've been through. I tried to help but I was robbed of that chance. I could even see that you were digging a hole in this part of yourself, me, by using hope. Hope is defeating to you in this situation, mostly because you gave me up so long ago. In that kind of environment, you are prey to an enormous amount of mugging. Do you see that? You said that you hoped your partner would be kinder tomorrow and then when it didn't happen, you hoped again. That perpetuated your pain so many times. And of course I was rendered helpless to benefit you. It has been a miserable existence for both of us.

Soul-mugged self: What am I to do now? I've finally gotten clear on at least an intellectual level that I must stop this hope habit, for sure. But what do you want me to do to be sure I don't abandon you ever again? I want you to be the strongest part of me, the part I call on to direct me through anything, anytime, anywhere, no matter what.

Innate wise self: Spend at least thirty minutes a day in quietude and silence, because I can speak to you and am more available to you when you release the incessant chatter of that busy mind of yours. From now on, you don't even have to analyze and dissect problems and challenges the way you used to. Turn to me and I will give you answers from a completely different angle. When you can actually join with your inner place that is me, as I said, your life will become much easier. I know that won't be immediate, but it is available to you now.

Soul-mugged self: I guess my biggest fear is that if I'm not going to be with this partner, then I won't ever hear those words I find so crucial, about how wonderful and necessary I am, how adored I am, how smart, how talented – you know, all the ways that my partner defines me at times. I'll be lost.

Innate wise self: That is one of the biggest hooks, isn't it, for your staying? What about when your partner invalidates you, takes all of that away by the toxic ways he talks to you and treats you? What then? You are impoverished, dislocated in a sense. You are without a home for me because you have blocked me out.

Soul-mugged self: I know. It is a horrible prison I've locked myself into. I lost the key long ago. I know you are right. I just hate to look at it directly. It's so ugly. When you used the words "without a home," they struck a chord in me. I sometimes have felt that my partner was trespassing, and that your rights were being invaded by someone who had no business being in that part of me. It was a weird image, but it came again when you said that. There were no boundaries I could keep private, and that started long before I got into this relationship.

Innate wise self: I'd like you to experiment with something. Pretend your partner has just said the kindest things you can remember being said. Now, instead of soaking them up like a dried up piece of toast that is getting needed moisture, say to this person "On a deep level, I understand now that you don't have the power to define whether I'm lovable or not. I have my own ways of knowing whether I am lovable and they don't depend on you at all. I get these lovable feelings from deep within my own soul, where I live now. I know I have permitted you to tell me that I exist for a long time. I'm really used to it, but it never actually filled that void, that hole in my soul. So now I'm taking back defining my essence. My essential being is mine to love, whether you tell me I am lovable or not." How would that feel to say?

Soul-mugged self: Whoa. That's a mouthful. Let me think about that. It is extremely empowering to consider. I certainly like hearing it from you. I notice I'm not feeling quite so frightened right now.

Staying Focused on the Inner You

You need to claim the events of your life to make yourself yours.
– Anne-Wilson Schaef

Have you ever been in a garden where you observed a caterpillar eating a petunia? The petunia shriveled up. But if you observed the garden closely through the succeeding weeks, at some point you would find a beautiful butterfly perched on another blooming petunia in the exact same spot. If you had never gone back into the garden that second time, you would have imagined that no petunia had replaced the one that had been eaten and that the caterpillar had only devoured more of the flowers. Just as nature restores itself, so in your life, out of seeming devastation, comes the renewed energy to begin and then continue your journey inward.

Everything you have experienced in your life has contributed to the person you are and each event has influenced the succeeding ones. Each incident in your life has led you to the present and, ultimately, to your desire to restore your soul. So you really are in the perfect place to move further ahead toward reclaiming your magnificent essence.

During your soul restoration, your commitment to restore your soul may fade in and out of focus. You will undoubtedly listen to your own voice at times, and at other times you will continue to be overly influenced by others' voices. As you notice that you have strayed, direct yourself back to the music of your own unadulterated voice. Just bring yourself back to your self, turning toward that inner light that wants so much to be renewed and restored to its rightful place. At times you may even feel a strong yearning from your soul to breathe free.

Soon after you were born you began what I call darkness conditioning. Your light was dimmed instead of honored, and your soul was diminished instead of allowed to expand. Others directed your actions based on their priorities and perceptions, often with minimal consideration of you. They may even have erroneously thought they had your best interests in mind.

Finally, you began to expect others to direct you. Darkness fell on your soul and you stopped tuning in to that vital essence for direction. These people were not wiser than your soul, but you were too young to make that distinction then. You did what you did in the way you did it because that is what you thought gave you the best chance of receiving what you needed. You now know, though, that you must rely on your inner self.

Soul Discovery

Making peace with that skeptic part of you is essential. Otherwise, you will be prevented from becoming a flourishing soul. Presently, your internal skeptic may be so strong that it overpowers whatever you attempt. First, give your skeptic a name. Choose one that is your least favorite name, one that you would never call yourself or your children. Now, speak to that skeptic within you with that name, saying: "_____, thank you for sharing, but I see it this way," or "... I am going to take this risk," or "... I will listen to my soul anyway... " The second step is to turn down the volume of your skeptic voice so that you can more distinctly hear the voice that is always speaking to you, your wise essence.

Over time you have no doubt developed a way to negate the positive steps that will take you ahead, even if you never thought of yourself as a skeptic. This often happens when the steps or the change they would create seem too frightening. Now, as you can imagine, your well developed negator must be quieted to clear the way for you to move toward soul restoration.

To find this sense of your soul, which is always speaking within you, begin to have moments of just being – not doing, not searching, not pleasing anyone else – just opening to your soul in silence. You will know when you have heard it because you will experience a deep sense of inner peace. If you become very still, you will hear a very wise person speaking: yourself.

Soul Discovery

Take a day when you stop making any judgments. Pretend you are prohibited from any judgmental thinking. You can only say, "I'm going to let that wise place, that divine wisdom inside of me, decide who I am, what I am to do, and who others are today." to anything that happens or any biased opinions you notice forming inside your head. As you go through your day with that prohibition, notice how relieved you are that you don't have to make a judgment today. You have taken the day off. A place deep within you that knows is now free to decide your life. Do this just for today. Tomorrow you can do the experiment again if you so choose.

You may notice you make many more judgments in one day than you thought you did. Patients I have given this assignment to were aghast at their process. What they concluded was that bringing day-to-day living into alignment with their authentic self was surprisingly challenging to them.

As a person whose soul has been mugged, you have used an arsenal of techniques which have led you to believe you could assess, judge and then control outcomes. Hope was a huge tool you used for this purpose. You can undoubtedly think of others.

To consider eliminating these ways as you reclaim your soul could be mystifying and terrifying to you. Allow these feelings to be. Give them room to move through you. While these questioning and fearful feelings will be useful for you to experience and hear, do not allow them to dominate you.

When you stop yourself at this point from falling back into your old accustomed ways, questions such as, "How am I going to make it?" will arise. At that point, say to yourself, "I don't exactly know, but I do know I am going to. I don't need to know the exact outcome at this moment. All I must do now is remember to stay present to what is occurring."

One important strategy to cope with your feelings of discomfort is to make a list of things you can do when doubts and fears come up. First, remind yourself to take your life hour by hour. Other suggestions which may be helpful to you are:

Call or be with comforting friends.

Write in your journal about how scared you feel.

Take walks to gain perspective.

Make up projects (like gathering unusual rocks and attaching meaning to each of them).

Surround yourself with beautiful flowers to remind yourself that they grow without any effort on your part but lovingly watering them.

Light a candle that symbolizes your faith in the process (there is light in the midst of this black darkness).

Tell yourself you are entering a new life.

These are just some of the many ways to handle uncomfortable feelings. You can begin to think of other peaceful and comforting activities, unique to your predilections. Once you keep moving through your disquieting times, you will notice that the process of going through these periods can reassure you that reclaiming your soul is possible and that your soul-tending activities are actually sustaining and anchoring you.

Like an ability or a muscle, hearing your inner wisdom is strengthened by doing it.
– Robbie Gass

Filling Yourself with Your Self

Once I was staying at a hotel for a meeting. I noticed it was also the site of a conference. As I watched people scurry about, I stopped a young woman and asked her what the conference was about. "Well," she said, "it's hard to describe. I brought a notebook to fill with this person's wisdom, but so far all we've done is sit in silence for two hours. I haven't written a thing in here except insights I had during the meditation." I was astounded that around 200 people were waiting for someone they had decided was an authority to tell them their truth. The leader was wise enough to turn that task over to the participants.

The privilege of a lifetime is being who you *are.*
– Sheldon Kopp

One of the obstacles to communicating freely with your soul is your persistence in thinking others have your answers. They don't. These reside in your soul. Another barrier is your attempt to understand reality by looking through a tiny opening. Your limited vista shuts out most of the landscape. What is the point of limiting the infinite possibilities of your self by using objects such as a toy telescope, an inexpensive throw-away camera, or even a pair of binoculars.

You must be willing to disregard your finite devices so you can permit the unlimited wisdom within you to guide you. The intuition from that pure and powerful spiritual place is not only yours now but has always been your crucial source for guidance and immense peace.

Soul Discovery

Create a visual image of the internal, unlimited, wise, intuitive, sacred place within. Give yourself several hours to do this project. Gather several different kinds of materials: watercolors, markers, crayons, different textures of materials, paste, magazines to cut up, writing tools, and other things you find in the house, on your walks on the beach, or in other natural settings. Get a huge piece of butcher paper. Lay it flat on the floor. If this revered place inside you had form and voice, how would it look? What are the many ways you can describe it visually? Fill your paper with all the many different expressions of this essential aspect of yourself that you can imagine.

You may have been disquieted by this experiment since you are seeing an abstract part of you converted into visual form. Just notice what your feelings are and allow them to tell you exactly what it is that disturbs you. Whatever you are feeling will dissipate more quickly if you pay attention to and acknowledge all of it.

You may also be experiencing some anxiety about how you are going to live all aspects of your life in your new way. You have been engaged in soul mugging for so long that the idea that you could live another way may be somewhat overwhelming, especially with your multidimensional essence clearly delineated. Again, note your feelings and be assured that it is natural to be unsettled. This new way of being is still tentative, yet to be proven, and certainly has not yet been woven into the fabric of your soul to the extent that it is an automatic part of you.

Viewing the Treasures of Your Inner Self

You are not only restoring and reclaiming your soul, but you are changing many other aspects of your life, including the way others interact with you. One of the ways you may accelerate this process is to become an acute observer of your thoughts. In your observation of them, do your thoughts freely enter and exit? Or, do you hang on to some of them, believing certain thoughts are truths you must adhere to? Do these truths identify and define you? Consider now that you do not need to hold on to your thoughts so tightly. Experiment with the idea that your thoughts are merely thoughts. One comes in, you notice it, and then it leaves as another enters.

Soul Discovery

For however long you can, but for at least twenty minutes a day, picture yourself without your partner at your side. In your image, feel totally peaceful, free, your spirit expanding and full of joy. Imagine this as if you are experiencing it. Be in a definite place, such as by the ocean or in a meadow. Smell the sea air or the honeysuckle. Use all your senses and let in the grandeur of it all. Feel the power you have within you to create this exact scene for yourself. See it happen and be in it as if you were there now. (This experience in no way implies that you must end your relationship. Its purpose is to show you that you can feel these magnificent feelings without involving your partner at all.)

Joan, a 40-year-old Caucasian woman who owned an international artifacts and jewelry store, came in for therapy several months ago. Jack, her husband of nine years, had left her.

She was completely surprised by this; she had not picked up a single clue which might have prepared her for his leaving. At first she worried that he had been kidnapped. After six weeks of therapy twice a week, she finally accepted the fact that he had left her, and most likely did so for several, long-standing reasons.

On this particular day Joan and I were handling an issue she had struggled with from the day Jack had departed her life. During her therapy she had become acutely aware that she had placed her sense of anchoring in Jack to such an extent that she felt she now had no place to go where she could feel safe. She said Jack took a huge portion of her with him when he left. He took not just her sense of self, she stated, but the sense that life had any order to it.

"Chaos has reined in my life since Jack left, Dr. Papillon. I have never known such disorienting and confusing feelings. I sometimes think I am going crazy because I can't calm down enough to even decide what to eat or where to eat it.

"I had no idea he had taken over so much of my life. Looking at it now, though, I'm glad he left that way. He opened my eyes to what I had let happen to me. Of course, it occurred way before he and I married. I mean, I had let others dictate who I was from almost as long ago as I can remember. But after Jack's leaving so abruptly, I could not mistake this deep neglect of my self, and the lack of connection I had with my intuition. I mean, I totally missed any indication he was even thinking of leaving the marriage. How cut off from my self is that?"

I suggested to Joan that she begin to notice places, people, and situations where she felt even a small amount of groundedness, preferably where she had helped to create this sense for herself and therefore was in charge of it. The next week Joan began her session by saying:

"That assignment was very difficult for me. I thought maybe the house itself would be a place I could choose, but that brought with it a whole set of uncomfortable feelings: criticisms, jarring jolts to my sense of self, and other unpleasant memories.

"I certainly became more acutely aware this week that I had put up with a lot of discomfort to get a little piece of what I called "security" feelings from Jack. What an eye-opener! I don't want another person to be my anchor for feeling the way I feel about my self, whether that person is the most loving man, the greatest friend, or anyone. That is just too precarious.

"I understand this now, and it has taken me a long time to settle down enough to begin to explore just what happened to me. I'm still amazed that it all happened without my knowledge.

"My stomach still isn't what I'd like it to be. I mean I get sick very easily. I've lost so much weight that none of my clothes fit. I see that I have been a mess. I can tell you for sure that when I choose to be with a partner again, it will be on very different terms. I will be my own anchor and will find my groundedness from within my own soul. My foundation stays here, with me. That feels so great, to claim that with you right now."

What have you given up, thinking it would make you feel safe? Did you believe your compromises were essential to get your needs met? You obviously thought so at one point, but what about now? You are beginning to perceive, I am sure, that your soul restoration process is taking you down many paths that you either have never traveled or have not gone toward for many years.

One of the most important revelations is that you do not need to sell your soul anymore as a trade for what you considered at times "security at its best" or "complete bliss." Within you, and you alone, is the treasure that you have been looking for. You were born with it. It will keep you alive even if all the extraneous delights are withheld, or offered only at a price which is too high.

Centering on Your Authentic Self

Can you knowingly restructure your thoughts and beliefs so that only you are the center around which you build your life? Yes, it is absolutely possible. It is also essential to your full restoration. This change, though radical, has nothing to do with whether you stay in this relationship. It has everything to do, though, with how you are willing to be with your soul, your partner and every other person in your life.

Soul Discovery

I was struck by the impact of a phrase used by a woman during a lecture. This phrase lingered in my mind like a headline over the next few days. It especially had meaning for me in the context of soul mugging. This phrase was "premature cognitive commitments." These are commitments you make very early in your life about people, your essence, and your abilities. These commitments still run your life unless you make them known to yourself and consciously re-evaluate each one of them. "Premature" refers to the early time you made them, "cognitive" means that you processed them as truths, and "commitment" says that you are devoted to them, and that they, not you, are in charge of your life. List at least five premature cognitive commitments you have made. How valid are they today? Answer this question several times a day for the next three weeks.

The commitments and decisions you made in your early years may still be more powerful that you are aware of. These were not consciously decided, but you may still be held by these forces in ways that you now can be conscious of.

Aligning With Your Spiritual Essence

You can view your situation from a tremendously expanded perspective if you know and trust that you have a spiritual side that can inform you of the vast possibilities for your life. As you begin to experience this realm of true knowing, you will realize that you are not just a physical being. In your journey out of the despair that the hole in your soul has caused you, you will be experiencing yourself as more than the limited existence represented by your physical presence.

You can imagine that if you perceive yourself as a person who does not have an inner voice, then you are bound in all kinds of ways. You become highly vulnerable in the most crucial areas of your life. In addition, you are considerably constricted by such a narrowed focus.

However, if you can see a grander vision of who you are, all sorts of options will open up. It will be as if someone gave you a much stronger telescope. Suddenly you will see stars and galaxies that were not visible to you before.

Once you experience the spiritual part of you, you will never want to go back to seeing yourself as anything less. Why would you choose to have a sparrow's wings once you've flown with the wings of an eagle? Once you catch this glimpse of who you really are at your core and see the fullness of your soul, you will want to explore the new possibilities now waiting for you.

Soul Discovery

Lie down outside in a wide open space. Pretend an airplane is making figures in the sky, when suddenly it writes you a message about your particular soul's journey. What does it say? How does the message match the glimpses you are beginning to have about your essence?

What do these additional choices and greater possibilities bring to you in the context of soul mugging? Certainly, you begin to ask a different set of questions. You do not say, "What is wrong with me or with the other person?" Rather, you ask, "What meaning can I get from this?" The lens through which you view your whole life is now changed.

I myself do nothing. The Holy Spirit accomplishes all through me.
– William Blake

Take some time now to contemplate your original self, the memory of your origin in God (or whatever word you use for your higher power). You will discover there is a divine aspect of yourself that was there before you ever even had a physical body.

A Child's Request

A three-year-old begged and pleaded with her parents to have a moment alone with her newborn sister. The parents were afraid to allow that, thinking perhaps the child was jealous of her sister and might harm her. The three-year-old kept insisting that she must have these moments alone with her sister. Finally, her parents agreed, and listening over a baby monitor they heard their older daughter say to her newborn sister, "Could you tell me about God? I'm beginning to forget."

Always remember that you came into this world whole, perfect and complete. Along the way, things happened which caused you to forget that magnificence. For instance, you may have sensed that you were a bother, a burden, or too much to handle for your caregivers, who seemed to have too many other responsibilities. At that point you began the robbing of your soul.

There is a brokenness
out of which comes the unbroken,
a shatteredness out of which blooms the
unshatterable.
There is a sorrow
beyond all grief which leads to joy

and a fragility
out of whose depths emerges strength.
There is a hollow space
too vast for words
through which we pass with each loss,
out of whose darkness we are sanctioned into
being.
There is a cry deeper than all sound
whose serrated edges cut the heart
as we break open
to the place inside which is unbreakable
and whole,
while learning to sing.
– Rashani

You will find it easier to love yourself once you can place yourself in the realm of your spiritual self (the unbreakable, unshakable, vast part of you), as well as your physical self. Both of these dimensions coexist and are always present to you. Staying aligned with your spiritual essence will provide the perspective needed to stay clear of soul mugging forever.

Betty was a 38-year-old Hispanic woman with a successful advertising business. She and her boyfriend had recently broken up after five years in a committed relationship. She came into my office for her first session stating that she felt as if she were going to die. She had no physical symptoms of disease, no doctor's diagnosis on which to base her claims, just an extremely strong feeling that she was about to die. That first day she stated:

"I feel plunged into the depths of despair. I think I will just expire any moment. I am preoccupied with death, how it might feel, what relief it would bring me.

"I can't imagine that I can keep living with this much desolation. It is as if I have a disassembled soul, decomposing as each day passes. It is terrible. I am beyond being able to cope with these horrible, terrifying feelings. The worst pain comes after a night of dreaming of death. It is the most vivid image of blackness and then blankness I have ever known."

A few sessions later, Betty reframed her experience:

"Doctor, I was so betrayed by Tony that I had nowhere to go but into death. It was the worst rejection I've ever experienced. I was forced, by the situation, into total isolation from my usual world and the community he and I hung out in. Now, though, I see that my death desires were really telling me that my old ways of being would have to die. It was a symbolic death of everything as I knew it.

"My life as I had experienced it did die. It had to before I could find the sacred part of myself that I had never paid much attention to.

"Believe me, that internal source of life has saved my life. I now think about what this death could teach me about accepting myself completely, including my experience of betrayal.

"Doctor, I realize as I am talking that I am welcoming back my soul. I am returning it to its rightful place in my life. Now that's what *I* call a miracle. Suddenly I'm energized beyond belief. It is all new territory for me. *I* get to explore my soul without a past, in a way, because I left it so early I can't recall ever being with it. Thank you, thank me, thank God."

Living From Your Core

Can you be truthful enough with yourself to permit yourself to live every moment in a way that honors your soul? Selling out to a partner has been devastating to you and now you realize that the most important being is the one inside of you. You cannot expect it to be ignored and then also be intact to benefit you.

Your primary concern in living from your core moment by moment is not to focus on what you are receiving, but on that which originates from your essential self and emanates from you. The difference is profound. It reverses your focus in governing your life.

Soul Discovery

After taking a hot shower, wait for the steam to leave the bathroom mirror. As it clears, the face of someone you admire emerges. You know this person cares for you. Who is it? What kind of expression does he or she have? What does this person say to you about your soul? Do not edit anything out. Write as you listen carefully to all you are hearing.

As you become acquainted with your soul, you may not know how to respond to feelings from such an unfamiliar place within you. This person in the mirror can speak words that you may have censored or even completely blocked out, for it is your wise essence.

Freedom will reign when all your thoughts and definitions of yourself come from your soul. You will replenish your energy by returning to that sacred place within. A patient once said to me: "I desired liberty. For liberty I grasped, and for liberty I uttered a prayer."

Soul Discovery

As you re-establish and deepen your new awareness of your soul, your foundation will grow stronger if you build into your daily schedule a few key soul workout routines.

Practice mindfulness. Be present and alive to each moment and to its opportunity to strengthen your commitment to your soul. For example:

Eat very slowly and notice the different tastes as your mouth takes the food in.

Become aware of the face of each person you pass in public.

Listen carefully to song lyrics, searching for the transformative line in each of them that could quicken the pace of your journey.

Learn how to enter the different dimensions of reality at every moment, noting whether you are perceiving it from your spiritual or physical being. Let yourself experience being in both within the same two or three-minute period. Switch back and forth so that you gain clarity about how each of these places feels throughout your whole body, mind, and soul.

Learn new ways to design a richer inner life that can infuse your work activities, your relationships, and the world which you alone inhabit.

Develop a dream that you are committed to fulfilling and find how your soul intends to guide you towards it each moment. Focus on the needs of your soul and give those needs top priority in your day.

Lightening Your Burden

Jerry, a 52-year-old African-American man married for thirty-five years, didn't know any way of life other than his relationship and his career as a teller in a bank. Jerry was extremely sad when he first came into therapy. He was stuck in his daily routine. In fact, he saw his life only in the past and felt it might as well be over.

One day, after four months of intense therapy, Jerry resolved to do something he had never tried before.

"Doctor, I'm so sick and tired of being sick and tired of my life that I decided some very important things. I read an article that gave me a new definition of commitment, and, for some reason, it triggered a whole set of resolutions I've decided to claim for my life. The definition was doing whatever it takes without harming anyone or going against your highest values to get what you want. Well, I'm committed to that way of being in the world now.

"I can't believe I was able to do this, but I let myself, for the first time in at least twenty years, cry over some past injuries I've had with Rose. She has reinforced so much of the hatred I have carried around since I was four or five years old. Well, once I cried, I couldn't stop. I picked up a piece of paper and I started writing her a letter, not one I'd give her, just one I'd love to be able to give her.

"It's not worth giving it to her now that I see that most of the damage is about what I've done to myself over these years. I've been so full of self-hatred that whatever she'd say to me I'd just add to my list of things to hate about myself. Anyway, I experienced that pain. I cried for a while, wrote for a while, and then cried some more.

"It felt so good. My chest opened up and I know I could breathe easier. I took my first deep breath in many years. I let go of so much that by the time I got up to go into the hallway, I hardly had to use my legs. I felt that light.

"I let myself be for the first time, just be. On into the night, I was just being, instead of fretting and fuming and feeling resigned to life."

Jerry had suffered most of his life, primarily because he wanted to avoid his pain. He said later that if he had known what would happen if he had just acknowledged his pain and let himself feel it, he would have done this much sooner. He realized through therapy that it frightened him to even consider feeling the pain. He said he'd then have to handle what that pain was and how deep it went. He stated he was not sure the pain or the fears would ever stop once he opened that door.

If soul mugging is ever again an unwelcome intruder, your resulting suffering can tell you where you are still being held captive. Your pain is without question a result of being tied to old ways you still believe will work. As long as you hold on to these, your pain will continue. And the tighter your grasp, the greater your pain.

Since you want to be free, un-imprisoned by anything that is holding you down from your grandest possibilities, turn your attention toward your pain, as well as all that is yet unsolved in your heart. Just move toward it, instead of hiding from it or saying it isn't really there. Be with it all, embracing it as you become more acutely aware of it. The way out of your pain is to go through it directly, not to fervently avoid it.

I can open to the pain of the world within in confidence that it can neither shatter nor isolate me, for I am not an object that can break. I am a resilient pattern within a vaster web of knowing.
– Joanna Macy

Have you ever been afraid to allow yourself all the time you need to experience whatever your pain is? Jerry thought he would either go crazy or his heart would break if he let the pain out. How about you? It is a bold act to become all that we are because it means feeling all that we feel, as well as owning all the power we have, all the choices we can make, and all our possibilities.

Faith is the bird that sings to the dawn while it is still dark.
– Kabir

Experiencing the New You

Did you know that your greatest power is to change your mind about who you are? Right now, you are aware of your soul and of allowing it to guide you, saying it is your divine core. Or you may state that you are a body with a certain history, past, roles, job, gender, mistakes, achievements, resume. Which have you chosen at this second? And now? And at this moment? Whenever you choose to be a spiritual essence, you place all of your life into a perspective you could not otherwise know.

Jody, a 24-year-old Caucasian woman who was working for a non-profit organization, was completely disgusted with herself when she began therapy. She said that, though she knew better, she was felt she was a complete victim in life. She related that her marriage was impossible and that her life seemed to be in ruins. That was eight months ago. On this particular day, Jody came in full of a joy I had not seen before. I commented about the change in her mood.

"Dr. Papillon, I read about this seminar in the paper last week and decided to go. It was the most important thing I've ever done for myself. First of all, let me get out some notes. Almost all of them are about being a victim.

"They said – just a second – oh yes, the root word of victim is *weik,* which they said was from the Indo-European language group, and it means 'to separate.' The word 'weak' also comes from the same root. So, they continued, if you feel weak, you are feeling powerless and separate from something.

"I have felt separated from other people for a long time. I haven't wanted to interact with anyone at work, and I've certainly been distancing from Lance for the past few months. Nothing seems to be going right with my relationships, so I've retreated. I have also felt separated from my power, with no creativity at all. I've even felt separated from nature. And, most importantly, as you know, I have experienced being separated from my source, from God, from my spirit, from my life. Cut off. That's it. Feeling like a victim is a combination of all those feelings.

"What I discovered, though, is that I had become so used to the label 'victim' that I decided, unintentionally, that I could never be normal because I was depressed, mistreated, and a mistake besides. You know how many ways I've labeled myself in here. But there was this one person in the seminar who asked if he could speak. He said, 'I don't see myself as anything but a creator.'

"Dr. Papillon, he was a paraplegic, but I soon forgot he was even in a wheelchair. He was so inspiring. He said, 'I allow for the possibilities of life at all times. I know magic happens. I believe all people must pursue their dream.'

"He was filled with life. Nothing was going to stop him, and yet I was letting myself be stopped by so many things. I was amazed. This guy was authoring his life by his choices and they were all such great ones. I didn't want him to stop talking. I'll never be the same again. That victim label is in the trash."

All the issues of soul mugging can be seen as having a spiritual dimension, as symptoms of alienation from one's true self or essential being. Moving your exquisite soul back into its rightful place is your main task. This essential part of your being holds your capacity for unconditional presence, wakefulness, openness, creativity and responsivity to life. It is a deeper connection and is more fundamental than any self-designed structure that it is possible to create in any other way.

Soul Discovery

The next time you are in a crowd, experiment with the idea that God is in every face. See what you can find as you walk along in public places. Do you find signs of God? Do you find messages from God? Allow yourself to play with this idea. It is a fascinating exercise in exploring where you think God is or isn't. Let yourself find God in everything just for that time. Then you may want to expand it to a week. Your soul will be especially nurtured by this experience. It has been yearning to have more of your time in your head to contemplate the multi-dimensional and multi-faceted aspects of itself.

Letting Your Soul Take Charge

Because you picked up this book and have read this far, you have provided a way to restore the being within you. If you have completed the Soul Discovery assignments, you are well on your way. It is very important that you remain open and inquisitive to your experience without bias or attempts to control the thoughts and feelings which come up for you. What appears is just what you need to be renewed, nourished, and revalidated and for your soul to flourish.

A Strong Faith

When I was in the midst of my own soul restoration, I found that rereading one of my father's journals gave me comfort. He had left them for his children when he passed away. In one entry he discussed his faith as a Christian:

> "When you stop to think about it, there have been, from time to time, some rather ridiculous notions advanced about where God is or isn't. For instance, some have tried to persuade me that there is something wrong with the religious faith of a woman who uses nail polish or lipstick or by the regularity with which a person goes to church. I do not understand the mystery. I have no answers. It is enough to know there is a power through which we can get out of a grave, any grave. 'Neither death, nor life, nor angels, nor principalities, nor powers, nor things present, nor things to come, nor height, nor depth, nor any other creature, shall be able to separate us from the love of God.' (Romans 8:38-39)."

I discovered that I had a way I could look at my own faith because my father had let me know how he looked at his. He had always been someone I looked up to. I didn't know he had such a strong sense of what he believed, no matter what anyone would say to him about it. His faith encouraged me in my own spiritual quest to restore my soul. His faith influenced how I would define my spirit in my life from then on.

Certainly there are countless ways to restore your soul. One way is by being silent for a period each day, so that you can hear what your essential being is saying. The soul can be restored by letting go of the familiar and safe, by constantly renewing and expressing yourself in the world, and by your being aware of what you give your attention to daily. Then the relationship with your soul becomes the model for the relationship you have with the world. When you have learned to be with that essential being more of the time, you will find that your decisions will become effortless. Take this now on faith. I have certainly found it to be true.

When you go to a therapist/spiritual advisor because you are feeling disheartened, desperate, or miserable, that person might ask such questions as: When did you stop singing? When did you stop dancing? When did you stop creating something that had meaning just for you? When did you begin finding discomfort in your quietude?

Everything that is presented to you is an avenue connecting you more intimately with your soul. Ask your soul what it thinks, what it feels about the experience. Certainly embracing all of yourself – the lovely, the marred, the mistakes, and the successes – is necessary to restore your precious soul. It is all the same to the soul, just you being you in all your glory.

With your soul restored to its rightful place, there is no effort. You will find you are being led gently as if you were being carried down a quiet path in the midst of spring.

Why should I wish to see God better than this day?
I see something of God each hour of the twenty-four, and each moment then,
In the faces of men and women I see God, and in my own face in the glass;
I find letters from God dropped in the street, and every one is signed by God's name,
And I leave them where they are, for I know that others will punctually come forever and ever.
– Walt Whitman

Chapter Eight

They Can't Take That Away From Me

Building Your Inner Sanctuary

The dark night of the soul comes just before revelation.
– Anonymous

My barn burned to the ground. I can now see the moon ...
– J. Stone

"I'm dying so I can have a new life."

More than anything, Judy wanted to regain a clear sense of her self. Immobilized by her belief that Brad held all the power in their relationship, Judy entered therapy more than a year ago. A 41-year-old Caucasian woman, she had devoted herself to being a housewife after marrying Brad fifteen years before. Up to that time she had been a successful real estate agent.

"I do feel as if I had to die. I couldn't be only what Brad needed me to be. You know how I used to sneak out of the house to come in for my sessions. I'm finally getting to the point where my actions match who I really am inside."

For the first time Judy was wearing a black business suit and carried a briefcase. She also had a new hair cut that dramatically changed the way she looked.

"I can't make myself wait on Brad the way I used to. I still bring him things to eat if I'm joining him in the den, but almost everything I used to do I did out of fear. What a way to live!

"I began to notice that everything that was not authentically me was dropping away. That's what I mean about dying. I know now that I had to die to the old me so I could live my own life, not Brad's idea of what my life had to be. I didn't know how much Brad's version of me had disappeared until you and I started talking about the way I was. As you pointed out, I had started down that path even before I met Brad.

"I've seen that I can and will stand up for my own ideas and preferences. It makes such a difference. I even feel different physically.

"I've certainly noticed that Brad is responding to these immense changes in me. Several times I've thought he would leave. You know he left before when I did small things that would make me feel visible. He still may leave, but I'm not going back to the way it was and I was.

"I died, but I came back. I so wanted to have integrity with my self, to be visible to myself, to be a being I can love and respect. That was worth dying for."

Are you willing to die to the lesser in yourself in order to be reborn into the greater being that you are? As Judy so clearly pointed out, her external environment now reflects her internal environment and not vice versa. Building your inner sanctuary will create a dwelling for your indwelling soul. Life for you can then be lived from your core within, outward.

Nothing and no one can divert you. Nothing and no one will be able to push you off. It will be your holy place where you alone abide.

As you align yourself with your soul, the truth in you is awakened and you can live fully from that place. Do not expect this guidebook to completely develop that place for you, though. Only you can do that.

As you continue to do the tasks suggested, even more aspects of your soul will reveal their magnificent and unique expressions. Use this book to inspire, perhaps even compel, you to do whatever inner soul work it takes for your soul to constantly and predictably flourish. Part of the wonder, the mystery, and the magic is your willingness to find your own way through the process, listening to your soul at each moment.

At times you will notice it is easy to free yourself to hear your soul. You may be most receptive to listening as you hike on a mountain path, or perhaps lean against a tree to feel its energy. At other times, though, it may seem difficult to let go of the interference that has prevented you from allowing your soul to speak for many years.

Judy's revelations about her dying in order to build her inner sanctuary showed that the stronger her sense of self became, the less vulnerable she became to Brad. Before she started on this restoration process, she had tremendous hunger for her partner to define her being. As a consequence, she was always at his mercy. During one of her sessions, she had blurted out, "I will never be that hungry again!" You may have reached this point, too. Can you sense how empowering this is for you?

It may be difficult to keep faith with what is occurring at an intuitive level, somewhat removed from your rational knowing. But trust what you know and that you will know more. In other words, practice doubting the doubt. Your knowing will claim itself into being in its own time and way. It is an emerging process, rather than a finite, concrete state that comes all at once.

Someone once described a poignant moment while in the presence of Mother Teresa:

"She doesn't look at you, she looks into you and restores you to your self." Only by being very connected to her soul could she touch another in that way.

You are in the midst of gathering pieces of your soul and connecting with your own power. You are recreating your self, that self that is firm and forceful, yet gentle, compassionate, and loving. Surrendering all those early, inculcated beliefs about who owns your soul and who has a right to define it is a challenge. It means giving up definitions of yourself that are based on what others once said about who you are.

I'll never forget being on a road similar to the one you are on now. I had no map to guide me. Finally I cried out to no one in particular: "I don't need someone to define my existence. The most profound relationship I'll ever have is the one with my self, my soul." It was a major turning point in the journey out of my dark blankness. In truth, this was a very sacred moment for me. You will have these moments, too. You will get a glimpse of light which you will not necessarily understand with your intellect, but you will feel inside of you. It is real, and it is you as you are reborn into a life that is yours.

You are literally building a dwelling for the soul you have been denying. At a young age it may have gotten you into trouble by expressing itself. At that time it was better ignored than acknowledged. Yet, only with your soul intact can you live in a way that is profoundly related to the realities in your life, not the illusions you allowed to rule your life earlier.

By now you know one thing for certain: hope cannot be permitted to extinguish your soul's guiding light. Your original soul has been retrieved now. You have moved your soul from being misplaced to being celebrated.

Solidifying your soul is the most powerful and restorative experience you will ever have. It is the source of miracles and the key to your inner peace. As you return to the wholeness and wonder of the world you came in with, the world where you were still one with your soul, continue to use your own eyes and cry out with your own voice while interacting with all aspects of your being.

The Interwoven Tapestry of Psychology and Spirituality

Both psychology and spirituality are essential in affirming the presence of a life within that is unbound, uncaught, limitless, and free. Unraveling psychological patterns activates your spirituality.

As patients integrate their concepts of spirituality with psychology, I often point out that the beliefs of major religions often honor the spiritual essence of each individual and recognize an eternal source. A concise way to express these fundamental truths is to say that God is everywhere, as well as within you. By revering the soul in yourself, you are joining with the omniscient, omnipresent, and omnipotent spiritual source.

Some patients have had a difficult time with the concept of divinity within. They have struggled with the idea that there was anything of value within them, much less something as highly revered as divinity.

In whatever ways you describe the essential essence within you, it is powerful, whole, intuitive, vital, wise, and perfect. You are free to use different words so semantics do not get in the way of building your inner sanctuary. Your own words and descriptions will help you take complete possession of your dwelling.

A patient had mentioned that at her next session she wanted to talk about coming to terms with where she saw God in her life. I received an unexpected call from her and upon returning it heard her say in an uncharacteristically apologetic tone of voice:

"All week I have felt a little nervous concerning talking about my early religious upbringing and the spiritual idea of my soul as divine and within me. I've been so set in how I see things, as you well know by now. I don't want you to be frustrated. The strangest thing has happened. I had a dream. It was so real to me that I was astonished when I woke up that I hadn't lived it. I want to tell you about it while it's fresh. Do you have any time before my scheduled appointment?"

Doris, a 54-year-old African-American woman, had grown up in a religious family, but had never reconciled her childhood beliefs with the ideas she had uncovered during the year she had been in therapy. She began:

"In my dream were all these people dressed in white. The space around them was all white, and it looked like heaven as I've pictured it. But there were all sorts of people there, ones I never expected to see and ones I've disagreed with strongly, and actually argued with many times because their beliefs were so opposite from mine.

"The message I got from the dream was how judgmental I have been about people's beliefs if they differed from mine. I tend to forget that we are all really just wanting to have a personal experience with God, however that can happen. Sometimes I get into thinking that a person has to see God the way I do or talk to God in a particular way, or that person is wrong.

"Until this dream I saw myself as separate from God, also: alone and weak, helpless and worthless. There is even a phrase I've used: 'I am a worm in the dust.' Even as I'm speaking, I realize I saw others exactly as I saw myself, unworthy of a closeness with God. The idea that God just might be within me and within them was way beyond me.

"I'm just beginning to get the idea that the presence, the power, and the love of God are within me. Can I really believe these qualities are all part of my soul, as well the souls of all people everywhere? I know I gave up my soul ages ago. Now I'm thinking that it just may be that God never left me, but I left God. I mean, I left that part of me where God could easily speak within me, my soul."

At that point Doris was crying as if she were pouring out her illusions and at the same time taking in the splendor of her discovery. She knew her life would never be the same. It was one of her major turning points toward building an inner dwelling of safety, love, and peace for her newly found soul.

Soul-Less To Soul-Full

If you asked me what I came
Into this world to do,
I will tell you:
I came to live out loud.
– Emile Zola

Meister Eckhart, a mystic who lived in the thirteenth century, described how you may experience making contact with your soul. "When we speak of divine matters, we have to stammer, because we are forced to express our experiences in words." By now, if you don't know all *about* your soul, you do *know* your soul and its wisdom, its love, and its ability to guide you.

Soul Enrichment

Write down some of the times in your journal when you knew your soul was speaking. You might think of setting up a special book (similar to a book for a newborn) which chronicles the important moments when you feel your renewed being express itself. As the building of your inner dwelling progresses, you will continue to have new experiences of coming into being from within.

As you build this sanctuary for your soul, there are no rules for what you are to do. There is no single way or path. You are pursuing your essence in a direct manner now. Avoid paralyzing yourself by waiting for perfection. Simply start. And if necessary, start again. The greatest power you have now is to tune into your soul, to live in harmony with the new guidance you hear.

Also, there is no reason to understate or constrain your being. You are here to do great things. Become a pilgrim, as it were, with the intention of never letting your inner sanctuary be torn down by another.

Soul Enrichment

Pause for a moment to breathe in a sense of accomplishment for all you have achieved. Sense how empowering it is to be building your inner sanctuary.

As the designer and the weaver of a new type of dwelling, you can re-enchant your world. You are much richer, deeper, and stronger than you know. You are the mystery unfolding, free to open to your own depth.

Soul Enrichment

At this moment, see yourself as a cathedral. Sketch it into your journal. What kinds of furnishings do you choose for it? What colors do you select? What gardens and landscaping do you surround your cathedral with? It is your sacred site. Perhaps you can visualize your favorite trees, waterfalls, stones of unusual colors and shapes, hills or mountains in the background – whatever brings you comfort and honors your soul. As you envision your cathedral, know that your soul will totally flourish.

You are increasingly manifesting your internal while regenerating and blossoming in external ways also. You create these moment by moment. You will invariably change, even before you have a chance to be fully conscious of it.

Soul Enrichment

Building your inner sanctuary calls for you to continually see yourself as you are in the present. Find new ways to experience your essence, inventing new possibilities as you go through the day:

Be like a sunflower, not complaining, just open, with your little seeds, and your yellow petals. And turn your face to the sun (the light), following it around. At night (the dark times) just stay there, quiet and content, solid and sure. Imagine yourself as a peaceful soul – just being – no matter what the external world says as it passes by. If this image does not fit, find one that has meaning for you, one that readily portrays a peaceful way you could be in the world at this moment. That's the fun of all this. You get to make up whatever you want and let it match you completely.

Search for your original soul face. Let that be your only face, the one with which you entered this world. You may not actually remember it, but imagine it and create a visual sense of it. Remove all your masks and return to your original source, the deepest core of your being, that unknown, remembered gate of your first dwelling.

Reclaim your voice through poetry, chants, and nonsensical sounds. When you free your voice, you free your self. You have been silenced since childhood: by your parents, by teachers, by the bully in the school yard. As you reconnect with the voice you were born with, you will sing in triumph.

Think of your essence as a closet mystic. You may certainly be one. A mystic is someone who, through the soul, has a naked, direct relationship with the Divine Presence.

Appreciate deep glimpses of the divine in your dreams, during lovemaking, from exalted moments of friendship, and as you feel aesthetic ecstasy while looking at a great painting or listening to music. You may not have been taught to recognize these as profound encounters with the Divine Presence in you.

Focused Soul Attention

As you transform your foundation into one that is sacred, you are owning responsibility for living within the integrity and harmony of your relationship with the Divine. Bring your soul into its dwelling and allow it to be the primary voice in your life. Your flourishing soul, if it could speak directly, might say:

I direct my attention.

I lean towards risk.

I try on difference.

I manifest miracles.

I hunt value.

I live truth.

I honor others.

I connect with source.

Add any others which your soul would express. Look for a sense that someone is holding you with one hand and leading you with the other.

As you pay close attention to your soul, you will know when it, rather than other elements of you, is speaking. Often your soul will say, "Just pay attention," "Be at peace and trust," and "You are not alone." When you listen, you are living by faith, which is the daring of the soul to go farther than it can see.

Soul Enrichment

When you are opening to unlimited possibility, what is your life about? How are you designing it? What is authentically you? Are you willing to let the inauthentic part of you go? If not now, when? You are standing at a threshold from which you can step in any direction. You can choose to live this way all the time. Visualize one scenario of your life with unlimited possibilities. How do you feel inside? What would you do to manifest it first? Next? Have you ever tried the creative expression you chose?

To build my own faith, strengthen my soul connection, and lessen my fear, I have used a statement the minister of a small community church said as each person left the service:

"If you knew who walked beside you at all times on this path that you have chosen, you would never experience fear again." I will never forget what a sense of peace that sentence created each week.

I was also moved by a profound statement I read in an art gallery one day. I later met the creator, who is a great artist, sculptor, and author

Spirit of Self-Reliance
It is appropriate to regret misunderstandings,
And to be sad, if you care to be,
That they occur.
But do not regret your part of them
When you know that you have acted properly.
To regret, that is to commit treason to yourself
To barter your soul
To deny your heart
And to lose your integrity.
You might straighten the misunderstanding,
But you surely cannot un-betray yourself.
Remember the words,
'For what shall it profit a man
If he shall gain the whole world
And lose his own soul?'
– Bill Worrell

Soul Tools for Completing Your Inner Sanctuary

We are the mirror as well as the face in it.
... We are pain
and what cures pain, both. We are
the sweet cold water and the jar that pours.
– Rumi

As you exult with a sense of triumph, you are free to move and change. An invisible band around your essence has burst, allowing you to know what Rumi is saying. Feel as if you are soaring into a new-found, newborn liberty.

From Chrysalis to Freedom

Freedom is an essential tool for building a sacred temple that no one else can enter without your permission. You are coming out of hiding to express yourself, perhaps for the first time. It is absolutely imperative that you know you have the freedom to achieve this. If you are to live from the center of the authenticity that is truly you, others' opinions must no longer dominate.

Real freedom is the melody of your soul and is actually a requisite to your wholeness. As you tune in to your inner self, you inevitably learn that you have been imprisoning long-held desires to unfold and to reveal previously unexplored facets of yourself.

Imagine the feelings of inner freedom. What if you let go of just one element of self-doubt right now? What if you overcame one worry? Releasing these is difficult, but it becomes easier with practice. Freedom is only experienced by living in the world without being in bondage in any way.

One of James Joyce's heroes describes a process similar to transformation after soul mugging: "When the soul of a man is born in this country there are nets flung at it to hold it back from flight. You talk to me of nationality, language, religion. I shall try to fly by those nets. For what to the soul are nets, 'flung at it to hold it back from flight' can become for the one who has found his own center the garment, freely chosen, of his further adventure."

Start first with this tool of freedom, for if you find you have no freedom within you, no flexibility to move around without major consequences, you will find that the remaining elements for completing your inner sanctuary cannot be developed.

Suzanne, a 46-year-old Hispanic woman, was an executive in a computer company. After having been in therapy for eight months, she came in one day exclaiming:

"Last night I walked into the house full of all the joy that I so easily express at work. I suddenly realized I didn't need to be put off by Tony's nasty looks. I never saw that I automatically cut off that spontaneity when I came through my front door.

"The contrast hit me straight on. I said, 'No way!' I decided to take a bold approach. I thought, 'What is that? Here I am, so powerful one place, yet so timid and withdrawn in the other.' Tony just didn't seem as big and foreboding as before. It was all in my changed perceptions of what I know I am now.

"Dr. Papillon, when we talked about how much I had bought into my belief that I was Tony's little woman, I had never seen it as a belief before. What a sense of freedom I got by that awareness. I could start expressing that bound-up self inside of me and not shake as much. I was wild.

"There's no other way to say it. I just began to say things about what I planned to do over the weekend and mentioned to Tony that he could either join me or not. I told him my desires and didn't apologize or ask if they were okay.

"Now, that's like being let out of a dank, dark prison. I know now that nothing can stop me from being connected to my own soul. I still feel the surge of energy from living through this last night. I'm so thankful."

From Blindness to Vision

Another essential tool for transforming your inner realm is to generate a vision for your self. As you seek the wisdom of your soul, listen carefully. It has something specific to say. Indeed it has a solid plan, anchored in the dimension of life you are now embracing. Your vision will come with specific ways to carry it out. It may not happen all at once, but rather, may unfold as you start following the first inklings of that vision. Again, faith is essential each step of the way.

As you follow your vision, expect to step outside your familiar way of approaching situations in your life. This will be especially true for you, since you gave up sovereignty of your soul long ago.

After a time you will see how necessary this approach is to building an unshakable foundation from which you can live, move, and replenish your being. Your expanded vision is capable of overcoming your feeling of being robbed of your essence. Within you resides a tremendous capability for actualizing your vision and eclipsing the former narrow existence you called your life. The force is transcendent.

Soul Enrichment

Who are you within your deepest, most reverent self? How can you best honor your soul at this very moment? Whatever your answer, give yourself the time to actually accomplish that. What would be the next most empowering thing you could do for your soul? Do it also.

Robert, a 26-year-old African-American man, worked for the transit authority. He had been in treatment for more than a year when he came into a session with a package under his arm.

"Dr. Papillon, I've got to show you what I found. After our talk last week about developing a vision for my life, I immediately knew what you were saying when I saw this poster. I just had to get it framed. It's perfect for what I plan to do for the rest of my life.

"Jessie thought I had flipped out when I came home with the poster. She can be so critical and so negative about any creative ideas I have. Several months ago I stopped bothering to even tell her what I thought. It just hadn't worked to do that. Well, now that I have this wonderful new sense of never allowing my soul to be lessened by her, I am starting to show her parts of myself I hid.

"It is interesting to feel so different inside as I reveal things like this poster. I just didn't let her put-down attitude detract me from my excitement over finding it. In fact, it made me want to do it more. I know that the person I choose to be now can never be pushed aside by Jessie or anyone. My soul is the most precious part of me. I feel my chest expanding as I say this aloud. I'm claiming something. My heart feels more open, too. I've widened and deepened from the inside out. Is it noticeable when you look at me?

"Let me just read a few of the lines from the poster. It's titled: How to be Really Alive. 'Live juicy. Find snails making love. Develop an astounding appetite for books. Draw out your feelings. Amaze yourself. Make "yes" your favorite word. Hang upside down.' It goes on, but the thing that excites me is knowing that I can be that unlimited. My vision for my being is to be as one-of-a-kind as I possibly can, and to have fun doing it."

Robert's vision may be very different from your own. Notice how absolutely transformed he was when he realized he could have his own perspective, his own way of being in the world. That's how you can be. Be as a child, discovering that a chair is not just a chair, but maybe a fort to crawl under, a wall to hide behind or an object to explore by turning it upside down. Only a child's awe of the world can move you to a place where you explore wonder and spontaneity.

Soul Enrichment

Make your own personal Bill of Rights for your soul. Be wild and outrageous with it. Have fun with it and be unlimited in your thinking about it. Add to it from the depths of your soul. It is a guiding document that you will be changing and adding to as you gain more ability to stay in the sacred home you are building.

From Fright to Courage

Courage is another essential tool. It takes great daring to move away from those invisible fences you placed around yourself. You are now overcoming the powerful forces that have prevented you from fully and freely unfolding. You may have to continue walking forward when every fiber in your being says, "No, this is too terrifying. I want to crawl back within my safe haven of smallness." Your intention to keep walking is vital and will lead you to the courage you already possess.

From Separation to Connection

Your inner sanctuary will only be complete when you maintain a sense of connectedness with your soul at all times. This is a pivotal tool. The bond with your soul must be indelible and impenetrable. The power of the connection comes from your willingness to pause, permitting you to take in the whole design of your inner realm. This tool is crucial in fully completing your soul's home.

Soul Enrichment

Build an altar for your inner sanctuary. Begin by placing on it a picture of yourself as a small child. Choose one from a time before your soul mugging began, when you seemed to still be aware of that divine place within. Put a lily or another flower beside your picture. Remind yourself that the flower has neither to toil nor fret, but opens in its own time and in its own way without controlling any of the process. Other reminders you may wish to include are a dream catcher from the Native American culture for all the possibilities that you are now aware of, unusual rocks and objects you find in nature, a candle that you keep lit to represent your soul's presence, small pictures that appeal to you. Actually, the list is long. Create your altar from that place within that is totally aware of who you truly are.

From Compromise to Integrity

A profound pillar of your inner sanctuary is integrity. Think of this word in a very broad sense. It is much deeper than moral uprightness and a sense of steadfastness. In fact, it is allowing yourself to be formed and shaped entirely by your soul. Even if you allow ninety percent of yourself to be molded by your soul, that will not be enough. Outside forces could then still render their impact upon your commitments.

Soul Enrichment

Even if you never show it to anyone, write at least three secrets you hold about yourself. They may be recent or very old secrets. There is something about sharing them, even on paper, that is freeing and will allow more space for your soul to live within you and speak its words of peace, love, truth, and light to you and through you.

From Adrift to Guided

A closely related tool to integrity involves your willingness to turn your life over to the guidance of your divine self. Each morning ask this wise advisor: What am I to do? Where am I to go? What am I to say and to whom? No longer will your intellect or your physical being alone drive your life. Now your soul will be at your center, integrating you and governing you.

Many patients have expressed a less burdened and more empowering life once they fully turned to their internal realm. They became so securely anchored that they were able to withstand outside forces, no matter how strong those were.

Sophie, a 41-year-old fashion industry salesperson, sought therapy for feelings of despair about her marriage:

"Joseph is so callous about the way I'm choosing to be in my life. I don't think he understands me even on a very basic level. I've told him I'm not like other people. I've also explained to him that now my values are different than when he met me in Italy fifteen years ago. He expects me to come to see you, but then not to change."

After six months of therapy Sophie came into a session very disturbed:

"Dr. Papillon, how do I get him to see that the world I once lived in with him is no longer the world I identify with? You know I live totally from inside of myself now. He thinks I've gotten worse when I try to explain this. I can't seem to get him to see that I have a deep, inner home which I tune into continuously and rely on to know what to do and how to be. I have a compass that is invisible.

"I get such terrible headaches by the time he and I finish a conversation. It is so frustrating. Sometimes I even give up talking. He has no idea what integrity is, for example. To be true to my soul, I have learned how I must be, and that is not his way. I love the integrity that I know now. It feels so right to me. I really have come home now, to my inner home.

"I want Joseph to honor my soul as I do. I know that is not asking too much. And whether he can do that or not, I will honor it no matter what the cost.

"It is much less stressful for me at work, at home, and everywhere to live this way. I have an inner steering ability. I never even question my inner wisdom. I can depend on it. My purpose is to have a peaceful existence all the time, everywhere I am."

From Disappointment to Gratefulness

Your sense of thankfulness is another essential tool in building your inner sanctuary. Even though Sophie never directly mentioned gratefulness in that session, you can tell that she appreciates her newfound home. As you build your inner home, remember to be thankful in your heart about everything in your life, even appreciating that all the mugging you endured got you to the place where you are now.

This element of thankfulness within your inner sanctuary will keep your soul at peace. T. S. Eliot must have known this when he stated that we will never cease exploring, but in the end we will arrive where we started and know our original home for the first time: that unknown, now remembered place.

Have you ever wondered why something has occurred in your life? Good came from it because it brought you here now. You are doing an extraordinary thing by building your inner sanctuary for your self. You probably never thought of yourself as an architect. Yet you certainly are the designer of your inner residence.

From Resentment to Forgiveness

Another needed tool is forgiveness. Your acts of forgiveness will strengthen you. By forgiving the other person, you are contributing more to your own inner sanctuary than you are benefiting them.

Forgiving can unburden you of the past so you can more readily move on with your life. You certainly do not want to carry around any unresolved feelings that can sabotage your inner temple. You must stay pure, open, innocent, and unconditionally loving within it.

All the tools you are using include their own roles and characteristics. You will want to appreciate them in their broadest perspective. And then you will want to balance these resources.

Each of these tools has spiritual and psychological aspects. Forgiveness, freedom, connectedness and guidance, for example, carry spiritual as well as psychological implications. You need all of these dimensions to fully build and furnish your sanctuary. Then it will completely serve you.

Soul Enrichment

Start a dream journal. Separate it from the journal you have been using for the soul explorations found in this guidebook. Your dreams can tell you where you are stuck, what your unconscious is working on, and where you are heading. Do not purchase a dream dictionary. Rather, let your soul interpret your dreams for you. Your own ideas can add magnificently to the building of your inner sanctuary.

From Chatter to Prayer

Although there are many others you will want to add to your own particular inner sanctuary, the last tool I will address is prayer. Prayer refocuses you on the activities that are the highest priority for a soul-full life. Some of my patients have reported that they have eventually ended up praying without ceasing. In a sense, if you look at all the elements included in your inner realm, you will frequently be in prayer as you incorporate them into living within your inner sanctuary.

In prayer you ask to be open to your soul, permitting it to relay its message to you. You are joining forces with God in that moment and thus with your unlimited and most sacred connection. Prayer allows you to look at any past, present, or future pain and refuse to believe it is the last word. I have never spoken with anyone who does not receive enrichment from the experience of prayer, including a sense of peace, bliss, and renewed energy for life. Prayer itself is a transformational experience.

It is not important what you pray or how you pray, or even when you pray, but that you pray. Prayer moves you back into knowing who you are at your deepest core. By connecting and reconnecting to your essence through prayer, you can restore the wreckage done to your precious soul. Actually, you can no longer not pray, for your soul will begin praying for you at some point, if it has not already. Through prayer you shift your perception from your outer to your inner world, from the appearances and circumstances of your life, to the reality of your inner core.

With that kind of shift, you can then live from a higher, more sacred perspective that provides a clearer and more powerful way of focusing on what is important to you now. Prayer is integral and crucial to you, especially after years of having that hole in your soul deepened by your use of hope. Prayer will help you know that the promise of getting back to the light, to the wholeness, to the truth of who you are, held more substance than mere words. You will experience an even brighter light because you have been in the blackest kind of darkness.

If you begin praying despite any misgivings, I assure you that you will find great solace. The openness to receive that occurs when you pray and listen is not a loss, but is a powerful joining. In prayer you are connecting with the spirit that has been longing to breathe free and to have its way with you.

To live always in the Secret Place of the Most High,
To think only those thoughts that are inspired from above,
To do all things in the conviction that God is with you,
To ask God for everything and in faith expect everything,
To live in perpetual gratitude to God who gives everything,
To love God so much that you can inwardly feel that you and
God are One, This is the prayer without ceasing, the true worship of your soul.
– Christian D. Larson

Nourishment for a Thriving Soul

We must learn to reawaken and keep ourselves awake, not by mechanical acts, but by an infinite expectation of the dawn, which does not forsake us even in our soundest sleep.
– Henry David Thoreau

Feel

The key element of keeping your soul nourished is to know that the most significant work you do in the world and in your life is done within your inner sanctuary. To live life fully from your soul you must be willing to feel all of your feelings and express them through laughing, grieving, joyous outbursts, cheering, frowning, animated activity, giving thanks, experiencing anger, and forgiving yourself and others. You may not have expressed some of these feelings in many years. I encourage you to accept and move through all of what you feel. However, do not try to evoke your feelings or hold onto them. As they pass through you, just recognize that they are the language of the soul, and represent only one of the endless ways your soul can relate to you.

Stay Present

Another nourishment for your divine core is to channel your energy into the present. Your soul cannot relate to you if you are fretting about the past or preoccupied with the future. If thoughts draw you back into the past, release them to pass on through you. Realize that letting them go reconnects you to your self.

Soul Enrichment

Write a poem which captures how you feel at the present moment. Let it create order out of the mixed feelings you may have inside. Allow it to flow out of you, expressing any emotions you are aware of. See if you can let your soul write the whole poem. It does not have to rhyme or even make logical sense. It is created out of your being in the present moment.

Embrace It All

Choose to place your essence in the presence of beauty, grace, and empathy. Seek the insights of people who are at the edge of life, those who are giving birth or dying.

Embrace whatever you are experiencing in your life at every moment. This is by far more beneficial to your soul's well-being than yearning for or wanting what you do not have. Acceptance will draw abundance of all kinds into your inner sanctuary.

Welcome Spontaneity

Rachel, a 38-year-old Caucasian woman, had been a buyer for a large department store but decided to be a housewife for a while. She had been in therapy for nine months when she came in for an extra session.

"I had to see you before I lost some of the peace I am currently feeling. It is bliss, really. I decided to experiment with what we had touched on last time.

"I surprised Brad by having a rope tied to the front door and a note which asked him to follow the string until it stopped. At the end of the string he found me lying on a quilt on the floor with flowers, candles and a set of symbols I had collected: a rock, a leaf, an acorn, a feather, an empty paper bag, and some rice.

"I had classical music playing softly in the background. He definitely looked puzzled. I had never acted unpredictably or presented him with anything he wasn't prepared for. I am very reasonable, organized, direct, traditional and … well, I used to be that way anyway, and I am sure he was still looking at me through those old eyes. Did I surprise him, though!

"I began by telling him that he and I were going to develop a ritual for our relationship. This ritual was to be totally made up as we went. I didn't have any preconceived notions about it. He was very skeptical and almost left the room. I told him to stay with me for a while and then he could leave if he still wanted to.

"We used every single one of those symbols and the meaning we got from some of them was ... inspired by God. What can I say? I couldn't have come up with them myself, but I know my soul was having the time of its life in that room. I had never felt so bonded with it.

"The beauty which developed from that one ritual will stay with me forever. It gave us a way of seeing what was going on between us, from the perplexing to the ecstatic."

Rachel expressed so well what a ritual can do for your soul. I strongly recommend that you not plan your ritual, whether it is with your soul or with your partner. The spontaneity of the experience will keep you present to what unfolds next. If you plan your ritual, it will be difficult to keep it from coming from that old place in you that limits you rather than allowing you to experience the unlimited possibilities within any situation.

Soul Enrichment

Practice the following each day:

Sit very still for at least eight minutes.

Notice details such as a leaf's veins.

Search for humor in tense situations.

Give up a rigid definition of something you have tenaciously held onto.

Listen to a tape of music that you have enjoyed in the past.

Break a habit (like taking a different way home or listening to hard rock or another type of music you have not been familiar with).

Write down ten things that happened yesterday and force yourself to find something positive about each one.

Make one day sacred and refuse to do anything unless you can find a way to see it in that light.

Celebrate your soul for one whole day.

Follow a small child.

Lie down on the grass or sand or meadow and watch clouds or birds for thirty minutes.

Hold hands with someone in silence.

Serve

Serving others in ways that you have not previously served them is another way to nourish your soul. You have rich gifts to offer, many of which you are not even aware of. Once you make a commitment that you are going to give of your essence in this way, though, many options will present themselves to you. The important thing is for you to be open and willing.

Receive

Related to serving is your ability to receive love. You may think that you already know how to both give and receive love. Yet, from mugging your self over many years and living with a hole in your soul, I suspect that you do not yet have a full sense of the feeling of receiving love. Your ability to receive love is as vitally important as your ability to give love.

Giving from your soul will help unlock your ability to receive love. Learn to absorb the precious words or the beautiful nonverbal gestures given to you. Receiving love is a crucial part of nourishing your soul and thus your inner sanctuary.

Soul Enrichment

Take a day in the week and say "yes" to whatever occurs, perhaps not aloud, and not in terms of taking on more projects, but rather in terms of what you experience that you would usually resist. Just say "yes" to it and go on. Watch what happens when you cease your struggle around it. You can always go back to "no" tomorrow.

Live in Truth

Nurturing your soul also involves living in truth all of the time. You were not honoring it in this way when you were ignoring it, mugging it, beating it down and allowing it to be mugged. You may also have tried to kill it when you thought it was getting you into trouble with its unwanted wisdom.

Now that you are building this inner dwelling for it, you need to acknowledge truths about your essence and about the way your situation and environment presently are, not as you wish they were. By living within truth you will find support from associating with others who hold to these same values.

To be authentic and honest with your self and with every other person you have any kind of contact with is to truly live from your soul. Your standard will be to stay true to that, never wavering, no matter what. The rewards for this kind of truthful living and being with others include always being in complete harmony with your restored soul.

Soul Enrichment

Take a moment each day to ask yourself this question: "If I were to use God's eyes to see myself, what would be reflected to me about me?" Utilize God as your mirror to see your essence today.

Allow Mystery

Actively becoming a part of the great mystery of life also nurtures your soul. You were conditioned from early in your life to calculate formulas and follow rules for life, to gather information and to attempt to understand everything that was going on. When you could not do that, you were particularly frustrated. However, life is not about finding the answers. Life is about seeing life's questions and being with them in such a way that you end up loving the questions themselves. Be completely at ease with not knowing, and your soul will thank you for eliminating the frantic activity that has been so unproductive for you.

Soul Enrichment

In your journal list as many ways as you can think of to replenish your soul in ways which will uniquely meet its needs. Create ideas, unusual foods, and your own expressions of humor. You possess a combination of ingredients that no one else on the planet has. Only you can express what your soul is saying.

Focus Your Attention

Ram Dass, a wonderful contemporary prophet, nurtures his soul by carrying a reminder with him at all times. When he is in a checkout line at the market, Ram Dass takes a string of beads out of his pocket and begins to play with them. In this way, just by feeling the beads in his fingers, he says he can remember that he is a soul rather than merely a body waiting for others to finish checking out and paying for their groceries.

He immediately tunes in to his essence, finds what it needs and proceeds to follow, once more, his inner voice rather than his external environment. During his focus on his inner self he is returning to the sacred place where he can draw forth patience, kindness, consideration, and receptivity. So, too, can you find that holy space within your inner self by placing some remembrance of your essence in your pocket or purse.

Placing your attention on the divine within you, whether through a physical object or not, is an important aspect of nurturing your soul. This maintains a strong link to the sacred realm within as you live through the ordinary, and helps to redirect your life toward extraordinary experiences. Ask yourself many times throughout the day: Where is my attention now? And now? Your energy goes to the place where your attention is focused. As you place more attention on your soul, you will increase your serenity. Anguish over things that have been bothersome to you will vanish.

Soul Enrichment

Initiate action or complete one thing each day in any area that in the past you did not think you could accomplish. Select a goal you have wanted and achieve it. You will be amazed at how empowered you feel after you do this.

Craig, a 59-year-old Hispanic man, was an attorney who was highly regarded in his legal specialty. He had been extremely successful from early in his career. However, when Craig entered therapy he was despondent. Not only had he grown apart from his wife of ten years, who was also a lawyer, but the relationship had deteriorated to such an extent that Craig had no idea how to repair it.

During a session eleven months after he began therapy, Craig reported a new awakening:

"I have never, ever paid any attention to my heart. I know I married Eva because of purely intellectual reasons. We were in the same field of law and we had similar interests as hobbies, you know, all those rational reasons. Well, last weekend I went to the desert alone. I had never seen the desert at this time of year.

"When I walked around at night, I began to have very strange physical sensations. My heart seemed to be ready to jump out of my chest. My knees were wobbly and my stomach felt uneasy. I didn't know what to think. I had never experienced such weird feelings. Well, I was simultaneously looking at some amazing colors in the sky. I'd never seen such an array of stars. I saw plants I'd never run across.

"I didn't think I was spiritual, but this was an opening to something supreme and larger than I am inside. I was too inspired to be frightened, even though I had to find a rock to sit down on. The only way I can express it is to say that I felt at one with everything I was seeing. There was no separateness between me, the plants, the stars, and all of it. It took me a long time to be able to move again.

"I was exhausted and exhilarated at the same time. I think for the first time I totally opened my heart to become one with nature, the oneness of life, and to the awesome source of it all. I will never be the same. I don't even want to be the same."

Craig was nurturing his soul, perhaps for the first time in his life. Now he was using his heart, not just his intellect, to experience life. Previously he had decided that he could think his way through life, think his way to happiness, and then find love and joy. It can never happen that way.

It may make you feel very vulnerable to consider living with your heart wide open, especially since for so much of your life your soul has been robbed of its essence. However, if you nourish it from an open heart, your soul is actually your life's best protector. Now you can let your soul protect you. Building your inner sanctuary gives you a secure place from which to move in the world. You will have this residing within you at all times. That is where your safety lies, not in closing off your heart.

Life –
Experience it ALL
and
let it go
Don't handle
life
as if it is an
accumulation
of all you've done
or said or been
It is
brand new
NOW
and
Now it is
new again
Be with it
as it happens
Be it
Release it
so you are
present. fully
for the next life
that is
ready to appear.
You are
all of God
in this
precious second
How is God presenting
God as you
this instant??
What a sight-sound-
smell-taste-
of life
You are, I am
I awaken
to more of me
as God
As I die
to each old
moment
ever being
born again.
Welcome to the
new.
– Lucy Papillon, Ph.D.

Experience Your Expanded Sacred Space

Dear Lord,
Free me of myself so that I may please You.
– Michelangelo

You will notice that your internal world speaks to you throughout your day, once you have provided it the time it needs to flourish. Despite significant changes you have made within yourself, you may still find that certain unacceptable aspects linger. These will reappear in myriad ways until you make peace with them. Experience each of these unacceptable aspects one by one. Your previous tendency to repress them and move them aside will not be effective. One helpful approach is to learn more about what each of these signifies to you by forming a visual image of it in your mind.

Soul Enrichment

Visualize an image for the aspect of you which you find most acceptable, in fact, the part of you that you like the most. Now, place this image in your left hand. Visualize an aspect of yourself you find despicable. Place this second image in your right hand. Allow yourself some time to get a clear picture of each of the two images. Now take these two images and form a new third image. This may not make intellectual sense at the moment, but allow your third image to fully enter your mind as you open your hands, merging the first and second images together to create this third one. If your soul has not yet whispered to you the meaning of your third image, just start writing about it in your journal. The ideas and elements of their meaning will unfold as you allow your pen to begin to write. Do not force a meaning, but let a meaning come to you. Observe what it may mean and go on from there. What implications can you draw from this third image? How can this third image be a new strength for you?

Lillie, a 39-year-old French woman who held a high position in an international peace organization, first sought my help because of her partner's abrupt departure. At one session a year after she first began therapy, she stated:

"Dr. Papillon, you know I had a very interesting time with the assignment you gave me. I wrote everything in my journal so that you could add to my interpretations. I think I received from my soul just what I needed to get, though.

"My first image was of a beautiful white butterfly, small, fragile, and very lively. The second image I had was of a murky, dark, sticky substance. It was ugly, seemed to have no use, and kept me from being able to open and close my hand.

"The first image is my spirit. It is free, full of joy, love, spontaneity, wisdom, and light. This image of my spirit shows the part of me that knows, and restores itself to new life when all around me looks black.

"I immediately understood that the second image I got was associated with how I get stuck in my head about how ugly I am, how unacceptable I feel, and how full of doubt, fear, and worry I am. That part of me is very dark, negative, and unpleasant.

"The third image was of a large black eagle. It was clearly a powerful bird, flying above the things of this world, landing when and where it chose. I immediately knew that the eagle represented taking the powerful part of that negative image of myself. Its blackness was my darkness. The wings of the eagle represented the flight of the butterfly.

"Through the merging of the two images, my inner spirit is grounded in a creature that incorporates my negative power, yet transforms it to energize my soul. I can now speak even more forcefully about who I am and what I am to do in this world.

"I was really happy with what emerged because I can see how my darkness has held me for a long time in a place that did not serve me at all. My new image empowers me to be all I know I can be now. It was amazing to uncover it all this way."

An important aspect of building your inner sanctuary is for you to experience times when your mind does not interfere with your being. You cannot actually stop your mind except by watching it do its thing. In watching it, it will eventually stop because its energy is on watching, not on thinking. Thoughts may still be present, but they have been rendered powerless by this method.

Soul Enrichment

Spend a complete day in silence. Eat in silence, walk in silence, and stay committed to not answering the phone or doing any work that distracts you from your day of silence. If possible, find a place to be outside, and listen only to nature's sounds. You will be amazed at how much you have missed by not being silent long enough to hear every sound in the environment which you select.

Ask your soul a simple question about something that has been bothering you: "What will it take for me to have peace about this?" Choose the answer you think will bring you the most peace and then quit thinking about the issue. If that answer does not bring peace after two days, ask the question again. Keep asking your essence this question.

What are you doing to enrich your soul on a continuing basis? Some choices now might include: catching falling light, gardening at least once a day, taking off pointless masks you continue to wear and armor you do not need, pursuing new arenas for self-expression, learning about new subjects you have been interested in, and being a miracle worker in some capacity.

Soul Enrichment

Have a tape recorder available so that you can make a recording that you can play many times. Select a time and place where you will not be interrupted. Take a few deep breaths and record yourself as you read the following words:

"You, my precious soul, are to be honored and respected. You have endured a tremendous amount of neglect in the past, although I did not do this consciously. I am now freeing your energy for you to come into the foreground of my life. I will listen to you speak. I will let you guide me through unfamiliar and familiar spaces. I will allow you to provide the wind for my wings to glide on. You, in all your un-imprisoned splendor, are right here, present to offer me all my unlimited possibilities. Life begins anew today. This is your moment in time where you can carry me farther than I ever expected. I acknowledge you, appreciate you, and celebrate you. Thank you for all you are in my life, my everything from now on."

Those who seek the Light are merely covering their eyes. The Light is in them now.
– Course in Miracles

Chapter Nine

Ode to Joy

Sustaining Your Inner Realm

The soul is the sense of something higher than ourselves, something that stirs in us thoughts and aspirations…
The soul is a burning desire to … remain children of light.
– Albert Schweitzer

"I never thought I could get so much by letting go."

John, a 42-year-old Caucasian man, held a position of considerable power in the entertainment industry. He was accustomed to thinking quickly, controlling many facets of a situation simultaneously, and solving many, seemingly unsolvable, issues at once. After nine months in therapy/spiritual guidance, John said:

"Doctor, I had the most amazing experience last night. I could hardly wait to get here. I have never let myself be what I would call 'out of control.' I mean, I was never comfortable with not being in control: in business, in relationships, or anywhere, really. I know you have strongly suggested that I at least give it a try.

"Well, for a week now I have been getting up at 4:30 instead of 5:30 each morning. I go into my garden room right off my library and I focus on one particular flower. I look at it, experience the beauty of it, and eventually I can just stare at it with no thoughts about it, or anything else for that matter.

"I watch my thoughts, as we talked about, but I don't stay with any of them. That has helped me the most. Eventually they stop on their own. Anyway, back to last night. I went into the garden room and decided to calm myself from the turmoil I'd experienced.

"Sally was away at her weekly meeting so I didn't have to explain my actions. She has really been grilling me about some of the changes she is noticing. She's having a hard time understanding them. I am having a difficult time coming up with ways to describe the internal realm you and I are building, so the communication is strained between Sally and me now. We had been doing so much better, but I am concerned about how quickly I am evolving out of my old controlling ways with her. Even though she says she hates it, she's used to it.

"Last night, I was sitting in the garden room and I felt this loosening of the hold I have felt about who I am as an executive in the social world and at work. I just sensed a weakening of the notion that I am only and irrevocably 'John' who does this and that. I began to see that 'John' is an object, a role, rather than the sum total of who I am. I am so much more than that small image that I am astounded.

"I had never thought in these expanded terms before. It was as if I had a flashlight in my hand and I was shining it on all the various aspects of who I truly am. I am the one, I realized, who holds this flashlight and now allows myself to see my soul. I am so much more than my narrow view of this 'John' person. It's an amazing awareness.

"I was not able to sleep well that night because I kept coming back to what that opening created for me. I am so much more than the life I put on a suit for each day. In fact, that part of me has shriveled as I connect with so many other parts. Whew, this is more than I can take in. It is big, real big."

John related how he had glimpsed the divine core of his being in that experience. Within each of you is a reservoir of this divine wisdom. It is only a matter of taking the time to step out of your usual realm of existence and into this grander, inner realm to sense the magnificence of it.

Connecting with your divinity brings you to the very center of your sacredness. As you connect with the center of your sacredness, you will be able to access this place that can absolutely break you open to a brand new, miraculous understanding of all that you are. To some of my patients, this process has seemed like surrendering to the completely restored soul deep within them.

> *Thought is a tool to take you to the gate.*
> *Then you must leave your tools behind.*
> – Emmanuel

Listening to your soul takes you through the "gate" into the wisdom that is beyond. You have been introduced to many ways to build and fortify your inner sanctuary. Now to keep it alive you need to enter your inner silence. This is where your truth can speak. Meditation is a path that will help you release the treasures that rest within the depths of your inner being.

There are as many ways to attain this inner experience as there are souls. Whatever means will illuminate your inner essence will be your particular avenues. Some patients take a quiet walk each day, focusing on each step to take them to a deeper place within their inner sanctuary. Others use firelight, candlelight, or a phrase from a spiritual book they are reading at the time.

Whatever causes you to reach into your depth, the joy, the unconditional love of your divine being-ness and remove you from the discordant clamoring of your intellectualized thinking, will be your way.

Soul Enrichment

As you move through your life, think of yourself as doing a sacred dance of light and love. Tune in to the idea that as you walk in the world this week, you are not just walking, but dancing in a sacred ceremony of life. Your vision of this notion will, by itself, open up new paths for you to explore. Nature is ablaze with that sacred dance. Notice different aspects of nature such as the sea, the trees in the wind, the blades of grass when it rains and how they dance.

You will begin to see that your meditative practice permits you to experience a broader light, a wider sense of your soul as well as of reality. This expansion is limitless as long as you do not allow your conscious thought processes to control your communication with your inner self. As you let go of your thoughts, allow your soul to give substance, meaning, and relationship to the expanding inner realm you have entered.

Often the experience of meditation becomes one of going into a deeper, undifferentiated awareness of your essence which brings you a sense of unity and connectedness with other people, nature, God, and the universe. Through the time you spend in communing with that divine place in you, you overcome your mind's natural tendency to think it is separate and apart from all other things. Thus, you reclaim your connection with an infinite intelligence that can more readily serve your soul than using your own ability alone can do.

There is a sense of relief that comes over you once you profoundly understand your inner self and your linkages through it to the outer world. You are not alone and you do not have to constantly consider everything. It will become natural for you eventually to abide for extended periods of time in this inner realm each day.

Meditation is an excellent method for getting out of God's way so that this natural unfolding and restoration of your soul can occur. The re-energizing of the soul is nourished by your willingness to go consciously into your inner realm at a designated time each day. Your meditative moments permit you to view yourself in ways that are normally hidden from you.

Meditation aids your soul in moving into its rightful place. You will find peace, contentment, love, and creativity in the place previously ruled by fear and reactivity. Rekindling your original relationship with your essence prior to the time any mugging took place will greatly enrich and replenish your entire life.

Soul Enrichment

Get a timer and set it for one hour. Fill a bowl with spiritual quotes, sayings, inspirations or sources of strength and solace that you have gathered over your life. Find new ideas or add your own to this bowl. When the bowl has at least fifty quotes in it, pull out a quote every hour, read it, and see how it applies to the thoughts that you had as you took it out of the bowl.

As you no doubt know by now, you must have quiet within yourself to sense your soul. It has been said that silence is God's one and only voice. Your overriding spiritual focus is to tune in only to the present moment. Then you begin to experience God, where in the past you only knew about God.

There are many ways of meditating, but one very simple method is to focus your attention totally on your breathing. As you breathe in, just say "in" and as you breathe out, just say, "out." Place your full concentration on inhaling and exhaling. That is all. Since your thoughts block your encounter with your soul, completely focusing on your breathing is a useful way to stop other mind activity.

As you meditate, at times you may notice that you hear noises in the environment. These can easily interrupt your process, but only if you let them. Instead, allow the noises to be signals to go deeper into your meditation. You can actually use the clamor or clanging to remind yourself to refocus your attention onto the present moment.

Let go of any thought you find yourself attached to, whether it is a thought of other activities or a feeling of annoyance. Any of these can keep you from connecting deeply with your soul.

There is nothing mysterious about meditation. It is an act of contemplation that enables you to achieve a higher state of consciousness than you normally experience. To achieve this state you can also focus on a word, a sound, a phrase you repeat, a prayer you utter, something that clears your mind and guides you to a path of complete inner stillness. Some patients have found that physical movement is helpful in achieving a meditative state. Drumming, running or tai chi chuan (a controlled, symbolic dance) add repetition. This rhythm will often aid in meditation.

Soul Enrichment

Dedicate a day to consciously allowing your soul to have its way. Do this without disclosing your purpose to anyone. No one is to know what you are listening to within yourself or what the day is about. This day is for you to get more acquainted with your soul. Remember to spend a day like this at least once a week.

Jeannie, a 39-year-old Caucasian woman, had been in therapy for ten months. She had lost her job selling cosmetics in a department store because her supervisors felt she was not serving customers properly. She had been unable to concentrate on her customers, repeatedly bringing out the wrong items.

Once in therapy, Jeannie realized that she was feeling overwhelmed by the chaos of her relationship with Allan. Their frequent fights often lasted into the night, leaving her anxious and exhausted the following day.

Jeannie and Allan had also been coming in together for therapy, and they were beginning to find a sense of peace between them. This particular day, still without a job, Jeannie came in for her regular session:

"I find that the only time during the day when I completely know everything is going to be okay – not just with Allan, but with my whole world – is when I go into my room, sit in my chair by the window, and get very still for at least twenty minutes. You know, it is not so much the quietness of the room or the comfort of that same chair, but the focus on something I don't pay attention to at any other time.

"I have ignored my inner realm as if there were nothing in there. That seems foolish now since we've talked so much about my impoverished soul. No wonder it's been in that state with my attitude about it.

"Anyway, two days ago I was sitting in that chair and I got this wonderful image. I was opening a door. As I walked through the door I got the strong sense that I was seeing myself in a brand new way I had never even considered before. It was just indescribable. It brings chills up and down my arms to tell you about this. The rest of the day, I would ask myself: Am I seeing myself in this exalted way?

"That whole day was magical for me. Nothing could have disturbed my peace. I felt soothed, as if I were immersed in warm, fragrant oil. It was a bliss I never wanted to end. I am now convinced that I must sit still and listen to my inner voice so that I can flourish in my world once more. Allan certainly noticed a difference when he came home. He loved how I was. I was so much more attuned to him, but much more importantly, to my essence."

Jeannie related a very important aspect of meditation. The present moment contains the seeds of all things, including liberation from all that limits you. Whatever suffering, fear, worry, anger, pain, misery, and despair you may feel, the seeds of your peace do not primarily lie in resolving a situation which triggered those feelings.

If you nurture your soul, it can more readily nurture you. You are transcending, for the moment, the feelings that you have been burdened with. When you return from your inner sanctuary to the environment where those feelings arose, you bring a different perspective. It is not your feelings that have changed; it's you.

You have shifted your way of perceiving things, and your insights are fresh. Can you see that the impact of this shift can be powerful for you? You no longer need to figure things out in your old ways because you now have access to a new world, your inner sanctuary, where intuition, a limitless source of possibilities, and deep wisdom, live.

Meditation is the art of paying attention to the divinity within you. It is an effective way to make qualitative changes to your soul, for it helps you connect with your soul, and it launches you on an exciting journey into uncharted territory. As you explore the unknown within, you learn more about your essence. There is no other way to fully discover who you are.

Besides the meditation suggestions presented in this chapter, a guided meditation can also be valuable.

Soul Enrichment

Tape record yourself saying the following:

You are in a sunlit field with flowers everywhere, and trees along the edge of a meadow. The air is just right, with only a slight breeze. Feel the warmth of the sun as it shines down and permeates through you. The light fills every cell, every organ right now.

Feel this light stream through you, for you are now a bridge between heaven and earth. See the light surround you and see yourself entering that light. See yourself coming from the beams of light as a newly born infant. Look into your eyes at this newborn age. See love, untainted and unharmed. See love filling that newborn baby: your self. See your self as that baby in all your innocence. Knowing now what you know, tell your essence as that newborn: 'I know you are there and have always been there, and I will get back to you. After all this exploration, I will arrive where I started, and I will know you as an unknown but still remembered gate to heaven. Thank you for helping me remember there is a part of me which is still untainted. I am reclaiming you now as I go through whatever it takes to be more conscious of you, for you are the soul of me.'

It is important to point out that meditation is not a complete answer. A flourishing life is based on a comprehensive approach. Throughout this guidebook you have been exposed to many aspects of a comprehensive approach to life: psychological understanding; spiritual connectedness; self-examination; assessment of different stages of your life concerning where, when and how soul mugging started; and physical awareness including the holding of your pain and stress. A synthesis of these many facets is needed in a comprehensive approach to your life.

Something opens our wings. Something
makes boredom and hurt disappear.
Someone fills the cup in front of us.
We taste only sacredness.
– Rumi

Ways of Viewing Your Relationship from within Your Sanctuary

Genuine beginnings begin within us, even when they are brought to our attention by external opportunities.
– W. Bridges

You have gone through many stages to get to where you are now. Building and sustaining your inner sanctuary are similar in many ways to the stages of the caterpillar transforming into a butterfly. Obviously, the butterfly cannot skip the chrysalis part, even if the caterpillar perceives that it is spinning a place of death for itself. It must continue if it is to emerge as a creature that is free, expanded, and limitless within its newly transformed self.

You are also moving through a process that is similar to a seed turning into its next stage of development. That seed needs darkness to turn into new life. Your own journey had to include a period of darkness for you to gain all you are now capable of. Your experience, whatever it has been, has taken you to this point. You could not have passed over any portion of it or you would not have all the possibilities that are available to you now.

Therefore, it is extremely important that you acknowledge gratitude to yourself for your situation with your partner. Although it may not feel like a gift, those challenges solidified your new self. In fact, they led to your soul restoration. This person became the mirror you needed to attain the insight necessary to comprehend your soul mugging and its reverberating impact on your life. You could never have known the extent of its damage, the compromises and even the annihilation you were perpetrating on your soul without exactly this person as your romantic partner.

Whether you stay in this relationship or not is less relevant than is your solid, unwavering commitment to sustain your inner sanctuary. The question of your partner's place in your life must be resolved in the context of this fervent promise to your soul.

I cannot make this kind of decision for you. Neither do I make a recommendation of this type to my private patients. That would be dishonoring of all your effort and achievement in restoring your soul. You are now able to listen carefully to your essence, that divine being who does know what is best for you. Let it speak to you about your partner and your relationship. In fact, listen especially carefully to your soul's wisdom about this aspect of your life. You already know the risk of reverting back to some of the old habits with this person. Is your foundation firm enough to maintain and nurture your soul while you share a life with this partner? Only you can answer that.

An Example Based on My Relationship

After Jonathan and I had been apart for several months, I wrote him a letter. In it I requested that we meet in a place comfortable to both of us. I told him that I had some things I needed to say to him. He agreed, and when we met I began with:

"Jonathan, I have become aware over time that your love for me was one of the most important things I have ever experienced in my life. You were able to give me the kind of love that I had never had. Because of the particular ways that you showed your love – from holding me for hours to looking at me in such a way that I felt worthy of being seen for the first time in my life – I felt wanted, that I mattered. Thank you for that gift to me. At the same time, through our interactions I experienced devastation deep within my soul that I could never have fathomed. I would not have stayed without the relentless hope that my love would make the difference. The sense I had of being repeatedly dishonored, plus your unwillingness to be honest with me and with that other woman, freed me to become who I am today. I had to move beyond my anger to explore my own unnamed, unacknowledged, unexamined and certainly unhealed pain. If I had not done this, I'm sure I would have died inside. The agony was too great. When I did turn within to find some answers, I began to see what I had done to my soul over a long period of time. Our relationship was the catalyst for the most tremendous growth I have ever experienced. In this way it was a blessing. Instead of dying inside, I chose to renew my connection with my core and to re-establish my spiritual foundation, which I now depend on to guide me. It wasn't easy. But I had to do it. I had to learn to honor my soul in a way I otherwise never would have. The experiences I had in my relationship with you forced me to do that. The mirror you provided helped me to see clearly that I was completely invalidating my soul. Now, after having done all this work on my essence, I would like us to consider having a relationship in which we would both be completely conscious of and respectful of our most precious possessions, our souls. I will never again violate mine by ignoring its messages to me. I will never allow you to denigrate it by what you say or do. I'm far beyond that. However, I'm also aware that you are capable of sharing great love. To experience our love without my being desecrated would be a wonderful experience."

Jonathan seemed to appreciate hearing about my discoveries. We resumed our relationship, but after a period of time, it became clear that my soul could not thrive in this relationship. From that experience I knew that I could look to my soul, seek its counsel, and, most of all, rely on it in all situations.

Can you give yourself the space and time necessary to sustain the foundation for your inner sanctuary while in your relationship? Do you need to separate from your partner in order to do this? That depends on how the two of you are adapting to each other or how effectively you are relating to each other. Do you have a living area large enough to provide you with ample space and privacy for focused, intense work on your restoration? If not, you may want to consider the possibility of you or your partner moving to another place, so that you can dedicate yourself to what you need for your soul to thrive.

You must completely strengthen your inner core now. And do not fool yourself into thinking that you can do this half-way. Nor will it serve you to fear you will lose your partner if you take too much time. Which is more important: having a restored soul the rest of your life, or an impoverished soul that you carry into another relationship? Think seriously about these matters. Your life does depend on it.

Here are several considerations and questions to ponder while making your decision:

Kindness and closeness never justify betraying your own feelings and needs.

Are you being honest with your feelings when you think about making changes in the relationship?

Are you tempted to empathize with your partner's desire to be with you, rather than honor the value of your own soul?

Are you inappropriately influenced by anything your partner may be saying versus your intuitive knowledge of your truth?

How strong is your partner's commitment to the kind of relationship you envision?

Is your partner willing to examine his or her contribution to what has happened?

Is your partner committed to his or her own growth, as well as supporting your growth wherever it takes you and for as long as it takes?

Are you willing to make a decision now, or are you acquiescing to a status quo in your relationship?

When you and your partner have a discussion, do your old behavior patterns come back?

Is your decision to be with your partner, or to have separate residences, or even to break up with your partner, based entirely on your soul's wisdom? Are you sacrificing your intuitive judgment and appeasing your partner? Or are you reacting too strongly against him or her?

Soul Enrichment

Become aware of what you say. Ask yourself the following question at least ten times each day: What part of me is talking now? My soul? My mugged soul? My hatred? My love? My anger? What part?

Remember that cooperation is based on open and honest negotiations, not secret soul sacrificing losses or even both of you losing something in a compromise. Generosity in relationships is commendable, but giving up any of your long, difficult journey toward your soul is certainly to be avoided. This would violate your vow to your essence. Your decisions need to be reached in complete honesty with your self. Deciding something as important as your future with or without this partner will only be resolved when it is grounded in your intuition and inner wisdom. Authenticity with your partner must then follow. Again, it must be grounded in your inner self.

Although the process of deciding what to do about your relationship is difficult, it can be part of your continuing growth towards total renewal of your soul. See it as a process which is necessary to fortify your sacred inner realm. Then it will be a refreshing challenge rather than a dreaded dilemma. Some couples emerge from a time of difficulty much stronger and more committed than ever. Other times the partners move on in their lives without each other.

Your ultimate decision concerning your relationship depends on many factors. Your degree of commitment to the relationship must be considered. The question of your partner's commitment embraces many aspects of the characteristics of each of you in addition to the qualities of your relationship. Can each of you stay committed to people, projects, jobs, friends, and family for years, despite certain inevitable challenges?

Another factor is strength of mind. In other words, how well will your partnership handle separation? Is there enough individual independence that each person can provide the other with a clear sense of their needs individually and within the relationship?

Because your soul, not your relationship, has top priority at this point, the quality of your communication is vital when sustaining your inner sanctuary. Your soul has been homeless for many years. As you fortify this necessary sacred shelter, it must be the focus of your attention.

As you evaluate your relationship, consider whether the attitude of trust is sufficient in each of you. Although you and your partner may have lost a great deal of trust, if trust was established before you became aware of your soul disparaging experiences, then perhaps trust can be renewed. Your first priority is to have trust in the world at large, not just within your partnership. It is possible that for you trust is a quality which has been lacking for a long time.

The capacity to love intimately and to stay vulnerable is an important factor in your decision. If you sense obstacles are present to this openness, consider this factor carefully.

Do not let others discourage you during this critical time in your growth. Someone may suggest that taking separate vacations will give you enough time. Consider carefully the time involved in originally dislocating your soul from its rightful place. The amount of time for soul restoration varies by individual and is impossible to predict.

Several years ago I received three caterpillars as a gift. If I wanted the caterpillars to transform into butterflies, I had to follow the instructions specified. First I built a box for them. I placed elements from their natural environment – sticks, leaves, and dirt – around them. After a few weeks, each caterpillar began to build its chrysalis. It was magnificent to observe. The instructions stated that while they were in the chrysalis it was imperative that the box not be touched, not even accidentally nudged. The chrysalis was not to be disturbed in any way.

At last the magical moment came when the first chrysalis began to move on its own and a butterfly began to emerge. I remember how tearful I became. I knew I was experiencing the miracle of life once more.

This shows precisely what you must do. You have completed the building of your inner sanctuary. This is a sacred time for you. Sustaining and honoring it now is as much a part of the process as building it. This is your soul's home. Do not jostle it, disturb it, or permit stress to enter it at any time during this crucial stage. Your becoming that butterfly, a person free, open, resilient, and transformed, depends upon guarding the entire process of your restoration, not just part of it.

There is nothing more redemptive than an authentic relationship with another human/spiritual being. However, there is also nothing more demanding and more spiritually transforming, because in order to attain that quality of relationship, you need to take responsibility for your every attitude, feeling, and action.

Your relationship profoundly influences whether your soul thrives or shrivels. Within your relationship you must be able to completely be yourself and allow your partner that same centeredness. Are you prepared for that level of relationship?

What can eventually be revealed within the experience of deep love (of your partner or another later in your life) is the inherent sacredness of everything in life. In an authentic, trusting, completely honoring partnership, you sense that everything, at every moment, is aligned, attuned, and in unique interactive harmony.

And that, of course, is exactly the way life is. At every moment you are either reverent towards all that is present and living in the moment of that experience, or you have fallen back to sleep, into a sort of emotional dormancy or passive hibernation.

What is love, anyway?
More than a feeling –
a way of being,
being close to God,
being God in form.
Love is the light
glowing in that
dark room.
All else can shrivel
But love expands
the shrivelled
the despairing.
Love is
whispering
wonder-filled phrases
into the ear,
saying
"ALL IS WELL"
when nothing
seems right.
Love is
yellow umbrellas
scattered
across barren
lands,
saying
"Look beyond
the normal,
the everyday.
Be a yellow,

176

scattering,
brightening,
blossom."
Love
shows there is
no final despair necessary.
Love says
"I am with You always."
Love is
Presence,
a Comfort,
a Safe Womb
we climb into
to heal and protect
and save us
when
all else betrays
us.
There love is, yea,
there God is
surrounding us
being us
breathing us
as
we kneel
not in prayer
but in
utter helplessness –
there God is.
"Love is who You are,"
God says,
"Be Love NOW
turn around towards
Your Self, you've
left You in all this
storm, you've walked
away from Me, stomped
on that magnificent
blossom
thinking It/You
weren't Love
at all but rather
an unworthy, shallow,
sorry specimen.
No! Never speak of
God – You that way

You are describing God
and God cannot be
less than God is.
God is.
Do you hear Me?
God – Love is and
that is all.
Speak again, dear One,
in words worthy of You,
God in form.
You are the wonder
happening
now as You awaken to
more Love,
expanded Being,
God expressing
so beautifully."
How can We be other than
our Selves as God
We are all one.
Images
coming from God;
Love,
Love born anew
each moment
in the manger of
Our heart.
So,
what is Love
It is Me
and You
at Our fullest,
deepest,
grandest.
Love is
here.
Be still and know
IT
Me
You.
– Lucy Papillon, Ph.D.

Practices for Showing Devotion to Your Inner Realm

When peace, like a river, attendeth my way,
when sorrows like sea billows roll;
whatever my lot, thou hast taught me to say,
It is well, it is well with my soul.
It is well with my soul,
it is well, it is well with my soul.
– Horatio Spafford, 1873 (hymn)

Your ever-present task is to attune and align yourself with that marvelous power that is deep within you, always present for you, that wants only the best and the highest possibilities for you. Eventually you will begin to realize that you are like a child in a lighted room who once closed his or her eyes long ago out of fear of the dark. You now sense more and more clearly that you have prevented yourself from being the authentic self you have always been.

You know that you diminished, reviled, neglected, and negated a vital part of you so that you could be seen as acceptable. Now you have decided not only to claim this part of you again, but never to let it be less than completely revered at all times.

He [God] is nearer to you than yourself. Why look outside? Become like melting snow.
Wash yourself of yourself. With love your inner voice will find its tongue growing like a
silent white lily in the heart.
– Rumi

Janie, a 49-year-old Caucasian woman, came into therapy and spiritual guidance nearly two years ago. She had been married for sixteen years to a man who more often than not had been, as she put it, "absent to her presence." Janie had started a job two months before she came into therapy. She was a manager for a gift shop in a large shopping mall. She thought if she had a stable income, she would feel freer to make a decision about the relationship.

One day Janie came into therapy with a journal tucked under her left arm. She had a twinkle in her eye that I had only begun to see in the previous two weeks.

"I have so much to tell you that I feel like I need a double session today. I am moving so fast in this transformational phase. I had no idea where my therapy would lead me. Only now can I begin to appreciate my journey.

"I'll admit it has been hell to face all that unresolved stuff inside of me. Of course, I can say that I am grateful to you and to myself that I stayed with it. Sometimes, though – yikes! – it was *so* excruciatingly painful. I'm glad life doesn't show me ahead of time what I must do to change. I mean, what fool would say 'yes' to that much agony? Oh well, I can't wait to tell you what's been happening.

"I brought the journal just to remind me of the different stages I went through these past five days. First, I was so angry that Jeff broke our agreement about contacting me in person. He just popped in on Friday morning to see if I needed anything. I was very proud of myself. I did not yell or even get mad. I firmly said, 'Jeff, this is a breach. I expect you to honor our agreements. Call me on Sunday evening as we had planned.'

"I then walked back into the house and wrote in my journal about all the different emotions I had. I miss him terribly. I wanted to have him come in and hold me, to be with me and tell me all his thoughts and, you know … the old part of me was alive once again. I could see that part pulling at me. I didn't give over to the powerful pull it had on me, though.

"I kept thinking of the image I described at our last therapy session. I was intent on holding on to that image of me: a tall oak tree with deep roots, planted in sumptuous soil. Nothing could push that tree over or even lean it in a direction in which it was not already growing. I certainly don't want to be rigid. I just want to be unwavering.

"Anyway, he left, and I had a bunch of conflicting feelings. Mostly, I knew I wanted to move on through this part of my spiritual/psychological growth so that he and I could meet more frequently.

"What I am so excited about today, though, Dr. Papillon, is that I realized two very different, but I'm sure related, things. Let me read you the two lines I wrote in my journal. One was on Friday night:

I know what I am, I know that I am, I know who I am, I AM.

"I felt so close to my soul, that kingdom of God within me that night. I was present to the Presence within me for sure. It was glorious. I also wrote on Saturday morning on the back of my checkbook at the store: 'I am already so, so I will just allow me to be.'"

"The other thing I have to tell you is that I had a wonderful dawning of a new way of being with Jeff. I have to be willing to be aligned with my soul's mysterious ways. I must also be willing to tolerate unpredictability as I continue to cultivate this awe-inspiring part of me. I realize this is a continuing process, this business of allowing my soul to have its say.

"I need to let Jeff be truly individual, without laying on my expectations. Then I got this image (I love the way I think in images now) of how the soul of our partnership could look. It certainly has a life to honor, too.

"Besides Jeff's soul longings and my own, I know that our marriage has certain unknown but necessary yearnings of its own. I got this notion that it had its own divinity. To signify the full reverence of our marriage, I saw this antique bookcase.

"There were gifts from all over the world on every shelf except one. This shelf was reserved for the present moment. To keep our relationship fresh, that shelf would always be reserved. It would remind us that the present is a treasure which can only be held for that moment and then released to vanish for the next. Nothing can mar the present (like the baggage of the past or the fears of the future) if we both keep the shelf (our relationship) clear to receive the present.

"I have thought of other things we can do to make our marriage a more sacred experience, but that one image stands out for me as just the right way for me to envision possibilities for my sacred, soul-filled marriage.

"It is extraordinary being in the space I live in these days. My life is so far removed from the way it used to be that I barely recognize myself. I don't even want to remember. I like being brand new."

Janie was expressing her transformed experience and her vision of a new future in her partnership. You, too, may be experiencing similar changes if you have been willing to stay attuned to your soul at all times. Note that Janie has soul energy, soul creativity, soul wisdom, and soul replenishment that can be found in no other place but within her. She has become her own guide in each moment. So can you. Your soul, not the external world, becomes your navigator.

Your shift from being dislodged by the confusing signals of the external world to the newly clarified guidance from within becomes available through continual practice. You will be able to differentiate between impulses which are tied to past beliefs and the intuitive sensations you receive from your soul. If the sensing of your soul brings relief and peace to you, it is your essence aligning you with your true path.

I've known rivers:
I've known rivers ancient as the world and older than the flow of human blood in human veins. My soul has grown deep like the rivers.
– Langston Hughes

You can get to that point where your soul feels flourishing, deep, and vital. Be patient and give yourself time.

Through my personal and professional experience, I have come to value my soul more than anything else in my life. If I had not had all the pain, the challenges, the tears, the despair, the terrible agony, and the deep sorrows of having to give up parts of me I thought were important, I would have never developed my essence. I also would not have experienced the joy of serving you. I would not be perceived as authentic unless my message came from a heart profoundly wounded by the suffering about which I have spoken.

I have, some time in the past, gone through all the various stages of this journey back to my original home, from which I will never depart. I choose to make my sacred wounds known to you so that you may have solidly placed stepping stones for your own journey home, in any way which shows itself to you and along any roads you choose to chart your unique path.

I wrote the following poem a few years ago as I was in the process of consecrating my inner sanctuary. I was also moved to offer a tribute to the connection I felt with nature because of the lessons it taught me as well as the nurturing it dependably offered me as I sanctified this, my soul's home. I present it to you in its fullness on the next page; I bless and honor you as you continue your soul's journey, allowing it to guide you always in all ways.

I am the Wave that sparks the ocean shore,
pushing inward and outward at the same moment,
finding Its own rhythm, Its own Truth.

I am the Sun, making diamonds of that blue, magnificent sea,
lighting the way through all the darkness
to the only Presence there is.

I am the Moon, reflecting its own Soul back
onto Itself, to learn to grow, to be,
to stay forever within Its own Oneness.

I am that Flower, wanting to live, to
show Its beauty, Its divinity, only
by Being, never by performing.

It is only Itself,
this Ocean Wave, this Sun, this Moon, this Flower,
never trying to imitate,
never wanting to compete.

All work perfectly
because they stay in their own
brilliant Essence,
their own
Spiritual Home.
– Lucy Papillon, Ph.D.

Printed in the United States
200970BV00002B/1-42/A